MIDDLE EASTERN Cooking

by Rose Dosti

Contents

ANOTHER BESTSELLING VOLUME FROM HPBOOKS
Publishers: Bill and Helen Fisher; Executive Editor: Rick Bailey; Editorial Director: Veronica Durie; Editor: Carlene Tejada; Art Director: Don Burton; Book Design: Dana Martin; Food Stylist: Mable Hoffman; Photography: George deGennaro Studios.

Published by HPBooks
P.O. Box 5367, Tucson, AZ 85703   602/888-2150
ISBN 0-89586-184-4
Library of Congress Catalog Card Number 82-82196
©1982 Fisher Publishing Inc. Printed in U.S.A.

Acknowledgments

The author is grateful to the following people for their assistance:
Catherine Fenady, Joseph Haiek, The Most Reverend John Chedid, Rabbi Yale Butler, Father Spencer Kezios, Ahmet Alpman and Sylva Manoogian. The author thanks Marya Dosti for her research assistance and the numerous fine cooks and store-keepers who graciously shared recipes.
Accessories used in photographs supplied by *Berber Imports* of Los Angeles.

Cover: Latin Quarter Kebabs, page 150; Shish Kebab, page 132; Barbecued Chicken Kebabs, page 142; Arabic Chopped Salad, page 60; and Arabic Pocket Bread, page 74.

Middle Eastern Cuisines

How It Began

Origins of many Middle Eastern dishes are lost in history. They are buried under layers of thousands of years of civilization, waves of immigrations and the overlapping of many cultures. Perhaps someday a historian will uncover their mysteries.

Earliest civilizations began in the areas fertilized by the Euphrates and Tigris Rivers in Iraq and by the Nile River in Egypt. Early man tended wheat fields, made bread from seeds, and domesticated animals. His diet was mainly grains.

Later, Indo-European tribes such as the Hittites, Persians and Armenians settled in Asia Minor. They brought with them a meat-eating culture, adding barbecued meats and preserved dairy products such as yogurt and cheese to the diet of grains.

Arabs journeying throughout the Middle East spread not only their language, philosophy, medicine, mathematics and Islamic faith, but new agricultural methods and spices from the Orient. New foods and cooking methods were a vast improvement on the existing simple cuisines.

About the same time the Byzantine, or Eastern branch of the Roman Empire added its influence, bringing delicacy and brilliance to Middle Eastern cooking. This domination lasted from the 4th to the 15th century. Later, the Ottomans spread their empire from Middle East to the Balkan Peninsula in Europe. During their 500-year rule they helped to integrate and solidify Middle Eastern cuisine as we know it today.

Many dishes are found in more than one country. I have often chosen one representative example. My first consideration has been to maintain the integrity and authenticity of each recipe. ✄

The Five Cuisines

From a culinary point of view, the Middle East can be divided into five general areas: Iran, known historically as Persia; the Arab World, including Iraq, Syria, Lebanon, Jordan, Egypt and the Arabian Peninsula; the Near East, encompassing Turkey, Greece and Armenia; and North Africa, which includes Libya, Algeria, Tunisia and Morocco. Israel remains separate

from the other areas because its cuisine, based on the cuisines of scores of countries, is still forming.

Iranian Cuisine

Iran, once known as *Persia,* is the easternmost area in the Middle East. Its cuisine is probably the most sophisticated, elaborate and unusual of any in the Middle East. Similarities between Arabic cuisine and Iranian cuisine exist. But in the hands of Iranian cooks, staples and staple dishes become a framework for a highly complex, colorful and exotic cuisine. Influenced by neighboring India, the food of Iran centers around rice and the aromatic spices and herbs that enhance it.

The use of rice is unparalleled anywhere in the Middle East. Rice is the sun around which satellite dishes revolve and interplay. No meal is without rice and its role is specific, with no violations allowed. For example, *chelo,* or steamed rice, is an accompaniment for barbecued meats. It is not mixed with other foods. Rice combined with other foods is called *pollo.* Rice garnished with egg yolks may be served with barbecued meat, but not with chicken. Meat dishes, too, have specific functions. *Khoresht* are soup-stews that are served mixed with rice. Meat stews belong to the category of *khorak* and are never mixed with rice. Rice, as elsewhere in the Middle East, is not confined to savory dishes. It may be mixed with candied fruit or with dried fruit and nuts.

Use of yogurt in Iranian cooking is mind-expanding. Legend has attributed its discovery to Persians. Yogurt is the basis of an entire category of appetizer-salads called *borani.* A table is never set without yogurt in at least one of its many guises. It is spooned over rice, meat, fish, poultry and mixed into soups, stews and salads. The mealtime beverage is *dugh*—yogurt diluted with water or soda water and flavored with mint and salt. Yogurt is also used in breads and desserts.

No other cuisine has made more passionate or exotic use of herbs. You may find the Iranian approach to herbs rather startling. Herbs are used in unusual combinations in omelets, salads, soups and rice dishes. Herb & Nut Omelet is a classic example. Dill, parsley, cilantro, saffron and cinnamon are combined with eggs, raisins and nuts.

Fruit as an ingredient has exceeded anything imagined by Arabic or Ottoman cooks. Prunes are added to Picnic Meatballs. In Duckling in Walnut-Pomegranate Sauce, pomegranate-juice sauce is spooned over duckling. Pomegranate juice may also flavor soups and stews. Fruit and fruit juices are added to syrups used for flavoring afternoon drinks, sherberts, jams and jellies. Sour cherries are adored.

Nan-e lavash is the dinnertime bread of Iranians. The recipe is almost identical to Lebanese Soft Bread Sheets. Paper-thin bread dough is baked against the sides of a beehive-like oven called a *tanour.* For the inexperienced, it is difficult to make but worth a try for the sense of adventure and accomplishment. Flour tortillas are a good substitute. Persian Flat Bread, a lovely bread with ridges, is used for breakfast with cheese, butter, jam and tea. These breads are available at Middle Eastern grocery stores and bakeries. Bread is not eaten when rice is on the menu.

An Iranian meal may start with a plate of assorted herbs served with a white cheese, cucumbers in yogurt and bread. The meal always includes a rice dish, soup or a soup-stew, fresh green salad, bread, pickles and yogurt. Sherbets, fruit drinks and desserts are served at the end of a meal. Tea is served after meals and between meals.

Iran or Persia

The country of Iran used to be named *Persia.* The language spoken in Iran is Persian. References to *Iran* and *Iranian* in this book designate the country or nationality. References to *Persian* usually indicate the language, but may also indicate a cultural heritage.

The Middle East

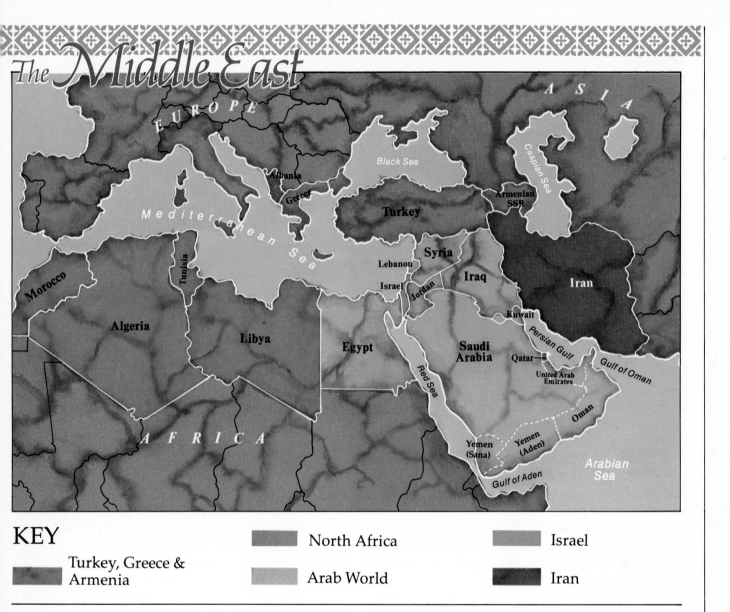

EUROPE

ASIA

Black Sea

Caspian Sea

Albania

Greece

Turkey

Armenian SSR

Mediterranean Sea

Tunisia

Syria

Lebanon

Israel

Iraq

Iran

Jordan

Morocco

Algeria

Libya

Egypt

Kuwait

Saudi Arabia

Persian Gulf

Qatar

Gulf of Oman

United Arab Emirates

Oman

Red Sea

Yemen (Sana)

Yemen (Aden)

Arabian Sea

AFRICA

Gulf of Aden

KEY

Turkey, Greece & Armenia

North Africa

Arab World

Israel

Iran

Arabic Cuisine

Islam solidified the Arab world and created a common language and culture. The cuisines of the Arabian Peninsula, Lebanon, Syria, Jordan and Egypt are dependably similar. Most foods are known by Arabic names, varying only in spelling and pronunciation. The seasonings, cooking method and presentation may differ, depending on the sophistication of the cook. Byzantine-Turkish influences have permeated and elaborated the dishes found in Lebanon and Syria. But in general, the peoples of the Arab world follow ancient eating habits and use common basic ingredients.

Spices introduced by caravan trade over thousands of years have been ingeniously incorporated into the otherwise simple cuisine. Arab cooks love seasonings. Heady spices such as saffron, cinnamon, cloves, ginger and cardamom are used in exotic combinations. Even desserts are distinctively flavored. Rose water or orange-blossom water, and cardamom are Arab-style flavorings frequently used in sweets.

Yogurt is known as *laban*. It is a favorite thirst-quencher when diluted with water and seasoned with salt. Sesame-Seed Sauce, or *Tahini,* is used over everything including bread, fish, meat, rice, bulgur, salad and soup. It provides a protein supplement in a chiefly carbohydrate diet.

Many ingredients are indigenous to each of the countries. Wheat and legumes, such as fava beans, white beans and garbanzo beans grow throughout the Arab world. Arab wheat provided food for the first civilizations of mankind. It is

still a staple from which various types of flat bread are made. It also provides bulgur and cracked wheat. Dates grow in the marshes of Southern Iraq and in the desert oases of the Arabian Peninsula and North Africa. Many Arabs start their day by eating dates and use them to break religious fasts.

Rice is imported from Pakistan, which supplies the best quality Basmati rice, or from the United States. It has become an important staple, frequently replacing bulgur or supplementing beans.

Beans, especially fava beans known as *fool,* go back to the days of the pharoahs. The national dish of Egypt is Egyptian Beans. It is eaten for breakfast, lunch and dinner. Beans frequently appear as an appetizer.

Arabic cooks may quibble over the preferred way to prepare or serve *kibbe,* but the basic ingredients and the dishes are virtually the same. This category of minced, molded, stuffed and layered ground meat is vast and basic to the Arabic cuisine. Lamb, the symbol of hospitality throughout the Middle East, is still served in honor of special guests. It may be roasted in vertical pits to serve whole on a tray with rice, salads, dates, bread and fruit, or made into stews and kibbes.

A wide range exists between a simple meal in a Bedouin's tent on the desert and the elaborate culinary style and presentations of Lebanese and Syrian mastercooks in metropolitan areas. An opulent culinary style was introduced to heavily populated areas by the Byzantines, then overlapped by the Ottomans, who ruled these Arab lands for over four centuries.

Throughout the Arabic world, dining while sitting on the floor is traditional. Dishes are placed on a floor tray or table all at once. In some countries, diners may eat standing up if the food is on a banquet table.

Foods are usually minced or cut up for easy enclosure in pieces of soft, chewy pocket bread. Eating is mostly communal-style except in restaurants and hotels and in Westernized cities. While forks and spoons are widely used, fingers are traditional. The Arabic custom of washing hands before and after meals is based on religious tenets of cleanliness which have been practiced for centuries.

Arab Gulf States

Occasionally, the countries which rim the Persian Gulf on the Arabian Peninsula need to be referred to as a group. They are commonly known as the *Arab Gulf States* to separate them from the rest of the Arab world and from Iran.

Near Eastern Cuisine

Turks, Greeks and Armenians share a culinary heritage rooted in Byzantine and Ottoman cultures. Dishes are almost identical except for a few indigenous ones and variations on names, pronunciations and seasonings.

Unlike the high-carbohydrate, pastoral diet of the Arab world, the Near East has a high-protein diet based on meat, cheese and yogurt. Meat, chiefly lamb, is roasted in a pit or on a spit. *Shish Kebab,* meaning *skewered meat,* is common. Numerous Greek meat stews, baked lamb dishes and soups are variations of one another.

As everywhere else in the Middle East, yogurt is a standard item on the menu and is used as a dressing for vegetables, rice, meats and soups. Turks and Greeks use pita bread and in Turkey's countryside, bulgur is as popular as rice. Cheese, especially feta cheese, is popular. It is often eaten for breakfast with olives and bread or served on the appetizer table.

Meals with sauces are always eaten with crusty bread. Greece and Turkey have the most-varied bread roster of all Middle Eastern countries.

Although rice is imported, it is considered an essential part of the cuisine. Long-grain rice is preferred. All rice is cooked so it is moist enough to savor and dry enough so that every grain is discernible. Sticky rice is abhorred. Rice accompanies meat, soups and stews and is sometimes sweetened to serve as dessert.

Greek and Turkish cooks make imaginative use of vegetables. Greeks love stewing vegetables in herbs and oil. Greek cooks lean toward a higher intensity of seasonings. Their favorites are dill, basil, mint, oregano, lemon, garlic and onion. Turks have recently acquired a passion for French fries and serve them with other vegetables, baked dishes, roasts and grilled meats.

Eggplant is native to India and was brought to the Mediterranean area by traveling Arabs. Eggplant Casserole, or *Mousakas* in Greece, is on page 83. Turkish dishes, such as Fainting Imam—stuffed eggplant, have captured the imagination of cooks throughout the Middle East.

Filo dishes are seasoned almost identically. Cinnamon, cloves and nutmeg is a favored blend. Savory pastries are eaten as appetizers or between courses. They are standard menu items for picnics, special occasions and holidays. Fillings are unlimited, and although filo has been around for centuries, new fillings continue to be discovered. In Istanbul, bakeries sell a pastry made with chocolate filling wrapped in chocolate filo sheets!

The dining style is similar to the rest of the Middle East. The *meze* table, or *appetizer course*, is a cultural habit with deep social implications. Meze is a social event, not merely part of a meal. And no one has a better grasp of its joyful aspects than Near Easterners. Greeks have an ancient legacy of aesthetic beauty, love of food and joy of life. This legacy is shared by the Turks and Armenians and is embodied in the meze. In Turkey, the meze may contain 40 dishes, appearing in a procession according to the cook's inclination. Greeks are content with fewer foods and more drink. Unlike the Arab world where adherence to Islamic prohibition of alcohol is strict, Moslems and Christians of the Near East have always enjoyed *ouzo, raki* and beer.

Meals are served as a series of courses, beginning with meze. If raki is served, Turks follow meze with grilled meats and a salad. Family meals may begin with a modified meze and proceed with soup, followed by meat, chicken or fish with rice or potatoes. Hot, savory filo pastry is a between-course dish. Beverages, such as wine, diluted yogurt, buttermilk, water or beer are consumed without any specific pattern.

Desserts, whether served after dinner or as an offering to guests with coffee, are lavish and varied. Deluxe Baklava, nut-filled Shredded-Pastry Dessert, and other pastries dripping with honey syrup reflect a Byzantine taste for sweets that is characteristic of the Middle East.

Armenia

The country once known as *Armenia* is now part of the Soviet Socialist Republic. It is referred to on the map on page 5 as *Armenian SSR*. Since ancient times, Armenians scattered throughout the world have retained their cultural and historical heritage as well as their identity with the Middle East. In this book, the origin of Armenian recipes and cooking methods are designated as being from the country of *Armenia*.

North African Cuisine

The countries of North Africa, Libya, Algeria, Morocco and Tunisia share a common Arabic heritage dating back to Islamic conquests in the seventh century. The cuisine has been influenced by both Arabs and Berbers. Egypt is geographically part of North Africa, but it is totally Arabic in culture. Other North African countries identify only partially with Arabic culture, even though Arabic is the language.

The heady cuisine of North Africa is full of color, beauty and simplicity. Marketplaces are aglow with preserved fruits, olives and pickles. Turkish-Byzantine influences are unmistakable in all the countries, even in Morocco where no Turkish rule existed. The French who left their language and an appreciation of French culture, made no inroads in altering the already rich Moroccan cuisine. French cuisine, although present, remains quite separate.

The Berbers are a major part of the populations of Libya, Algeria and Morocco. As Egyptian tomb paintings suggest, the Berbers are the aboriginal peoples of North Africa. They have managed to retain much of their language and culture

as well as many colorful elements of their cuisine. Couscous, for instance, is from the Berber word *kukus.* It is actually semolina, the heart of durum wheat, which has been processed into a pasta grain similar to fine bulgur in texture. It is eaten much the same way as bulgur, but many cooks in North Africa prefer it steamed in a double-boiler pot called a *keskes* or *couscousière.*

Tajine, another category of dishes highly influenced by Arabs and the colorful Berbers, is common to all North Africans. In Morocco, the word *tajine* also refers to the cone-shaped ceramic dish in which foods are cooked and served. Tajines are made with fish, meat, vegetables, fresh and dried fruits, nuts and seeds in colorful combinations. Lemon Chicken is a tajine recipe.

Turkish-style, savory filo pastries are known as *briouats* in Morocco, *breik* in Tunisia, and *bourek* in Algeria. They may be filled with meat, vegetables, chicken, salads and even eggs. The Tunisian national dish is Eggs in a Package, a filo pastry filled with a whole egg, parsley and sometimes cilantro. It is fried and served as an appetizer. In Morocco, Chicken Pastry is filled with egg and chicken and powdered heavily with sugar and cinnamon. It is usually served after the soup course. The dish is so basic to Moroccan menus that it has become a test for a new bride. Her mother-in-law closely watches the preparation.

Seasonings set each cuisine apart from the others. Algerians think Tunisian cooking is too hot and fiery. Tunisians regard Moroccan cooking as richer and far more complex. All the cuisines use similar seasonings, varying only in amounts and combinations.

Coffee is flavored with rose water in Algeria and orange-blossom water in Tunisia. Tea is king in Morocco, although French-style *café noir* or *cafe au lait* are favorites. The ceremonial tea service famous in Morocco is fast disappearing from the modern scene. It is still revered by the older generation who preside at tea, mixing in the mint leaves and tasting the tea before it is served.

Dining takes place in opulent comfort with Arabesque-designed backdrops. *Arab rooms,* as they are generally called in Morocco, are lined with divans. A round table is placed in the corner where the divans meet. Algerians surround their tables with mattresses or cushions. In traditional families, dining is done without utensils. Foods are delicately enclosed with bread and eaten slowly and leisurely. A meal is not complete without a tray of seasonal fruit, even when dessert is served. The trays are artfully adorned with leaves, blossoms and flowers.

In cities, Western ways of dining prevail. In Morocco, plates may be stacked at each setting, according to the number of courses expected. The appropriate plate is removed after each course. Otherwise, tablecloths layered one over the other are whisked away one by one until the final course is gone.

At a North African Arabic-style meal, you begin by washing your hands in a brass, silver or pewter basin. The meal may end with a few drops of rose water or orange-blossom water splashed on the palms of your hands.

Israeli Cuisine

Israeli cooking has an international approach because of the many groups of immigrants that make up Israel's population. Only a small percentage of the population is native. The remainder is made up of immigrants from about 100 different countries. Sephardic Jews from Greece, Turkey, Spain and North Africa have added a rich roster of dishes. Eastern European Ashkenazi Jews have brought *borscht,* potato dumplings, *gefilte* fish, noodle pudding and Egg Braid. Northern European bagels and pretzels could be forms of Sesame Bread Rings, the chewy bread sold by street vendors throughout the Middle East. *Matzo,* flat unleavened cracker-like bread used for Passover meals, may be a form of Cracker Bread. Savory pastries, like knishes, were named by Russian and Polish cooks from the Polish word *knyss,* meaning a piece of thin, rolled dough folded over a filling.

Yemenite Jews brought their own ancient culinary traditions like Brown Dyed Eggs which are cooked overnight for Sabbath brunch.

Dietary laws, called *kashrut,* place many restrictions on food habits. Pork and crustaceans are forbidden. Dairy dishes must be cooked and eaten separately from meat dishes. Dairy foods and meats require separate dishes that must also be used, cleaned and stored separately. Only "neutral" or *pareve* foods, such as fish and eggs, may be eaten with either meat or milk. The Sabbath is considered a day of rest and no cooking is done on that day. Foods that contain no dairy products and may withstand hours of cooking over low heat are prepared overnight to be eaten on the Sabbath. Such foods are Sabbath Stew, fish dumplings, *gefilte* fish and noodle pudding.

Meals in Israel tend to be European in style but Middle Eastern in content. Breakfast may include a chopped salad, olives, cheese, pickles, a flat bread for wrapping, and coffee with hot milk. The main meal is at midday with the entire family assembling after shops and schools close. The evening meal may be a light supper of sardines, dairy products, eggs and salad. Egg & Tomato Scramble is a favorite.

1

1/Vegetables for Tunisian Couscous, page 98

2/Parsley-Wheat Salad, page 58.

3/Sourdough-Crumb Soup, page 38.

2

3

Shown on the following pages: Tunisian Couscous, page 98, and French Cigarettes, page 164.

Holiday Foods & Celebrations

Eid al Udr

The Feast of the Sacrifice based on the story of Abraham falls on the 12th day of the Moslem year. The sacrificing of the lamb is commemorated with solemn church services and tributes to the dead. Actual slaughtering and cooking of the lamb is required of pilgrims to Mecca and has become customary among other Moslems. The sacrifice has several important rituals, including the slaughtering according to dietary law, or *halal*, and the distribution of the lamb in three parts: one for the poor, one for friends, and the last for a festive family meal. Families visit, share candies, sweets, tea and other favorite foods.

Eid al Fitr

Moslems throughout the world celebrate Eid al Fitr which ends a month of fasting during the holy month of Ramadan. Ramadan commemorates the time when the words of the Koran were revealed to the Prophet Mohammed through the archangel Gabriel. Fasting from sunrise to sunset during the month is considered a reminder that self-discipline is a lesson in submission. It is also an expression of gratitude for the good things in life. Eid al Fitr is begun when the new moon appears. It is a joyous time for giving to the poor and sharing gifts with friends and relatives. Favorite sweets, such as Pistachio Baklava and Butterflies are among the traditional desserts.

Easter

Greeks, Armenians and other followers of the Eastern-Orthodox faith consider Easter the most important holiday. The celebration commemorating the rising of Christ is preceded by religious observances during Holy Week. Dying eggs and baking holiday breads and cakes are part of Easter preparations. The first feast of Easter after Midnight begins with Red Dyed Eggs and Greek Easter Soup. A salad, roast lamb, fragrant breads and sweets are also part of the feast.

Rosh Hashanah

For the holiday that begins the Jewish New Year, Israeli cooks bake round Egg Bread to symbolize a smooth new cycle. *Charoset*, a sweet fruit mixture, representing sweetness, is also served.

Passover (Pesach)

Passover is the happiest holiday of the year for Jews throughout the world. The holiday, which falls in the spring in the Hebrew month of Nisan and lasts for eight days, recalls the exodus of Jews from Egypt and their liberation from bondage. The traditional substitute for bread during Passover is the unleavened bread called *matzo*. This symbolizes the hasty flight of Israelites from Egypt when there was not time to wait for the bread to rise before they set off. Before Passover, many Jewish families cleanse their homes of all traces of leavened foods.

The first two nights, or in Israel only the first night, are spent over an elaborate ceremonial supper called *Seder*. The Seder table is set with a symbolic plate of foods. This might include three whole matzos, a roasted egg, a roasted lamb bone, a sweet apple condiment, bitter herbs, a dish of salt water, and parsley or similar herb to be dipped in the salt water during the service. A glass of wine is placed before each person.

The story of the exodus is read from the Haggadah, a book utilizing song and ceremony to recall the tale.

Nowruz

The most important Iranian festival falls on March 21st, between dusk and darkness. It celebrates the New Year at the vernal equinox and marks the arrival of spring and a new life. According to legend, the celestial bull stands on a fish while balancing Earth on the tip of one horn. The moment spring arrives, the bull shifts his weight and tosses Earth to his other horn. Earlier in the day, Iranians place a sheaf of wheat in a bowl of water. The sheaf supposedly trembles at the moment the New Year begins.

Seven different foods beginning with the letter **S** appear on the table known as *haftsin*, the counterpart of the Christmas tree. A mirror, candles, goldfish, an orange, a bowl of water, the Koran, a tray of silver coins, yogurt, cheese and colored eggs also make up the symbolic table. At the arrival of the New Year, shouts of joy and congratulations fill the room.

The celebration lasts for 15 days. It is consid-

ered unlucky to stay home on the 13th day, so Iranians traditionally go on a picnic. Families stream to the countryside, meet with friends and relatives and dine on huge Picnic Meatballs filled with walnuts, raisins and prunes.

New Year's Eve

New Year's Eve in Greece is a day of reunion for family and friends. A charming tradition involving card-playing and bread containing a hidden coin prevails among Greeks. A legend stemming from the Ottoman occupation of Greece tells of a Greek bishop named Vasilios.

The bishop attempted to win back his parishioners' money and jewelry from a Turkish tax collector by challenging him to a game of cards. The bishop won the game but his parishioners fought over ownership of the jewelery. To solve the argument, the bishop asked the parishioners to bake bread in which all the jewelry had been placed. Those who found jewelry in their pieces of bread could keep it. So goes the custom of card-playing and the bread which is called *Vasilopita* after the bishop. New Year's Eve, for the most part, is filled with games, jokes, dancing, music and song. ✄

Rose Dosti

Rose Dosti's Balkan heritage gave her an early look at the cuisine of the Middle East. Although born and raised in New York City, she sat down to a table laden with traditionally prepared foods. She frequently observed her Albanian mother and friends as they prepared filo pastries, dolmas, kebabs and other dishes which had their origins in the Near East.

A seasoned world traveler, Rose became fascinated with the variety and beauty of Middle Eastern cuisines. She discovered that each cuisine has basic ingredients in common, but the methods of preparing and style of serving often differ. After each trip to the Middle East, Rose became more aware of the interest and curiosity shown by cooks in the Western world. And with this increased awareness came the realization that here was a basis for a new cuisine for entertaining! It was at that point that *Middle Eastern Cookery* began.

Rose has been a food and nutrition writer for the *Los Angeles Times* for almost 20 years. She writes on a variety of food-related topics, including a restaurant-review column and a reader-request column. She is a co-author of two other cookbooks. ✄

Shopping for Middle Eastern

Arabic Pocket Bread, khubz Arabi (Arabic): the ancient flat bread of the Arabic world. May be opened to form a pocket. Used for sandwiches or to pinch off for scooping up foods. See Arabic Pocket Bread, page 74.

Arack (Arabic); raki (Turkish): a liquor made from grape juice, grains or fruit in southeast Europe and the Middle East.

Avgolemono (Greek): a sauce made with egg and lemon and used in soups or sauces for vegetables, meat or fish. See Egg & Lemon Sauce, page 63.

Ayran (Turkish, Arabic); dugh (Persian): yogurt diluted with water and seasoned with salt or sugar.

Baklava (Greek, Turkish); baklawa (Arabic), paklava (Armenian): a dessert made with layers of filo pastry, filled with nuts and steeped in syrup.

Basterma (Armenian); pastourma (Greek); pastirma (Turkish): dried beef thickly coated with spices such as fenugreek, chiles, garlic and paprika. Thinly sliced and used in sandwiches, appetizers or with eggs. Prosciutto may be substituted.

Borek (Turkish); boureki (Greek); bourek (Algerian); breik (Tunisian); briouats (Moroccan), beoreg (Armenian): pastries made with filo pastry and filled with meats, vegetables, cheese and other savory fillings. See Layered Cheese Pie, page 112, Onion Pie, page 119, and Pumpkin Custard Pie, page 114.

Bulgur, burghul (Arabic): parboiled and dried wheat processed into grains of varying sizes from fine-grade to coarse-grade. Used like rice.

Chemen, chaimen (Armenian): see fenugreek.

Coffee, kahwa (Arabic); kafes (Greek); kahve (Turkish): roasted and pulverized coffee beans made into a brew. Pulverized coffee is available in canned form.

Couscous, kuskus (Berber): grains of various sizes made from semolina, the heart of durum wheat, which is coarsely ground, parboiled and dried. Grains vary in size from fine to coarse pellets. The finest grade is used to make the dish called *couscous*. See Tunisian Couscous, page 98, and Moroccan Couscous, page 100. In stores, couscous is often labeled *couscous mix*.

Dolma (Turkish); dolmeh (Persian); dolmades (Greek): any food stuffed with meat, rice or other filling.

Fava Beans, fava (Turkish); fool (Arabic): a broad bean from the plant of the legume family that bears broad pods with large, flat seeds. Only small fava beans, known as *brown* or *Egyptian brown beans,* are used in making Egyptian Beans, page 93. Any large beans, such as kidney beans, may be substituted. See *fool.* **Some people with certain enzyme deficiencies may have a toxic reaction to fava beans. If you suspect such a deficiency, avoid eating fava beans.**

Falafel (Arabic); tameya (Egyptian): fried cakes or balls made with garbanzo or other beans and seasonings. Used mainly as appetizers or in pita-bread sandwiches. Falafel mix is available in package form.

Fenugreek: a plant of the legume family native to southeastern Europe and west Asia. Ground seeds called *chemen* in Armenian and *hilbeh* in Arabic are used as a seasoning. Ground seeds or powder are available.

Feta (Greek): a semi-soft salty white cheese made with goat's milk or sheep's milk. Sold in cans or cut in brick shapes. Usually stored in brine. Ricotta, dry-curd cottage cheese, hoop cheese, pot cheese or any semi-soft Mexican-style cheese may be substituted.

Filo, phyllo (Greek): a paper-thin sheet of dough used to make sweet and savory pastries. Available in rolls of 10 to 20 sheets at Middle Eastern grocery stores. May be purchased frozen in some supermarkets and gourmet grocery stores.

Fool, ful or foul (Arabic): see fava beans.

Garbanzo-Bean Flour, ard-e nokhod-chi (Persian): a high-protein flour used in place of flour in ground-meat mixtures and other dishes in place of flour. Each cup of garbanzo-bean flour is equivalent to 1/4 cup all-purpose flour.

Garbanzo beans, hummus (Arabic): small light-brown beans. Dried beans are cooked and used to make dips or falafel. Lima beans may be substituted. Garbanzo-bean mix for making *Hummus bi-Tahini,* a dip, is available in packaged form.

Grape Leaves: leaves of grape vines, parboiled or preserved to use as wrappers for various stuffings. See Preserved Grape Leaves, page 176.

Grenadine Syrup, robb-e anar (Persian); dibs roman (Arabic): a syrup made from extracting juice from pomegranates. Used to flavor drinks sauces and meat, poultry or game dishes.

Food & Drink

Halva (Turkish); halwa (Persian, Arabic): a pudding-like sweet made with flour, semolina, cornstarch or farina. Widely used in Middle Eastern cooking.

Harissa, heriseh (Arabic): a hot paste used as a condiment or dipping sauce in North African, Jordanian, Palestinian and Israeli cooking.

Hummus (Arabic): see garbanzo beans.

Kasseri (Greek): a firm, cream-colored cheese made from goat's milk or sheep's milk. Used as a table cheese or for frying. Provolone, Bulgarian *kashkaval* or Turkish *kaser* may be substituted.

Kaymak (Turkish): a clotted cream equivalent to English Devonshire cream or French *crème fraîche.* Used as a topping on sweet pastries. Devonshire cream, *crème fraîche* or whipped cream may be substituted. See Clotted Cream, page 177.

Kefalotiri (Greek): a hard cheese used chiefly for grating. Substitute Romano or Parmesan.

Khubz Arabi (Arabic): see Arabic Pocket Bread.

Laban (Arabic): see yogurt.

Lavash (Armenian, Persian): circular cracker bread. See Cracker Bread, page 69.

Mahlab (Arabic); mahlepi (Greek): ground kernels of cherry stones. Usually sold whole but may be ground to order. Used as a flavoring for pastries, cakes and cookies in Arabic and Greek cuisines.

Mast (Persian): see yogurt.

Mlookhiyah (Arabic): a plant from the jute family. Arabs use the leaves to make a gelatinous soup. In Egypt, the leaves are chopped, cooked with seasonings and served over rice. Leaves may be dried or fresh.

Orange-Blossom Water: a distilled liquid from orange blossoms. Used to flavor pastries, creams and syrups.

Orzo (Italian); kridaraki (Greek): small rice-shaped noodles used in soups and meat dishes in Greek cooking.

Ouzo (Greek); raki (Turkish): a colorless, aniseed-flavored cordial that becomes milky when water is added. Whiskey may be substituted.

Pita, pide (Turkish); pita (Greek); khubz Arabi (Arabic): see Arabic Pocket Bread.

Pomegranates: leathery-skinned red fruit of a small bush or tree. When the fruit is peeled, many tiny translucent edible seeds are revealed. Juice from seeds is extracted to make juices and syrups. Available fall through winter.

Raki (Turkish): see arack.

Retsina (Greek): a white or red wine, flavored with pine resin.

Rose Water: a solution of water and essence of roses. Used to flavor pastries and sweets in Arabic cooking; also used in making of perfumes. Rose syrup and essence are available at gourmet grocery stores and are used by the drop when substituting for rose water.

Saffron, za'afaran (Arabic): dried yellow stigmas of the purplish flower of the crocus family. Used as a seasoning, especially in stews and curries. Available at supermarkets and Middle Eastern grocery stores but very expensive. Mexican varieties are less expensive, but not as aromatic. Turmeric is sometimes substituted.

Sarma (Turkish): see dolma.

Semolina: the heart of durum wheat, processed to make macaroni products and couscous. Grains vary from very fine meal to pellets. The meal is used in pastries. See couscous. Sometimes rice or wheat farina may be substituted.

Sesame-Seed Paste, tahini paste (Arabic): an oily paste made from ground sesame seeds. Used to make dips and sauces.

Sesame-Seed Sauce: see tahini.

Sumac (Arabic): ground seeds of a non-poisonous plant of the cashew family used as a seasoning. Not to be confused with the poisonous plants of the cashew family such as poison ivy. Use only the seeds sold at Middle Eastern and gourmet grocery stores.

Syrian Cheese: also known as *mountain cheese.* Resembles Monterey Jack cheese or Munster in texture and flavor. They may be used interchangeably.

Tahini (Arabic): the sauce made from sesame-seed paste. Also refers to the oily paste sold in cans or jars at Middle Eastern grocery stores. See Sesame-Seed Sauce, page 64.

Tarama (Greek): red or white roe of carp. Used to make dips.

Taramosalata (Greek): dip made from red or white roe of carp *(tarama).*

Za'tar (Arabic): a blend of spices including thyme, marjoram, sumac and salt. ✄

Appetizers

If there is a meal course that best illuminates the spirit of Middle Eastern hospitality, it is the *meze* or *maza,* the Arabic pronunciation for the word *appetizer.*

It is abundant, lavish in content, always generously offered and often so varied that Westerners mistake it as dinner. It is without question a social event, whether a celebration with song, storytelling, arguing over politics, or a subdued occasion of quiet and repose.

Each country enjoys a unique style of dining over meze. Iranians sample a plate of mixed herbs, including coriander, parsley or mint with cheese and a dip of yogurt mixed with cucumbers called *Mast-o Khiar.* This is served with squares of chewy Persian Flat Bread known as *Nan-e Barbari.*

Lebanese and Syrians have elaborate meze tables, sometimes with as many as 40 hot and cold Arab and Turkish-style dishes arriving simultaneously or in a procession. Empty plates are replenished constantly.

The Gulf States Arabic maza can be as simple as a bowl of nuts, some cooked fava beans, a few herbs, such as mint or parsley, or crisp romaine leaves or green onions. This may be eaten in a tent in a reclining position over carpets and cushions, or in an elegant hotel dining room.

Turkish meze tables are a feast of dishes arriving on tiny plates, their contents depending on the chef's whim. The chef at the Abdullah restaurant on the Bosphorus dazzled us with an ongoing array of appetizers that included sauced meat balls, Eggplant Pickles, marinated beans, and liver brochettes.

In Morocco, we experienced numerous styles of meze from bourgeois French-style delicacies served at a coffee table before dinner to fragrant Grilled Spicy Liver which doubles as an entree. In a mountain tent, our host greeted us with a bowlful of honey and bread.

You will find Middle Eastern meze dishes highly suited to party planning. Most of them can

& Beverages

be easily increased in quantity and prepared ahead, then frozen or refrigerated. Don't hesitate to dip into the seafood, bread and salad chapters for recipes to adapt as appetizers.

Arabs from Saudi Arabia crossed the Red Sea and discovered coffee in East Africa. Its reputation as a pleasurable brew quickly spread through the Middle East. It was soon discovered that coffee stimulated the nervous system and kept sleepy Islamic priests awake during their devotions. The brew that Arabs called *kahwa,* is also known as *cafe, kaffee* or *kafes,* depending on the country. It is enjoyed in the Middle East with much the same ceremonial gestures and etiquette as it was centuries ago.

Most Middle Easterners make a strong brew from roasted coffee beans that have been pulverized and boiled. The long-handled pot for making coffee is called a *jezveh.* Most hosts will ask guests how they want their coffee brewed and sweetened. Flavor preferences differ from country to country. Arabs enjoy coffee flavored with cardamom, Yemenites add ginger, and Tunisians stir in rose water.

Tea, like coffee, undoubtedly was first used as a medicinal herb and attributed with healing powers. The Chinese emperor Shen Nung is credited with the discovery of tea in 2737 BC. Tea probably had been traded between India and China for centuries before traveling with spice caravans to the Middle East.

Tea is a favorite beverage in Iraq. The dark brew—generally a mixture of Ceylonese and English blends—is poured into glasses sitting on saucers. The procedure is much the same in Turkey and other Middle Eastern countries.

The tea ceremony in Morocco is not as complex as that of Japan, but it comes close. Every family—rich or poor—owns a tea service of brass, pewter, silver plate or sterling which stands on a short-legged tray. When tea is served for breakfast, lunch, snacks or dinner, the family elder presides on a cushion beside the tray. He or she makes and passes tea after sampling the first brew. Only the practiced elder knows the precise moment the tea is at perfection.

Other drinks to enjoy in the Middle East are the fruit drinks offered on a hot afternoon or served with or after a meal in place of coffee.

Almost every cuisine boasts a favorite yogurt drink. In Turkey, it may be flavored with garlic. Persian yogurt drinks are flavored with mint. Lebanese sometimes add sugar to taste. The basic recipe for Yogurt Drink is on page 28.

Menu

Arabic Cocktail Party

Baked Kibbe, page 23
Eggplant Dip, page 26
Garbanzo-Bean Dip, page 19
Arabic Pocket Bread, page 74
Arabic Chopped Salad, page 60
Parsley-Wheat Salad, page 58
Chilled Bean Salad, page 62
Stuffed Grape Leaves, page 18

Yogurt Cheese, page 178
Arabic Lamb Pies, page 76
Olives
Eggplant Pickles, page 180
Date Domes, page 158
Pistachio Baklava, page 161
Arabic Coffee, page 32

Meat-Stuffed Grape Leaves

Dolmades (Greece)

These aromatic appetizers are served with lemon juice and sometimes with Egg & Lemon Sauce.

1/4 cup olive oil	Salt and freshly ground pepper to taste
1 medium onion, minced	3/4 cup water
1 lb. ground lean lamb or beef	Juice of 1/2 lemon (1-1/2 tablespoons)
1/2 cup short-grain rice	50 to 60 Preserved Grape Leaves, page 176
2 tablespoons chopped fresh mint or	2 lemons, thinly sliced
2 teaspoons crushed dried leaf mint	Boiling water
2 tablespoons chopped fresh dill or	Lemon juice to taste
2 teaspoons dill weed	

Heat olive oil in a large skillet. Add onion. Sauté until onion is tender. Add meat. Cook until meat is crumbly and browned. Add rice, mint, dill, salt and pepper. Stir over medium heat until rice is glazed. Add 3/4 cup water. Bring to a simmer. Cook, uncovered, over medium heat 5 minutes or until liquid is absorbed. Stir in juice of 1/2 lemon. Cool. Cut stems from grape leaves. Place grape leaves in a large bowl. Pour boiling water over leaves. Drain and rinse. Cool. Line bottom of a large saucepan with 2 or 3 large leaves. Place each leaf shiny-side down on a flat surface. Spoon about 1 tablespoon meat mixture in center of each leaf. Roll up, tucking in ends as you roll. Stack rolls seam-side down in an even layer over grape leaves in saucepan. Arrange 2 or 3 lemon slices over rolls. Repeat layering rolls and lemon slices. Invert a heatproof plate on top of stuffed leaves to prevent rolls from sliding while cooking. Press plate down gently. Pour in water to come within 1 inch of saucepan rim. Cover and simmer over low heat 40 minutes or until rice is tender. Leaves should be tender but chewy. Cool slightly. Arrange stuffed grape leaves on a platter. Sprinkle with lemon juice to taste. Makes 50 to 60 appetizers.

TIP ✥✥✥✥✥✥✥✥✥✥✥✥✥✥✥✥✥✥✥✥✥✥✥✥✥✥

Greek cooks sometimes line the saucepan with lamb ribs or bones to form a rack for the stuffed grape leaves while cooking. Rhubarb stalks are sometimes used as a rack. They also add interesting flavor.

Eggplant-Sesame Dip

Baba Ghannouj (Arabic)

An enticing dip for Arabic bread or a distinctive topping for hamburgers.

1 large eggplant	2 garlic cloves, cut in halves
1/2 cup sesame-seed paste (tahini paste)	Salt and freshly ground white pepper to taste
2 tablespoons vegetable oil	Chopped parsley or pomegranate seeds,
Juice of 2 lemons (6 tablespoons)	if desired

Preheat oven to 400F (205C). Use a fork to pierce eggplant in several places. Place pierced eggplant on oven rack and bake 1 hour or until soft. If using microwave oven, bake pierced eggplant at full power (HIGH) 5 minutes or until soft. Cool. Peel. Dice pulp into a blender or food processor. Add sesame-seed paste, oil, lemon juice, garlic, salt and pepper. Process until mixture is smooth and pale. Spoon into a serving bowl. Garnish with parsley or pomegranate seeds, if desired. Makes 2 cups.

Whiskeyed Chicken Livers

Arnavut Ciğeri (Turkey)

Tasty liver and onions may be served as appetizers or as a main dish.

1 medium onion, sliced, separated in rings	1/2 cup all-purpose flour
1/4 cup chopped fresh parsley	1/4 teaspoon salt
1 garlic clove, minced	1/8 teaspoon freshly ground black pepper
1/2 teaspoon red-pepper flakes	1/4 cup olive oil
1/4 cup whiskey or ouzo	Freshly ground black pepper to taste
1 lb. chicken livers or calves' liver, cubed	Lemon wedges for garnish

In a large bowl, combine onion rings, parsley, garlic, red-pepper flakes, whiskey or ouzo and liver. Toss to mix well. Cover. Marinate 1 hour or overnight in refrigerator. In a shallow bowl, combine flour, salt and 1/8 teaspoon black pepper. Heat olive oil in a large skillet over medium-high heat. Drain liver. Roll lightly in seasoned flour. Add to hot oil. Do not crowd in skillet. Sauté until browned on all sides. Remove from skillet with a slotted spoon. Place on a platter or in a chafing dish and keep warm. Dip onion rings in remaining flour to coat lightly. Add to oil in skillet. Sauté 5 minutes or until tender. Spread onion rings over liver. Sprinkle with additional black pepper. Garnish with lemon wedges. Makes 8 appetizer servings or 4 main-dish servings.

Yogurt-Cheese Dip

Labanah (Arabic)

Piquant party dip can also be a refreshing wake-up breakfast spread.

1 cup Yogurt Cheese, page 178	2 teaspoons olive oil
1 teaspoon crushed dried leaf mint	1 or 2 garlic cloves, crushed

Combine all ingredients in a medium bowl. Mix well. Makes about 1 cup.

Yogurt cheese may be purchased at most Middle Eastern grocery stores.

Garbanzo-Bean Dip

Hummus bi-Tahini (Arabic)

Scoop up this mellow dip with pieces of Arabic pocket bread or raw vegetable dippers.

1 (1-lb.) can garbanzo beans, drained	Salt and freshly ground pepper to taste
2 tablespoons sesame-seed paste (tahini paste)	1 tablespoon vegetable oil
2 garlic cloves, minced	1 or 2 parsley sprigs
Juice of 1 lemon (3 tablespoons)	

Place garbanzo beans in blender or food processor. Process until smooth. Add sesame-seed paste, garlic, lemon juice, salt and pepper. Stir to blend. Shape mixture into a mound on a flat plate. Press your finger in center of mound to make an indentation. Fill indentation with oil. Garnish with parsley sprigs. Makes about 1 cup.

Meatless Stuffed Grape Leaves

Warak Arish (Lebanon/Syria)

Preserved grape leaves can be bought in 1-quart jars. Each jar contains about 90 grape leaves.

1/4 cup olive oil
2 medium onions, minced
1 cup short-grain rice
1/2 cup pine nuts
1/4 cup raisins
1 tablespoon chopped fresh dill or
   1 teaspoon dill weed

1/2 teaspoon ground allspice
Salt and freshly ground pepper to taste
50 to 60 Preserved Grape Leaves, page 176
2 lemons, thinly sliced
Boiling water
Juice of 1 lemon (3 tablespoons)
1 tablespoon olive oil

Heat 1/4 cup olive oil in a large skillet. Add onions. Sauté until tender. Add rice. Sauté until rice is glazed. Add pine nuts, raisins, dill, allspice, salt and pepper. Mix well. Cut stems from grape leaves. Place grape leaves in a large bowl. Pour boiling water over leaves. Drain and rinse. Cool. Line bottom of a large saucepan with 2 or 3 large leaves. Set aside. Place each leaf shiny-side down on a flat surface. Spoon about 1 tablespoon rice mixture onto center of each leaf. Roll up, tucking in ends as you roll. Stack rolls seam-side down in an even layer over grape leaves in saucepan. Arrange 2 or 3 lemon slices over rolls. Repeat layering rolls and lemon slices. Invert a heatproof plate on top of stuffed leaves to prevent rolls from sliding while cooking. Press plate down gently. Pour in water to come within 1 inch of saucepan rim. Cover and simmer over low heat 40 minutes or until rice is tender. Leaves should be tender but chewy. Cool slightly. Arrange stuffed graped leaves on a platter. Sprinkle with lemon juice and 1 tablespoon olive oil. Makes 50 to 60 appetizers.

Chicken Mold

Çerkes Tavuğu (Turkey)

Serve this attractive pâté-like spread with toast and crackers.

1 (2- to 3-1b.) chicken
Water
1 medium onion, halved
1 medium carrot, cut in 1-inch pieces
2 parsley sprigs
Salt and freshly ground pepper to taste

2 slices white bread, crusts removed
1 cup finely chopped walnuts (5 oz.)
1 garlic clove, minced
Dash of paprika
Chopped parsley for garnish

Place chicken in a large saucepan. Pour in water to cover. Add onion, carrot, parsley sprigs, salt and pepper. Bring to a boil. Reduce heat. Cover and simmer over low heat 1 hour or until chicken falls away from bones and skin. Remove and discard bones, skin and vegetables. Reserve broth. Shred or dice meat. Place in a large bowl. Add 2 tablespoons reserved broth. Refrigerate to chill. Soak bread in remaining chicken broth. Squeeze dry, reserving broth, and place bread in blender or food processor. Add walnuts, garlic and paprika. Process until smooth, gradually adding 1/4 cup remaining broth until mixture is a thick sauce. Mix a third of the sauce into chicken in bowl. Shape into an oval mound on a platter. Spread remaining sauce evenly over mold. Cover and refrigerate to chill. Sprinkle with paprika and garnish with chopped parsley. Makes 8 to 12 servings.

How to Make Stuffed Grape Leaves

1/Trim stem end from grape leaves. Blanch leaves, then place shiny-side down on a flat surface. Spoon about 1 tablespoon stuffing mixture onto center of each leaf. Roll up, tucking in ends as you roll.

2/Stack rolled stuffed leaves seam-side down in an even layer over grape leaves in saucepan. Arrange 2 or 3 lemon slices over rolls. Repeat layering rolls and lemon slices. Invert a heatproof plate on top of rolls. Press plate down gently. Add water and simmer.

Fish-Roe Dip

Taramosalata (Greece)

Serve this snappy dip with crackers or spread it on toast.

1/3 (8-oz.) jar carp roe	4 slices firm white bread
1 small onion, grated	Water
1 garlic clove, cut	2 tablespoons red-wine vinegar or
1 cup olive oil	lemon juice

In blender, combine roe, onion, garlic and 2 tablespoons olive oil. Blend until smooth. Place bread in water to cover. Lift bread from water and squeeze dry. Bread should have the consistency of wet cotton. Add to roe mixture in blender alternately with remaining olive oil and vinegar or lemon juice. Blend until thickened and smooth. Cover and refrigerate to chill. Makes about 1-1/2 cups.

How to Make Baked Kibbe

1/Sprinkle pine nuts over meat layer. Cover with remaining meat mixture and pat smooth.

2/Before baking, cut meat mixture into 1-1/2-inch squares or diamond shapes without removing from pan.

Middle Eastern Pizza

Lahmajun (Armenia)

You'll like this easy version—it uses frozen dough.

1 lb. ground lean beef or lamb
3 tablespoons tomato sauce
3 tablespoons Grenadine Syrup, page 179
1 teaspoon salt

1/4 cup minced onion
2 tablespoons sugar
1 tablespoon toasted pine nuts, page 67
1 (1-lb.) loaf frozen bread dough, thawed

Preheat oven to 350F (175C). Lightly grease baking sheets. In a large bowl, combine meat, tomato sauce, grenadine syrup, salt, onion, sugar and pine nuts. Mix well. Divide dough into 6 equal portions. On a lightly floured surface, roll out each portion to a 4-inch circle. Place on prepared baking sheets. Divide meat mixture into 6 equal portions. Place 1 portion on each dough circle. Spread to within 1/2 inch of edge of dough. Bake 20 to 25 minutes or until dough is golden. Makes 6 pizzas.

Variation

Substitute Arabic Pocket-Bread dough, page 74, for frozen dough.

Baked Kibbe

Kibbe bi-Sainieh (Lebanon/Syria)

Pronounciation of kibbe varies from country to country and so do methods of preparing it.

1 lb. ground lean beef or lamb	**1/2 teaspoon ground allspice**
1/2 cup fine- to medium-grade bulgur	**Salt and freshly ground pepper to taste**
1 small onion, minced	**2 tablespoons pine nuts**
1/2 teaspoon crushed dried leaf mint	**2 tablespoons butter or margarine, melted**

Combine meat, bulgur, onion, mint, allspice, salt and pepper in food processor. Process until doughy. Preheat oven to 350F (175C). Grease an 8-inch square baking pan or a round 9-inch cake pan. Pat half the meat mixture into pan. Moisten your hands and pat surface smooth. Sprinkle with pine nuts. Cover with remaining meat mixture. Pat smooth. Cut into 1-1/2-inch squares or diamond shapes without removing from pan. Brush with butter or margarine. Bake 30 to 35 minutes or until firm and browned well. Serve kibbe from pan or invert on a tray or platter. Makes 48 appetizers.

Steak Tartar

Kibbe Naiyeh (Lebanon/Syria)

Raw kibbe is served like steak tartar—as a spread for crackers or toasted pocket-bread triangles.

1 cup fine- to medium-grade bulgur	**1/4 teaspoon ground cinnamon**
Water	**Salt and freshly ground pepper to taste**
1 lb. ground lean beef or lamb	**2 tablespoons ice water**
1 small onion, chopped	**1 tablespoon olive oil**
Pinch of chili powder	**2 or 3 parsley sprigs**

Place bulgur in a medium bowl. Add water to cover. Let stand 30 minutes or until water is absorbed. Squeeze any excess water from bulgur. Fluff with a fork. Combine softened bulgur, meat, onion, chili powder, cinnamon, salt and pepper in a large bowl. Knead, gradually adding ice water, until mixture has a buttery texture. If desired, place meat mixture in food processor or blender and process until texture resembles dough. Shape into a mound on a platter. Serve immediately or refrigerate and serve chilled. To serve, press center to make an indentation. Fill indentation with olive oil. Garnish with parsley. Makes 12 appetizer servings.

Variation

Armenian Steak-Tartar Patties (Chi Keofte): Pinch off pieces of meat 2 inches in diameter. Shape into oval patties, pressing your fingers into meat along one side to scallop edges. Arrange patties on a platter. Mix 2 tablespoons each of chopped green onion, green pepper and parsley. Add salt to taste. Sprinkle parsley mixture over patties. Sprinkle patties with red-pepper flakes.

Flaming Fried Cheese

Saganaki Feta (Greece)

Flaming adds a spectacular touch to simple fried cheese.

1 lb. feta or kasseri cheese	1/4 cup Cognac or brandy
1/2 cup all-purpose flour	Marinated Greek Olives, page 181,
1/4 cup butter or margarine	for garnish
Juice of 1/2 lemon (1-1/2 tablespoons)	

Cut cheese into 1-inch cubes or 2" x 2-1/2" x 1/2" rectangles. Dredge in flour. Melt butter or margarine in a large skillet. Add flour-coated cheese and fry quickly, turning until golden on all sides but not melted. Overcooking will cause cheese to stick to skillet. Place cheese on a platter or in a chafing dish. Sprinkle with lemon juice. To flame, heat Cognac or brandy and pour over cheese. Carefully ignite. Let flames go out. Garnish cheese with olives. Serve cubes with wooden picks. Serve rectangles on individual plates with knife and fork. Makes 6 to 8 servings.

Garbanzo-Bean Balls

Falafel (Arabic)

A popular street food since ancient times.

1 cup dried garbanzo beans, sorted, rinsed	1 teaspoon ground cumin
Water	1/2 teaspoon baking soda
3 green onions	Salt and freshly ground pepper to taste
1/2 cup packed parsley sprigs	Oil for frying
4 garlic cloves	Sesame seeds, if desired
1 egg	

Soak beans in water to cover overnight. Drain. Place beans in food mill or processor. Add green onions, parsley, garlic, egg, cumin, baking soda, salt and pepper. Process until almost smooth. Let stand 15 minutes. Refrigerate to chill. Pour oil 1 inch deep into a large skillet. Heat to 370F (190C) on a deep-fry thermometer. Moisten your hands and pinch off pieces of bean mixture 3/4 inch in diameter. Shape into small balls with your hands, or use a wet melon-ball scoop. If patties are desired, use 1 tablespoon bean mixture for each 2-inch patty. Roll in sesame seeds, if desired. Fry in hot oil until browned on all sides, about 2 minutes. Serve with wooden picks. Makes about 24 balls or 12 patties.

Variation

Substitute 1 (1-pound) can garbanzo beans, drained, for soaked dried garbanzo beans.

TIP

Fill Arabic pocket-bread halves with Garbanzo-Bean Patties. Add shredded lettuce, diced tomato, pickles, sliced radishes, olives and green onions. Drizzle with Sesame-Seed Sauce. A dab of harissa or Hot Sauce is a must.

Mixed-Herb Plate

Sabzi Khordan (Iran)

A plate of fragrant, fresh herbs for nibbling with bread throughout the meal.

Mint sprigs
Green onions
Fresh Italian parsley (flat leaf)
Watercress sprigs

1/2 lb. feta cheese, if desired
Cherry tomatoes, if desired
Cucumber-Yogurt Sauce with Raisins, below,
    if desired

Arrange mint, green onions, parsley and watercress on a platter. If cheese is desired, cut into bite-size cubes. Place cheese cubes and cherry tomatoes on platter, if desired. Serve immediately. If sauce is desired, serve separately. Makes 6 servings.

Cucumber-Yogurt Sauce with Raisins

Mast-o Khiar (Iran)

Delightful Persian sauce can be served as a salad with Herbed Rice.

2 cucumbers, peeled, thinly sliced
2 tablespoons chopped green onion
1/2 cup raisins
1/4 cup chopped walnuts

2 cups plain yogurt
Salt and freshly ground white pepper to taste
1 tablespoon crushed dried leaf mint

Combine cucumbers, green onion, raisins and walnuts in a medium bowl. Stir in yogurt, salt, pepper and mint. Refrigerate to chill thoroughly. Makes 4 cups.

Eggplant Dip

Melintzanosalata (Greece)

Easy eggplant dip can be served as a salad. It's similar to Italian caponata.

1 large eggplant
2 medium tomatoes, chopped
2 tablespoons chopped fresh parsley
1 small onion, grated
2 garlic cloves, minced

1/2 cup olive oil
2 tablespoons red-wine vinegar or
    lemon juice
Salt and freshly ground pepper to taste

Preheat oven to 400F (205C). Use a fork to pierce eggplant in several places. Place pierced eggplant on oven rack and bake 1 hour or until soft. If using microwave oven, bake pierced eggplant at full power (HIGH) 5 minutes or until soft. Cool. Peel and chop. Place chopped eggplant in a large salad bowl. Add remaining ingredients. Mix well. Refrigerate to chill. Makes 6 to 8 servings.

Arabic Nachos

(Adapted Arabic)

Similar to Mexican nachos.

1 cup Garbanzo-Bean Dip, page 19
2 tablespoons butter or margarine
1 onion, chopped
1/2 lb. ground lean beef
4 small Arabic pocket breads

1/4 cup pine nuts
1/2 cup Beef Broth, page 36, or
   Chicken Broth, page 36
1/2 cup grated string cheese, Monterey
   Jack cheese or mozzarella cheese

Prepare Garbanzo-Bean Dip. Set aside. Preheat oven to broil. Melt butter or margarine in a large skillet. Add onion. Sauté until tender. Add beef. Cook until crumbly and browned. Cut each pocket bread into 6 triangles. Open triangles and pull apart to make 2 pieces. Place triangles split-side up under broiler. Toast until golden. Remove from oven. Reduce heat to 350F (175C). Line a large pizza pan or baking sheet with toasted triangles. Spread as evenly as possible with Garbanzo-Bean Dip. Spread beef mixture on bean layer. Sprinkle with pine nuts. Drizzle with broth. Sprinkle evenly with cheese. Bake 15 minutes or until cheese melts. If desired, brown under broiler. Makes 6 servings.

Spiced Olives

Meslalla (Morocco)

A touch of the casbah to go with cocktails, to garnish salads or to give as a gift from your kitchen.

1 cup black ripe olives or
   Marinated Greek Olives, page 181
Juice of 1 lemon (3 tablespoons)
1 teaspoon paprika
Pinch of chili powder
1/2 teaspoon ground cumin

1 garlic clove, minced
1 tablespoon walnut oil, almond oil or
   vegetable oil
2 tablespoons chopped fresh parsley
Salt and freshly ground pepper to taste

Combine all ingredients in a medium bowl. Mix well. Cover and marinate 2 hours or overnight. Makes about 1 cup.

TIP ◇◇◇◇◇◇◇◇◇◇◇◇◇◇◇◇◇◇◇◇◇◇◇◇◇◇◇◇◇◇◇

String cheese, walnut oil and almond oil are usually available at Middle Eastern or gourmet grocery stores.

Yogurt Drink

Ayran (Turkey)

A popular drink throughout the Middle Eastern world.

2 cups plain yogurt
2 cups iced water
Dash of salt

1 clove garlic, minced, or
    pinch of garlic powder

Place yogurt in a medium pitcher. Add water, salt and garlic. Stir until blended. Refrigerate to chill. Makes 4 servings.

Variations

Persian Yogurt Drink (Dugh): Substitute 1 teaspoon minced fresh mint or 1/4 teaspoon crushed dried leaf mint for garlic.
Yogurt Fizz: Substitute club soda for water.

Pomegranate Drink

Boisson à la Grenade (North Africa)

A thirst-quenching fruit drink served after a meal or in the afternoon.

2 cups pomegranate juice or
    1/2 cup Grenadine Syrup, page 179
Juice of 2 lemons (6 tablespoons)
Cold water

1 teaspoon orange-blossom water
Sugar to taste
Ice cubes, if desired

Place pomegranate juice or Grenadine Syrup in a 1-quart pitcher. Add lemon juice. Fill pitcher with cold water. Add orange-blossom water and sugar. Stir to mix well. Add ice cubes, if desired. Makes 4 servings.

Variation

Pomegranate Fizz: Substitute club soda for cold water. Add 1 jigger (3 tablespoons) vodka or gin, if desired.

Anise Drink

Yansoon (Arabic)

This hot and spicy toddy reputedly cures stomachaches and colds.

4 cups water (1 qt.)	**1 tablespoon whole star anise**
1 cinnamon stick	**4 whole cloves**
Sugar to taste	**1/4 cup toasted blanched almonds, page 67**
1 (1-inch) piece gingerroot, crushed	**Additional cinnamon sticks, if desired**

Combine water, 1 cinnamon stick and sugar in a large saucepan. Place gingerroot, anise and cloves on a square of cheesecloth. Bring corners up and tie, making a cheesecloth spice bag. Drop into water mixture. Bring to a boil and cover. Boil 5 minutes. Remove spice bag. Strain liquid into a pitcher. Pour into mugs. Sprinkle each serving with almonds. Add cinnamon sticks, if desired. Makes 4 cups.

Variations

Anise Tea: Prepare Anise Drink. Bring to a boil. Drop 1 or 2 teaspoons loose Ceylon or English Breakfast tea into hot mixture. Remove from heat. Cover and steep 5 minutes. Omit almonds. Serve with lemon wedges.

Anise Drink with Rum: Place 1 jigger rum (3 tablespoons) in each mug. Fill with Anise Drink.

Almond Milkshake

Lahlib bi-Looz (Morocco)

Add a drop or two of almond extract to give this nutritious milkshake a stronger almond flavor.

1/2 cup slivered blanched almonds	**2-1/2 cups milk**
1/3 cup sugar	**1/2 teaspoon orange-blossom water,**
1 cup water	**if desired**

Combine almonds, sugar and water in blender. Process until smooth. Add milk. Add orange-blossom water, if desired. Process until slightly thickened. Makes about 4 cups.

Variation

Thick Almond Milkshake: Add 1 large scoop vanilla ice cream with milk. Process until frothy and thick.

Mint Tea

Atai (Morocco)

A simplified version of Moroccan ceremonial tea.

3 cups water
2 or 3 teaspoons green tea
Sugar to taste

1/2 cup mint sprigs, packed
2 cups water
Mint sprigs for garnish, if desired

Place 3 cups water in a 1-quart saucepan. Bring to a boil. Add green tea and sugar. Remove from heat. Pour into a teapot. Add 1/2 cup mint sprigs. Cover and steep 5 minutes. Place 2 cups water in a small saucepan. Bring to a boil. Remove from heat. Pour steeped tea and hot water simultaneously into each tea glass. Garnish with mint sprigs, if desired. Makes about 6 servings.

TIP

Tea glasses used for Moroccan mint tea are similar in size and shape to juice glasses. To prevent the glass from cracking, always place a metal spoon in the glass before pouring in hot liquid.

Floral Tea

Zhoor Finjan (Arabic)

These delightful teas are often used as cold remedies, but I recommend them anytime.

1/2 cup packed jasmine or rose petals
4 cups water

Honey to taste

Wash jasmine or rose petals. Use only fresh, young petals that are not bruised and have not been exposed to pesticides or chemicals. Place water in a medium saucepan. Bring to a boil. Add washed petals. Cover. Boil 5 minutes. Petals will discolor. Strain into tea cups. Allow each guest to add honey to taste. Makes 4 cups.

Iraqi Tea

Chai (Iraq)

Strong tea is served in shot-size glass cups with or without saucers.

2 cups water
2 tablespoons English Breakfast or
  Ceylon tea-leaf blend

Sugar to taste

Heat water in a tea kettle or medium saucepan. Add tea leaves. Cover and let steep 5 minutes or longer until very strong. Add sugar. Pour into small glass cups. Makes 8 servings.

Turkish Coffee

Kahve (Turkey)

For a foamy topping, the procedure for boiling and removing from heat must be followed exactly.

2 tablespoons pulverized Turkish coffee
1 cup water

Place coffee in a 2-cup coffee pot, or *jezve*. Add water. Stir to mix well. Bring to a boil, stirring occasionally. Remove from heat. Bring again to a boil, stirring occasionally. Repeat once more, stirring occasionally. Do not let coffee boil over. Pour into 2 demitasse cups. Distribute foamy topping equally on each cup of coffee. Let grounds settle at bottom 1 or 2 minutes before drinking. Makes 2 demitasse servings.

Variations

Arabic Coffee (Kahwa): Add a pinch of ground cardamom to mixture before bringing to a boil. Add sugar, if desired. For medium-sweet coffee, add 2 teaspoons sugar; for extra-sweet coffee add 1-1/2 tablespoons sugar.
Greek Coffee (Kafes): Identical to Turkish coffee, but if sugar is desired, the amounts vary. Add 2 teaspoons sugar for medium-sweet coffee. Add 4 teaspoons sugar for extra-sweet coffee.
Yemen Coffee: Add a pinch of ground ginger to coffee mixture before bringing to a boil. Add sugar to taste.
Algerian Coffee: Add a few drops rose water to coffee mixture after bringing to a boil. Add sugar, if desired.
Tunisian Coffee: Add a few drops orange-blossom water to coffee mixture after bringing to a boil. Do not add sugar.

Middle Eastern Lemonade

Lamoonada (Arabic)

Drinks like this appear as an afternoon refresher throughout the Middle East.

1 lemon
Sugar to taste
Cold water

Few drops of orange-blossom water
Ice cubes
Mint sprig

Squeeze lemon into a tall glass. Add sugar to taste. Fill with cold water. Add orange-blossom water and ice cubes. Garnish with mint sprig. Makes 1 serving.

Variation
Lemon Fizz: Substitute club soda for cold water.

How to Make Turkish Coffee

1/Bring coffee to a boil and remove from heat 3 times. Stir coffee occasionally as it comes to a boil each time. Do not let coffee boil over.

2/Pour coffee into 2 demitasses. Distribute foamy topping equally on each cup. Let grounds settle at bottom before drinking coffee.

Orange Drink

Sharbat-e Porteghal (Iran)

Here's a citrus refresher for a hot afternoon.

**1 cup freshly squeezed orange juice
   (2 oranges)**
Sugar to taste

Few drops orange-blossom water
Ice cubes
Mint sprig

Place orange juice in a tall glass. Add sugar, orange-blossom water and ice cubes. Stir to mix well. Garnish with mint sprig. Makes 1 serving.

Variations
Orange Fizz: Substitute 1/2 cup club soda for 1/2 cup orange juice.
Orange Oasis: Add 2 tablespoons orange-flavored liqueur. Omit sugar if desired.

Soups

Beans are a mainstay ingredient in soups throughout the Middle East. Soups made with beans are eaten hot and cold, morning, noon or night, with bread and sometimes with nothing more.

In Greece and Turkey, bean soups are usually given a final touch of lemon juice or vinegar. They may include meat. With meat added, bean soup becomes a robust meal for a chilly night or the main course for a supper party.

If beans are basic, lentils run a close second. Lentils dressed with lemon juice, and perhaps with a little meat, are often a main-dish meal in Middle Eastern households. Lentils combined with rice need only a salad and bread to round out the menu. Moroccan Soup, or *Harira,* the national dish of Morocco, is a fine example of how artful a soup made with lentils can be.

In metropolitan areas of Turkey and Greece, you will find a number of delicate and elegant versions of Egg & Lemon Soup. No wedding or special event is complete without one of these soups. The beef version, Wedding Soup contains chunks of meat.

Yogurt soups are another major soup category. Each region—indeed each cook—boasts a favorite recipe. Some yogurt soups, generally with a chicken or meat base, are served hot. Others are served cold as a summer refreshment before, during or after a meal.

From a culinary point of view, Iranian soups created by Persians over the centuries are by far the most sophisticated and perhaps the most interesting. Who else would think of combining lentils with pomegranates? Pomegranate Soup is delightful!

Another unusual soup is Sourdough-Crumb Soup. It is made with crumbs of sourdough. Although few people make sourdough crumbs today, they are available in packages at most Middle Eastern grocery stores. Many people in the Near East start their day with a nourishing bowl of Sourdough-Crumb Soup topped with feta cheese.

Soup recipes in this book make use of fresh ingredients. I recommend that you make your own stock. Soup is only as good as the stock that goes into it. Save chicken gizzards and necks from whole chickens. Freeze them in a freezer container until you have about two pounds. Add a few vegetables and herbs and you can make a stock that cannot be duplicated by canned broths. The recipe for Chicken Broth follows. Freeze cooked stock in 4-, 6- or 8-cup batches to use whenever you want to make homemade soup.

Fresh vegetables are preferred over canned or frozen. They often take no longer to cook and the flavor is more satisfying. An exception is canned tomatoes. With their distinctive texture and taste, they are sometimes preferred over fresh.

Yogurt soups such as Minted Yogurt Soup and Chilled Cucumber-Yogurt Soup are ideal appetizers. Egg & Lemon Soup is also a frequent appetizer. Soups made with beans and lentils are excellent main-course soups—even for parties. They are easy and fun to do. Serve them with one of the breads on pages 66 to 79. ✳

How to Sauté

To sauté means to cook rapidly in a small amount of fat over medium-high heat. In Middle Eastern cookery, oil or butter is often flavored by adding onion or garlic and sautéing until tender or golden. To promote even cooking and prevent burning, stir the onion or garlic frequently.

Menu

Persian Carpet Dinner

Mixed-Herb Plate, page 26
Yogurt Drink, page 28
Barbecued Lamb Kebabs with
Rice, page 132
Stuffed Peppers, page 90

Tossed Green Salad
Butterflies, page 169
Sherbet
Tea

Although simple traditional meals are served on a carpet, you can use tables, chairs and your best china for this meal, as do most Iranians.

Chicken Broth

A basic chicken broth to use in recipes throughout this book.

2 lbs. chicken necks, backs or gizzards
8 cups water (2 qts.)
2 celery stalks with leaves
2 small carrots
1 small parsnip, quartered
1 large onion, quartered

Few parsley sprigs
2 bay leaves
Salt to taste
6 whole peppercorns
Few dill sprigs, if desired

Combine all ingredients in a large saucepan. Bring to a boil. Reduce heat and cover. Simmer over low heat 2 to 2-1/2 hours. Cool uncovered. Strain. Reserve meat and vegetables for use in other soups or sauces. Pour into a clean jar or jars. Use immediately or cover and refrigerate up to 2 days. Broth may be frozen in freezer containers with lids, leaving 1 inch headspace. Makes 1 quart.

Beef Broth

Use this basic recipe whenever a recipe calls for beef broth.

3 lbs. beef bones with meat or
   chuck beef with bones
8 cups water (2 qts.)
1 medium onion, quartered
1 garlic clove
2 celery stalks with leaves

2 small carrots
2 bay leaves
Few parsley sprigs
Salt to taste
6 whole peppercorns

Combine all ingredients in a large saucepan. Bring to a boil. Reduce heat and cover. Simmer over low heat 2 to 2-1/2 hours. Cool uncovered. Strain. Reserve meat and vegetables for use in other soups or sauces. Pour into a clean jar or jars. Use immediately or cover and refrigerate up to 2 days. Broth may be frozen in freezer containers with lids, leaving 1 inch headspace. Makes 1 quart.

Pomegranate Soup

Ash-e Anar (Iran)

If using fresh pomegranates, extract the juice with an orange juicer.

3/4 cup lentils
2 tablespoons butter or margarine
1 medium onion, chopped
8 cups water (2 qts.)
1 cup long-grain rice
1 teaspoon turmeric
Salt and freshly ground pepper to taste
1/2 cup chopped fresh parsley

1/2 cup chopped green onions
1 cup pomegranate juice or
   1/4 cup Grenadine Syrup, page 179
1 tablespoon butter or margarine
2 tablespoons chopped fresh mint or
   2 teaspoons crushed dried leaf mint
1 tablespoon raisins

Rinse lentils several times. Set aside to drain. Melt 2 tablespoons butter or margarine in a large saucepan. Add onion. Sauté until onion is tender. Add water, drained lentils, rice, turmeric, salt and pepper. Bring to a boil. Reduce heat and cover. Simmer over low heat 40 minutes or until lentils and rice are tender. Add parsley, green onions and pomegranate juice or Grenadine Syrup. Simmer 15 minutes longer. Melt 1 tablespoon butter or margarine in a small skillet. Add mint. Sauté until butter or margarine is golden brown. Pour over soup. Sprinkle with raisins. Makes 6 to 8 servings.

Zucchini Soup

Sup-e Kadu (Iran)

Soup with lentils, rice and zucchini is a nutritionally balanced main dish.

2 tablespoons butter or margarine
1 large onion, chopped
1 cup long-grain rice
1 cup lentils, sorted, rinsed
Salt and freshly ground pepper to taste

10 cups water (2-1/2 qts.)
Juice of 2 lemons (6 tablespoons)
1 lb. zucchini, cut in pieces
1 tablespoon butter or margarine
1 tablespoon crushed dried leaf mint

Melt 2 tablespoons butter or margarine in a large saucepan. Add onion. Sauté until onion is tender. Add rice, lentils, salt and pepper. Sauté 1 minute. Add water. Bring to a boil. Add lemon juice. Reduce heat and cover. Cook over medium-low heat 30 minutes. Add zucchini. Cover and cook over medium-low heat 30 minutes longer, stirring once or twice. Melt 1 tablespoon butter or margarine in a small saucepan. Add mint. Sauté until butter or margarine is golden brown. Pour over soup. Makes 6 to 8 servings.

Variation

Substitute yellow squash or patty-pan squash for the zucchini.

Sourdough-Crumb Soup

Trahana (Greece)

An unusual, tart soup to serve for breakfast or with a salad or sandwich for a light supper.

2 tablespoons olive oil	6 cups water (1-1/2 qts.)
1 medium onion, chopped	1/2 cup sourdough crumbs (trahanas)
2 tablespoons tomato paste	1/2 cup crumbled feta cheese (2 oz.)
Salt and freshly ground pepper to taste	Additional freshly ground pepper

Heat olive oil in a large saucepan. Add onion. Sauté until onion is golden. Blend in tomato paste, salt and pepper. Add water. Bring to a boil. Add sourdough crumbs. Bring to a boil. Reduce heat and cover. Cook over medium-low heat 20 minutes or until crumbs are soft. Ladle into bowls. Sprinkle each serving with feta cheese and additional pepper. Makes 6 to 8 servings.

TIP

Sourdough crumbs, or trahanas, have a yogurt base and are dried over a long period. The packaged dry crumbs are available. When cooked, they resemble miniature dumplings.

Lentil Soup

Faki (Greece)

Regional seasonings can change the character of this soup. See the variations below.

1 cup lentils	1 small turnip or parsnip, if desired,
1/4 cup olive oil	peeled, diced
2 medium onions, chopped	8 cups Beef Broth (2 qts.), page 36
2 garlic cloves, minced	3 parsley sprigs
2 medium carrots, sliced	Salt and pepper to taste
1 celery stalk, thinly sliced	1 tablespoon lemon juice or vinegar

Rinse lentils several times. Set aside to drain. Heat olive oil in a large saucepan. Add onions and garlic. Sauté until onions are tender. Add carrots and celery. Add turnip or parsnip, if desired. Cook 10 minutes over low heat. Add drained lentils, broth, parsley, salt and pepper. Bring to a boil. Reduce heat and cover. Simmer over low heat 1 to 1-1/2 hours or until lentils are tender and broth is slightly thickened. Remove parsley sprigs and discard. Add lemon juice or vinegar just before serving. Makes 6 servings.

Variations

Arabic Lentil Soup: Add 1/2 teaspoon ground cumin and 2 bay leaves with other seasonings.
North African Lentil Soup: Add 1/2 teaspoon crushed saffron threads or powder with onion and 1 (8-ounce) can whole tomatoes, crushed, with broth.
Persian Lentil Soup: Add 2 tablespoons orange juice or 2 teaspoons grated orange peel or lemon peel just before serving.

How to Make Sourdough-Crumb Soup

1/Add sourdough crumbs to soup.

2/Sprinkle each serving with crumbled feta cheese.

Bulgur & Yogurt Soup

Tanabur (Armenia)

Yogurt and bulgur make this soup especially wholesome.

1/2 cup fine- to medium-grade bulgur
Water
6 cups Beef Broth (1-1/2 qts.), page 36
3 cups plain yogurt
1 egg, beaten

Salt and freshly ground white pepper to taste
2 tablespoons butter or margarine
1 small onion, minced
1/4 cup chopped fresh mint or
     1 tablespoon crushed dried leaf mint

Place bulgur in a medium bowl. Cover with water. Soak until water is absorbed, about 1 hour. Squeeze dry. Pour broth into a large saucepan. Bring to a boil. Add softened bulgur. Stir to mix well. Simmer, uncovered, over low heat until bulgur is tender, about 30 minutes. Beat yogurt, egg, salt and pepper in a medium bowl. Gradually stir into bulgur mixture. Reduce heat to very low to prevent yogurt from separating. Melt butter or margarine in a small skillet. Add onion. Sauté until onion is tender. Add mint. Sauté 1 minute. Stir into soup just before serving. Makes 8 servings.

Bean Soup   Photo on page 43.

Fasoulada (Greece)

A little olive oil and lemon juice or vinegar adds the final touch.

1/4 cup olive oil
3 medium onions, sliced
2 tablespoons tomato paste
2 medium carrots, diced
2 medium celery stalks, sliced
2 tablespoons chopped fresh parsley
1 teaspoon dill weed

8 cups water (2 qts.)
1 lb. Great Northern beans
Salt and freshly ground pepper to taste
1 tablespoon olive oil, if desired
2 tablespoons lemon juice or vinegar,
  if desired

Heat 1/4 cup olive oil in a large saucepan. Add onions. Sauté until tender. Stir in tomato paste. Cook 1 minute to blend flavors. Add carrots, celery, parsley and dill weed. Cook and stir until carrots are glazed, about 5 minutes. Add water, beans, salt and pepper. Bring to a boil. Reduce heat and cover. Simmer over low heat 1 hour or longer until beans are tender. Sprinkle 1 tablespoon olive oil, lemon juice or vinegar over soup before serving or serve separately. Makes 8 to 10 servings.

Variation

Bean Soup with Meat: Sauté 2 pounds short ribs of beef or 1 pound chuck beef, cubed, in olive oil until browned on all sides. Add onions. Continue with recipe, cooking soup 1-1/2 to 2 hours or until beef is tender.

Moroccan Soup

Harira (Morocco)

The national soup of Morocco is eaten for breakfast, lunch or dinner.

8 cups Beef Broth (2 qts.), page 36
1/2 lb. boneless lamb, diced
1 large carrot, cut up
Salt and freshly ground pepper to taste
1 (1-lb.) can whole tomatoes, drained
1 cup lentils, sorted, rinsed
1/2 teaspoon saffron threads or powder
4 small onions, quartered

1 cup chopped cilantro
1 cup chopped fresh parsley
Juice of 1 lemon (3 tablespoons)
2 tablespoons butter or margarine
1/4 cup all-purpose flour
Freshly ground pepper
Chopped parsley for garnish

Combine broth, lamb, carrot, salt and pepper in a large saucepan. Bring to a boil. Reduce heat and cover. Simmer over low heat 1 hour. Crush tomatoes with the back of a spoon. Add lentils, saffron, onions and crushed tomatoes to soup. Simmer, covered, over low heat 40 minutes or until lentils are tender. Add cilantro, 1 cup parsley and lemon juice. Knead butter or margarine into flour to make a ball. Add to soup. Stir occasionally over medium heat until flour ball melts, about 5 minutes. Sprinkle with additional pepper and parsley. Makes 6 to 8 servings.

Egg & Lemon Soup

Avgolemono Soupa (Greece)

Orzo, the noodle that looks like rice, is available at most Middle Eastern grocery stores.

10 cups Chicken Broth (2-1/2 qts.), page 36	**Giblets from 1 chicken, if desired**
1 small onion, halved	**2/3 cup orzo**
4 garlic cloves, crushed	**Salt and freshly ground pepper to taste**
2 celery stalks with leaves	**4 eggs**
3 parsley sprigs	**Juice of 2 lemons (6 tablespoons)**
1 carrot, quartered	**Additional freshly ground pepper**
2 bay leaves	

Combine broth, onion, garlic, celery, parsley, carrot and bay leaves in a large saucepan. Add giblets, if desired. Bring to a boil. Reduce heat and cover. Simmer over low heat 20 minutes or until giblets are tender. If not using giblets, just bring to a boil. Strain broth into a bowl. Return broth to saucepan and discard vegetables. Add orzo, salt and pepper to broth. Bring to a boil. Reduce heat and cover. Simmer over low heat 15 to 20 minutes or until orzo is soft. Place eggs and lemon juice in blender. Process until smooth. Add about 1 cup soup to egg mixture in blender. Blend until frothy. Add another 1 cup soup to mixture in blender. Process to blend. Add to soup in saucepan. If desired, dice giblets and add to soup. Stir constantly over low heat to bring to serving temperature. Do not boil or mixture will curdle. Sprinkle with additional pepper. Makes 6 to 8 servings.

Variations

Chilled Egg & Lemon Soup: Process cooked soup in blender until smooth. Refrigerate to chill. When ready to serve, beat 1 cup whipping cream until soft peaks form. Fold thoroughly into soup. Sprinkle with freshly ground pepper. Garnish with lemon slices.

Greek Easter Soup (Mayeritsa): Substitute 1 lamb heart, 1/2 pound calf's liver and 1/2 pound lamb honeycomb tripe for giblets. Simmer, covered, 2 hours over low heat. Remove organ meats. Dice and return to soup. Bring to a boil. Add 1/2 cup short-grain rice, 1 tablespoon chopped fresh dill or 1 teaspoon dill weed and additional pepper to taste. Reduce heat and cover. Simmer over low heat 20 minutes or until rice is tender. Add egg and lemon as directed above.

Beef Soup

Marak Basar Temani (Israel)

Yemenites eat this soup by dipping bread into broth, then into fiery Hot Sauce.

1-1/2 lbs. chuck beef, cubed	**2 celery stalks**
1 large onion	**2 parsley sprigs**
1 medium tomato	**Salt to taste**
2 medium potatoes	**1 teaspoon Black-Pepper Spice, page 188**
2 medium carrots	**Water**

Place beef, onion, tomato, potatoes, carrots, celery, parsley, salt and Black-Pepper Spice in a large saucepan. Add water to cover. Bring to a boil. Reduce heat and cover. Simmer over low heat 2 hours. Ladle broth into bowls. Break up vegetables and meat and spoon some into each bowl. Makes 6 servings.

Minted Yogurt Soup

Yayla Çorbası (Turkey)

An elegant first-course soup for a dinner party. To serve chilled, see below.

8 cups strong Chicken Broth (2 qts.), **page 36**	**1 cup plain yogurt**
1/2 cup long-grain rice	**2 egg yolks**
Salt and freshly ground white pepper **to taste**	**1/2 cup all-purpose flour**
	3 tablespoons butter or margarine
	2 tablespoons crushed dried leaf mint

Pour broth into a large saucepan. Bring to a boil. Add rice. Reduce heat and cover. Simmer over low heat 30 minutes or until rice is soft. Add salt and pepper. Combine yogurt, egg yolks and flour in a medium bowl. Stir until blended. Pour about 1 cup hot liquid from saucepan into yogurt mixture. Stir to blend. Add to soup in saucepan. Stir 1 minute over low heat. Melt butter or margarine in a small skillet. Stir in mint. Sauté 1 minute. Pour over soup. Makes 6 to 8 servings.

Variation

Chilled Minted Yogurt Soup: Process cooked soup in blender until smooth. Refrigerate to chill. Omit butter or margarine. Garnish with mint leaves just before serving.

Potherb Soup

Mlookhiyah (Arabic)

Potherb means a wild plant or herb which is cooked and used as a vegetable.

1 lb. fresh mlookhiyah or **1-1/2 cups dried mlookhiyah**	**1/4 cup chopped cilantro**
2 tablespoons butter or margarine	**6 cups Chicken Broth (1-1/2 qts.), page 36**
1 small onion, chopped	**1 teaspoon cumin**
2 garlic cloves, minced	**Salt and freshly ground pepper to taste**

Place fresh mlookhiyah leaves in food processor. Process to a smooth paste. If using dried leaves, reserve and add as directed. Melt butter or margarine in a large saucepan. Add onion and garlic. Sauté until onion is tender. Add cilantro and mlookhiyah paste or dried mlookhiyah leaves. Stir to mix well. Add broth, cumin, salt and pepper. Bring to a boil. Reduce heat and cover. Simmer over low heat 15 minutes or until soup is dark green. Makes 4 to 6 servings.

TIP ◈◈◈◈◈◈◈◈◈◈◈◈◈◈◈◈◈◈◈◈◈◈◈◈◈◈◈◈◈◈

This beloved soup of Egyptians, Jordanians and Palestinians is served over rice with lamb, chicken or fish. Fresh mlookhiyah, a spinach-like herb of the jute family, is sometimes available in Middle Eastern grocery stores. Dried mlookhiyah is more often available. Dried or fresh, the herb gives a thick, okra-like texture to the soup.

Clockwise from the top: Bean Soup, page 40; Meatball Soup, page 45; and Chilled Minted Yogurt Soup.

Barley-Yogurt Soup

Dzedzadz Tanabur (Armenia)

Hearty meat and vegetable broth is enriched with yogurt and egg, then flavored with mint.

1-1/2 lbs. beef soup bones or lamb shanks
8 cups water (2 qts.)
2 celery stalks with leaves,
   cut in 1-inch pieces
Few parsley sprigs
2 garlic cloves
1 onion, halved
1 carrot

Salt and freshly ground pepper to taste
1/2 cup barley
1 egg
2 cups plain yogurt
2 tablespoons butter or margarine
1 tablespoon fresh mint or
   1 teaspoon crushed dried leaf mint
Additional freshly ground pepper to taste

Place beef bones or lamb shanks in a large saucepan. Add water, celery, parsley, garlic, onion, carrot, salt and pepper. Bring to a boil. Reduce heat and cover. Cook over medium-low heat 1 hour 30 minutes or until meat falls away from bones. Remove bones or lamb shanks from soup and set aside to cool. Strain broth into a clean saucepan. Discard vegetables. Remove cooled meat from bones. Discard bones. Dice meat and return to soup. Bring to a boil. Add barley. Reduce heat and cover. Simmer over low heat 1 to 1-1/2 hours or until barley is tender. Beat egg in a medium bowl. Stir in yogurt. Stir about 1 cup hot broth from saucepan into yogurt mixture. Add to soup in saucepan. Bring to serving temperature over low heat, about 5 minutes. Melt butter or margarine in a small skillet. Stir in mint. Sauté 1 minute. Pour over hot soup. Sprinkle with additional pepper. Serve immediately or cool and refrigerate. May be served hot or cold. Makes 6 to 8 servings.

Chilled Cucumber-Yogurt Soup

Tsatsaki (Greece)

This refreshing summer soup can begin or end a meal.

2 large cucumbers, peeled, coarsely shredded
2 garlic cloves, crushed
1 tablespoon chopped fresh mint or
   1 teaspoon crushed dried leaf mint
2 cups plain yogurt

2 cups buttermilk
Salt to taste
1 tablespoon olive oil, if desired
1 tablespoon vinegar, if desired

Combine cucumber, garlic, mint and yogurt in a large bowl. Stir gently to mix well. Stir in buttermilk and salt. Sprinkle with oil and vinegar, if desired. Makes 6 to 8 servings.

Variations

Arabic Cucumber-Yogurt Soup (Khyar bi-Laban): Omit oil and vinegar.

Israeli Cucumber-Yogurt Soup (Tarato): Omit mint. Top soup with 2 or 3 tablespoons chopped almonds.

Persian Cucumber-Yogurt Soup (Dugh Khiar): Omit oil and vinegar. Add 1 tablespoon chopped green onion and 1/4 cup raisins to yogurt mixture.

Turkish Cucumber-Yogurt Soup (Cacik): Add 1 teaspoon dill weed or 1 tablespoon minced fresh dill.

Wedding Soup
Düğün Çorbası (Turkey)

In Turkey, a wedding or festive meal is not complete without this soup or one of its variations.

10 cups water (2-1/2 qts.)	**2 tablespoons all-purpose flour**
1 lb. chuck beef with bones, cut up	**1 tablespoon water**
2 medium onions, quartered	**3 egg yolks**
1 celery stalk with leaves, halved	**Juice of 1 lemon (3 tablespoons)**
1 medium carrot, cut up	**2 tablespoons butter or margarine**
Salt and freshly ground pepper to taste	**Paprika to taste**

In a large saucepan, combine 10 cups water, beef, onions, celery, carrot, salt and pepper. Bring to a boil. Reduce heat and cover. Simmer over low heat 1-1/2 to 2 hours or until meat is tender. Strain into a large bowl. Return liquid to pan. Remove meat from bones. Dice meat and return to soup. Discard vegetables. In a cup, mix flour with 1 tablespoon water. Stir into soup. Stir over medium heat 5 minutes or until slightly thickened. Beat egg yolks with lemon juice in a small bowl. Stir 1 tablespoon hot soup liquid into yolk mixture. Stir into soup in saucepan. Bring to serving temperature over low heat, about 5 minutes. Do not boil or mixture will curdle. Melt butter or margarine in a small skillet. Cook until golden brown. Pour over soup. Sprinkle with paprika. Makes 6 to 8 servings.

Variations
Rice Soup: Omit meat. Add 1/3 cup rice to hot broth. Simmer, covered, 30 minutes or until rice is tender. Continue with recipe.
Fish Soup: Omit meat. Add 1/2 pound any kind of fish to hot broth. Simmer, covered, 30 minutes. Continue with recipe.

Meatball Soup   Photo on page 43.
Youvarlakia (Greece)

One of the many versions of a favorite Balkan soup.

1 lb. ground lean beef	**8 cups strong Chicken Broth (2 qts.),**
1 medium onion, chopped	**page 36**
1/4 cup long-grain rice	**Salt and freshly ground pepper to taste**
2 tablespoons chopped fresh parsley	**2 egg yolks**
1 egg, beaten	**Juice of 1-1/2 lemons (4-1/2 tablespoons)**
Salt and freshly ground pepper to taste	**Chopped parsley for garnish**

Combine beef, onion, rice, 2 tablespoons parsley, egg, salt and pepper in a large bowl. Mix well. Pinch off pieces of meat mixture 1/2 inch in diameter. Shape into balls. Pour broth into a large saucepan. Bring to a boil. Add salt and pepper and meatballs. Reduce heat and cover. Simmer over low heat 45 minutes or until meatballs are tender. Beat egg yolks with lemon juice in a small bowl. Stir about 1 cup hot broth from saucepan into egg mixture. Add to soup in saucepan. Remove from heat. Garnish with additional parsley. Makes 6 servings.

Eggs

An egg is nature's most bountiful package of nutrients. Eggs are high in essential nutrients, including protein. In Middle Eastern cooking, eggs are used both to accompany other foods and as a main dish for breakfast, lunch or dinner. There is little or no concern over cholesterol and fat content. Eggs are simply accepted in sensible portions for their high food value.

Omelets are found in numerous forms. Persian omelets, called *kuku,* are probably the most unusual omelets in Middle Eastern cuisines. Filled with vegetables and herbs, they are eaten as a side dish or as a main dish with yogurt and salad. They are cooked over very low heat or baked until they are relatively dry and browned.

Arab Herb Omelet is eaten in pocket bread. It may be made in the form of a large fluffy omelet or several small ones, depending on the cook's preference. I like them small enough to fit into pocket bread with lettuce and tomato slices.

Eggs in a Package from Tunisia, is a fascinating egg dish. An egg is broken onto filo dough and topped with chopped onion and cilantro. The filo is folded over the egg and the whole package is fried. The result is a neat individual breakfast.

Scrambled eggs are universal. My favorite is Scrambled Eggs with Feta Cheese. Many versions appear in cheese-producing areas of the Middle East. Egg & Tomato Scramble, common from North Africa to Jerusulem, is called *leshakshek,* meaning *to shake* in Hebrew. Known as *lecho* by Hungarian Israelis, it is an excellent main dish for a lunch or light supper.

Armenians enjoy Pastrami with Eggs for breakfast or a light lunch. Eggs are cooked on top of a pastrami-like cured beef, popularly known as *basterma.* This cured beef resembles beef jerky in dryness and flavor. Basterma is found at most Middle Eastern grocery stores. It is easily recognized by its pungent coating which contains the ground seeds of fenugreek, or *chemen,* an important ingredient in many curry blends.

If you want to go the natural way when coloring eggs for Easter or to use as a Thanksgiving centerpiece, try the dyed-egg recipes in this section. You can achieve lovely warm colors with yellow or red onion skins. Collect onion skins from the bottom of a supermarket bin. Red onion skins will color eggs a deep russet. Yellow onion skins will dye eggs a rich golden color. The method is the same as was probably used by the ancient Byzantines and Greeks during Easter week.

There are red dyes called *vafi* for coloring Greek Easter eggs red. They may be purchased at Greek grocery stores during the holiday season. The dye comes in packets with instructions in Greek, so ask the clerk to translate the instructions for you. Most dyes of this type are dissolved in hot water before adding the eggs.

Sephardic Jews from Southern Europe and the Middle East continue the tradition of dying and cooking Brown Dyed Eggs overnight to serve on special occasions and Sabbath brunch. There are many versions for preparing these eggs. This recipe, from a Yemenite in Israel, is a simplified version using coffee and vegetable oil. This combination works together to color the whites of eggs as well as the shells. The color ranges from dove-brown to brown, depending on the strength of the coffee. ✄

Menu

Winter Fireside Supper	Christmas Dinner
Arabic Nachos, page 27	Stuffed Eggs Tarama, page 48
Bean Soup with Meat, page 40	Duckling in Walnut-Pomegranate Sauce, page 148
Sesame Baguettes, page 76	Persian Steamed Rice, page 104
Tomato & Cilantro Salad, page 59	Mixed Salad, page 57
Sponge Cake, page 163	Persian Flat Bread, page 70
Turkish Coffee, page 32	Sweet Bastela, page 168
	Algerian Coffee, page 32

Stuffed Eggs Tarama

(Adapted Greek)

Salty sharp-flavored stuffed eggs are excellent with cocktails.

12 eggs
Salted water
1/2 (8-oz.) jar caviar spread (taramosalata)
1/8 teaspoon ground red pepper

Freshly ground white pepper to taste
1 tablespoon lemon juice
Dill sprigs for garnish

Fill a large saucepan with salted water. Bring to a boil. Carefully lower eggs into boiling water with a slotted spoon. Boil rapidly 11 to 15 minutes, depending on size of eggs. Drain. Rinse in cold water. Fill pan with cold water. Add a few ice cubes. Add eggs. Let stand until eggs are completely cool. Drain. Eggs will peel easily. Peel eggs. Cut each egg in half lengthwise. Remove yolks. Place yolks in a medium bowl. Add caviar spread, red pepper, white pepper and lemon juice. Mix well. Mound into egg halves. Garnish with dill sprigs. Makes 24 stuffed eggs.

Variation
Yogurt-Stuffed Eggs: Omit caviar spread. Substitute 1/2 cup plain yogurt. Add salt to taste.

How to Make Stuffed Eggs Tarama

1/Place cooked eggs in a pan filled with cold water and some ice cubes. Let stand until cool, then peel eggs.

2/Mound caviar mixture into egg halves. Garnish with dill sprigs.

Skillet Eggs & Meat

Kıymalı Yumurta (Turkey)

A quick and simple dish to serve on busy days.

2 tablespoons butter or margarine
1 small onion, minced
1 lb. ground lean beef
1 tablespoon chopped fresh parsley
1 tablespoon tomato paste

1/4 cup water
Salt and freshly ground pepper to taste
6 eggs
Paprika to taste

Melt butter or margarine in a large skillet. Add onion. Sauté until onion is tender. Add ground beef. Cook until beef is crumbly and browned. Stir in parsley, tomato paste, water, salt and pepper. Mix well. Cover and simmer over low heat 10 minutes. Break eggs over meat mixture, spacing evenly around skillet. Cover and simmer over low heat 4 minutes or until eggs are done as desired. Sprinkle eggs with paprika. Makes 6 servings.

Pastrami with Eggs

Abukhd Havgitov (Armenia)

Armenian pastrami, or basterma, resembles beef jerky in texture and flavor.

2 tablespoons butter or margarine
1/2 lb. basterma or prosciutto, sliced

6 eggs
Salt and freshly ground pepper to taste

Melt butter or margarine in a large skillet over low heat. Arrange basterma or prosciutto in a single layer in skillet. Cook over low heat until browned. Break eggs into skillet over meat. Cook until eggs are set. If desired, cover pan a few minutes to steam eggs. Makes 6 servings.

Scrambled Eggs with Feta Cheese

Avga me Feta (Greece)

Try this easy dish for a different Sunday breakfast.

6 eggs
3/4 cup crumbled feta cheese (3 oz.)

2 tablespoons butter or margarine
Freshly ground pepper to taste

Beat eggs in a large bowl. Stir in cheese. Melt butter or margarine in a medium skillet over medium heat. Add egg mixture. Cook and stir until mixture is scrambled and partially set, but still moist. Sprinkle with pepper. Makes 6 servings.

Variation

Scrambled Eggs with Herbs & Feta: Add 2 tablespoons chopped fresh parsley, 2 tablespoons chopped fresh dill or 2 teaspoons dill weed to egg mixture before cooking.

Eggs in a Package

La Breik à l'Oeuf (Tunisia)

Surprise your family with neat packages of eggs in filo for breakfast, lunch or a light supper.

1/2 cup chopped onion,
1/4 cup chopped cilantro
6 filo pastry sheets
6 eggs

Salt and freshly ground pepper to taste
Paprika to taste
Oil for frying

Combine onion and cilantro in a small bowl. Place 1 filo sheet on a clean flat surface. Cover remaining filo sheets with plastic wrap to prevent drying. Fold filo sheet into thirds lengthwise, making a long rectangle. Break 1 egg onto center of rectangle. Sprinkle with 2 tablespoons onion-cilantro mixture, salt, pepper and paprika. Fold filo over egg envelope-fashion, enclosing egg. Moisten seams with water and press lightly with your fingers to seal. Pierce in several places with a wooden pick to let steam escape while frying. Working with 1 filo sheet at a time, repeat with remaining filo sheets and eggs. Pour oil 1 inch deep into a large skillet. Heat to 350F (175C) on a deep-fry thermometer. At this temperature, a 1-inch cube of bread will turn golden brown in 65 seconds. Carefully lower each egg package into hot oil. Fry, turning frequently to cook evenly, until golden on both sides, 1 to 2 minutes. Serve hot. Remove from hot oil with a slotted spoon. Drain on paper towels. Makes 6 servings.

Variations

Egg & Cheese in a Package: Add 1/4 cup crumbled feta cheese (about 1 ounce) or cottage cheese (about 2 ounces) to onion-cilantro mixture.
Egg & Vegetables in a Package: Add 1/2 cup any diced cooked vegetable to onion-cilantro mixture.
Ham & Egg in a Package: Add 1/4 cup chopped ham to onion-cilantro mixture.

Egg & Tomato Scramble

Leshakshek (Israel)

This quick egg-and-vegetable dish is commonly known as lecho by Israelis who came from Hungary.

2 tablespoons vegetable oil
1 large onion, chopped
1 small green or red pepper, diced

4 medium tomatoes, finely chopped
6 eggs
Salt and freshly ground black pepper to taste

Heat oil in a large skillet over medium heat. Add onion and green or red pepper. Sauté until vegetables are tender, about 5 minutes. Add tomatoes. Bring to a boil. Reduce heat. Simmer, uncovered, over low heat 10 minutes. Break eggs into tomato mixture. Break egg yolks with a fork. Mix lightly into tomato mixture. Cover and cook 3 to 4 minutes or until eggs are set. Sprinkle with salt and black pepper. Makes 6 servings.

Variations

Egg & Zucchini Scramble: Substitute 2 medium diced zucchini for tomatoes. Cook over medium-low heat with onion and oil until tender, about 10 minutes. Continue with recipe.
Egg & Eggplant Scramble: Substitute 1/2 eggplant, diced, for tomato.

Herb Omelet

Ijee (Arabic)

Prepare a single, large, thick omelet or several small thin omelets for filling Arabic pocket bread.

6 eggs
2 tablespoons chopped fresh parsley
1/4 cup chopped green onion
1 tablespoon chopped fresh mint or
   1 teaspoon crushed dried leaf mint

Salt and freshly ground white pepper to taste
2 tablespoons butter or margarine

Beat eggs in a large bowl. Stir in parsley, onion, mint, salt and pepper. Melt butter or margarine in an 8-inch skillet over medium heat. Add egg mixture. Cook, gently lifting edges so uncooked portion flows underneath. When eggs are browned underneath, 5 to 6 minutes, flip omelet. Cook until browned on other side, about 4 minutes. Cut into wedges and serve immediately. Makes 4 to 6 servings.

Variations

Individual Omelets: Prepare egg mixture. Melt 1-1/2 teaspoons butter or margarine in a 6-inch skillet. Add 1/4 to 1/3 cup egg mixture. Cook until golden brown underneath. Flip omelet. Cook until browned on other side. Continue to cook omelets with remaining egg mixture.
Arabic Omelet with Cheese: Beat in 1/2 cup crumbled or diced feta cheese or Syrian cheese (about 2 ounces) into egg mixture before cooking.
Arabic Omelet with Vegetables: Chop any leftover cooked vegetable to make 1 cup. Stir into egg mixture before cooking.

Herb & Nut Omelet

Kuku Sabzi (Iran)

You are in store for a flavor surprise when you bite into this exotic omelet.

2 tablespoons butter or margarine
4 green onions, finely chopped
1 or 2 lettuce leaves, chopped
1/4 cup chopped fresh dill or
   2 tablespoons dill weed
1/2 cup chopped fresh parsley
1/4 cup chopped cilantro
2 tablespoons butter or margarine

8 eggs
1/2 teaspoon baking soda
1/2 teaspoon crushed saffron threads or
   saffron powder
1/8 teaspoon ground cinnamon
Salt and freshly ground pepper to taste
3 tablespoons chopped walnuts
3 tablespoons raisins

Preheat oven to 350F (175C). Melt 2 tablespoons butter or margarine in a large skillet with an ovenproof handle. Add green onions, lettuce, dill, parsley and cilantro. Sauté until onion is tender. Add 2 tablespoons butter or margarine. Heat until melted. In a medium bowl, combine eggs, baking soda, saffron, cinnamon, salt and pepper. Stir in walnuts and raisins. Add to herb mixture in skillet. Do not stir. Cook over medium heat until set around edges. Place in oven. Bake 20 to 30 minutes or until golden and set. Cut into wedges and serve immediately. Makes 6 to 8 servings.

Naturally Dyed Eggs
(Greek-Style)

Armenian and Greek cooks often use this method to color eggs for the holidays.

3 cups packed brown, red or
   yellow onion skins
12 eggs

1 teaspoon salt
Cold water

Spread about a third of the onion skins in a large, deep saucepan. Arrange half the eggs over skins. Continue layering, making 2 more onion-skin layers and 1 more egg layer. Sprinkle with salt. Carefully pour in cold water to cover. Bring to a boil over high heat. Reduce heat. Cook, uncovered, over medium-high heat 15 to 20 minutes or until eggs are colored as desired. If using red or brown skins, eggs will be deep russet. If using yellow skins, eggs will be golden. Remove eggs from hot water with a slotted spoon and set aside to cool. Makes 12 dyed eggs.

TIP

Scoop up onion skins from the bottom of a supermarket onion bin or collect them throughout the year.

Red Dyed Eggs
Avga Kokkina (Greece)

Bright and shiny red eggs add cheer to Easter festivities.

12 eggs
1 pkg. red egg dye (vafi)
Water

1/2 cup vinegar
Olive oil

Dye eggs according to package directions using dye, water and vinegar. Do not overcook. Eggs will be cooked 15 to 20 minutes after water reaches boiling point. Carefully remove eggs and drain thoroughly on paper towels. Pat dry if necessary. Dip a soft cloth in olive oil. Rub each egg with cloth until shiny. Wipe with a dry, clean cloth to remove excess oil. Makes 12 dyed eggs.

Brown Dyed Eggs
Humidoes (Israel)

Yemenites serve these sand-colored, coffee-flavored eggs for brunch on the Sabbath.

12 eggs
Cold water

1 cup vegetable oil
1 cup strong coffee

Place eggs in a large saucepan. Add cold water to cover, oil and coffee. Bring to a boil. Reduce heat. Simmer, uncovered, over very low heat 2 hours or until shells are browned. Peeled eggs will be light brown. Makes 12 dyed eggs.

       Naturally Dyed Eggs; Red Dyed Eggs; and Brown Dyed Eggs

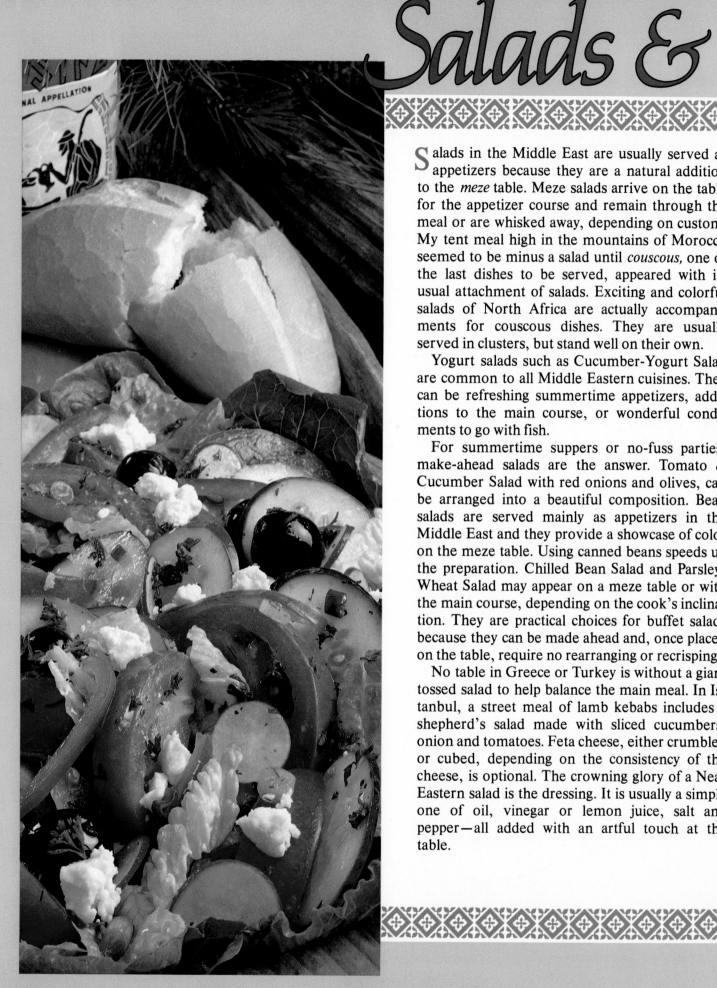

Salads &

S alads in the Middle East are usually served as appetizers because they are a natural addition to the *meze* table. Meze salads arrive on the table for the appetizer course and remain through the meal or are whisked away, depending on custom. My tent meal high in the mountains of Morocco seemed to be minus a salad until *couscous,* one of the last dishes to be served, appeared with its usual attachment of salads. Exciting and colorful salads of North Africa are actually accompaniments for couscous dishes. They are usually served in clusters, but stand well on their own.

Yogurt salads such as Cucumber-Yogurt Salad are common to all Middle Eastern cuisines. They can be refreshing summertime appetizers, additions to the main course, or wonderful condiments to go with fish.

For summertime suppers or no-fuss parties, make-ahead salads are the answer. Tomato & Cucumber Salad with red onions and olives, can be arranged into a beautiful composition. Bean salads are served mainly as appetizers in the Middle East and they provide a showcase of color on the meze table. Using canned beans speeds up the preparation. Chilled Bean Salad and Parsley-Wheat Salad may appear on a meze table or with the main course, depending on the cook's inclination. They are practical choices for buffet salads because they can be made ahead and, once placed on the table, require no rearranging or recrisping.

No table in Greece or Turkey is without a giant tossed salad to help balance the main meal. In Istanbul, a street meal of lamb kebabs includes a shepherd's salad made with sliced cucumbers, onion and tomatoes. Feta cheese, either crumbled or cubed, depending on the consistency of the cheese, is optional. The crowning glory of a Near Eastern salad is the dressing. It is usually a simple one of oil, vinegar or lemon juice, salt and pepper—all added with an artful touch at the table.

Sauces

Every cuisine has flavor superstars and in the Middle East, sesame seeds, garlic, yogurt and lemon seem to dominate the scene.

The most-adored sauce in the Arab world is sesame-seed sauce, generally known as *tahini*. It is made from ground seeds from a plant that has been cultivated in Syria and Egypt since ancient times. The sauce is made from seeds ground to an oily paste. It is used to flavor foods or added to pureed vegetables such as the popular Eggplant-Sesame Dip or Garbanzo-Bean Dip. Sesame-seed sauce may be diluted to spoon over fish, meat, vegetables and salads. Pocket-bread sandwiches are rarely without a smidgen of tahini. It is also used extensively in sweets. Tahini is used chiefly in the Arabic world.

Garlic is prized in many Middle Eastern countries. In some traditional families, a newborn boy wears a garland of garlic around his neck to ward off evil. The most outstanding of all garlic sauces in the Greek cuisine is Garlic Sauce, or *Skordalia*, made by combining moistened bread or mashed potatoes with lemon juice and oil. It is used on almost anything, but is especially good on fish or as a dip.

Garlic is a favorite ingredient in yogurt sauces.

The basic recipe for Yogurt Sauce is on page 64. The same ingredients are the basis for Chilled Cucumber-Yogurt Soup.

Egg and lemon, a favorite flavor duo in Greece, is found in sauces that go into soups or are added to meat, fish or poultry, vegetables and even eggs. Mixing egg and lemon into hot liquid is such a delicate process that even veteran cooks may say a few words of prayer to ward off curdling. The best method to avoid curdling is to mix a small amount of the hot liquid into the egg-and-lemon mixture in a small bowl before adding it to the bulk of the hot liquid. Avoid cooking the sauce over too-high heat or cooking it too long.

Oil-and-lemon dressing, another dominant sauce in Middle Eastern cooking, appears in salads everywhere. No sauce could be more deceptive in its simplicity. Middle Eastern cooks add oil and lemon juice to salads by eye and feel—never by measure. Vinegar is frequently substituted for the lemon juice. I suggest you practice adding dressings without precise measures even though measurements are given in the recipes. Every salad has individual requirements which no scientific measuring system can satisfy. Your eye and deft hand are far more reliable. ✖

Menu

Holiday Brunch	Patio Supper
Olives	Chilled Cucumber-Yogurt Soup, page 44
Yogurt-Cheese Dip, page 19	Ground-Meat Kebabs, page 126
Bread Sticks, page 72	Tomato & Cucumber Salad, page 56
Vegetarian Skillet, page 87	Arabic Pocket Bread, page 74
Lettuce & Orange Salad, page 56	Pistachio Ice Cream, page 187
Fresh Berries in Cream	Iced Mint Tea, page 30

Tomato & Cucumber Salad

Domates Salatası (Turkey)

Arrange tomatoes, black olives, crisp green vegetables and herbs in an artistic centerpiece salad.

4 or 5 romaine lettuce leaves
4 medium tomatoes, cut in 1/4-inch slices
2 large cucumbers, peeled, cut in
   1/4-inch slices
1 red onion, peeled, cut in 1/4-inch slices
12 black Marinated Greek Olives, page 181
1/4 cup olive oil

Juice of 1/2 lemon (1-1/2 tablespoons)
1 tablespoon chopped fresh parsley
1 tablespoon chopped fresh mint or
   1 teaspoon crushed dried leaf mint
1 garlic clove, crushed
Salt and freshly ground pepper to taste

Line a large platter with lettuce leaves. Overlap tomato slices in a circle around edge of platter. Overlap cucumber slices in another circle inside tomatoes. Overlap onion slices along center. Garnish between rows with olives. Combine remaining ingredients in a small bowl or jar. Stir or shake to mix well. Pour over salad. Refrigerate to chill. Makes 6 servings.

Carrot & Orange Salad   Photo on page 11.

Salatat Jazar w' Lamoon (Morocco)

This fragrant salad is often served with Moroccan Couscous.

1 lb. carrots, grated
Juice of 1 lemon (3 tablespoons)
1 tablespoon orange-blossom water
1/8 teaspoon sugar

Pinch of salt
2 oranges, peeled, sliced
Parsley sprigs, if desired

In a medium salad bowl, combine carrots, lemon juice, orange-blossom water, sugar and salt. Toss to mix well. Arrange orange slices around mixture. Garnish with parsley, if desired. Makes 6 servings.

Lettuce & Orange Salad

Salatat Khus w' Lamoon (Morocco)

A beautifully arranged salad is ideal for a buffet.

2 heads butter lettuce
Juice of 1 lemon (3 tablespoons)
1 tablespoon orange juice
2 tablespoons peanut oil or olive oil

1 tablespoon orange-blossom water
Pinch of sugar
Salt to taste
2 medium oranges, peeled, sliced

Rinse lettuce and remove large outer leaves. Tear remaining leaves into a large salad bowl. Add lemon juice, orange juice, oil, orange-blossom water, sugar and salt. Toss. Overlap orange slices to form a circle in center of salad. Refrigerate until ready to serve. Makes 6 servings.

Zucchini-Relish Salad   Photo on page 10.

Ajlouk (Tunisia)

One of the satellite salads for Tunisian Couscous also makes a tasty dip.

2 medium zucchini
1 cup water
Juice of 1/2 lemon (1-1/2 tablespoons)

1 garlic clove, minced
Dash of hot-pepper sauce
1/2 teaspoon caraway seeds

Place zucchini in a large skillet. Add water. Bring to a boil. Reduce heat and cover. Simmer over low heat 15 minutes or until zucchini is soft. Drain. Place zucchini in a medium bowl. Coarsely mash with a fork. Add remaining ingredients. Mix well. Refrigerate to chill. Makes 6 relish servings.

Sweet-Potato Salad

Salatat Batata Helwey (Morocco)

One of nature's most nutritious vegetables is the base for an exotic salad.

1/4 cup peanut oil or olive oil
1 medium onion, chopped
1/2 teaspoon ground ginger
Pinch of saffron threads or powder,
  if desired
1 lb. medium, sweet potatoes (about 2),
  peeled, sliced 1/4 inch thick

1/2 cup water
Pinch of ground cumin
1 teaspoon paprika
1 tablespoon chopped cilantro
1 tablespoon chopped fresh parsley
Juice of 1 lemon (3 tablespoons)
6 or 7 green olives

Heat oil in a large skillet. Add onion and ginger. Stir in saffron, if desired. Sauté until onion is tender. Add potatoes and water. Bring to a boil. Reduce heat and cover. Simmer over low heat 20 to 30 minutes or until potatoes are tender but still firm. Drain. Place in a large salad bowl. Refrigerate to chill. Before serving, add cumin, paprika, cilantro, parsley and lemon juice. Toss. Garnish with olives. Makes 6 servings.

Mixed Salad   Photo on pages 10 and 11.

Slata Jidda (Tunisia)

Serve in a small bowl as an accompaniment for Tunisian Couscous.

1 tomato, chopped
1/2 medium, green pepper, diced
1 small cucumber, peeled, diced
2 green onions, minced

1 garlic clove, minced
2 tablespoons lemon juice
Salt to taste

Combine all ingredients in a medium bowl. Toss to mix well. Refrigerate to chill. Makes 6 relish servings or 2 large servings.

Parsley-Wheat Salad

Taboulleh (Lebanon/Syria)

Make this traditional salad in the morning and it will be ready in time for dinner.

2 cups fine- to medium-grade bulgur
Water
3 cups finely chopped fresh parsley
   (about 6 bunches)
1/4 cup chopped fresh mint or
   2 tablespoons crushed dried leaf mint
1 tablespoon minced fresh dill or
   1 teaspoon dill weed
1 cup chopped green onions

4 medium tomatoes, diced
1 medium cucumber, peeled, chopped
1 cup olive oil
1 cup lemon juice
Salt and freshly ground pepper to taste
Romaine lettuce leaves
Black Marinated Greek Olives, page 181,
   for garnish
Tomato wedges and mint sprigs for garnish

Place bulgur in a large bowl. Add water to cover and let stand about 1 hour or until bulgur has doubled in size and most of the liquid is absorbed. Drain well and squeeze dry. Add parsley, mint, dill, green onions, tomatoes and cucumber. Toss gently. Add olive oil, lemon juice, salt and pepper. Toss to mix well. Refrigerate. To serve, line a salad bowl with lettuce leaves. Mound salad on lettuce leaves. Garnish with olives, tomato wedges and mint. Makes 12 servings.

How to Make Parsley-Wheat Salad

1/Drain soaked bulgur and squeeze dry.

2/Mound salad in a bowl lined with lettuce leaves. Garnish with olives, tomato wedges and mint.

Pocket-Bread Salad

Fattoush (Arabic)

Triangles of toasted pocket bread give distinction to a tossed salad.

2 (4-inch) or 1 (8-inch) Arabic pocket bread
8 hearts of romaine lettuce
1 medium cucumber, diced
2 large tomatoes, diced
4 green onions, sliced
1/4 cup chopped fresh parsley
1/2 cup chopped fresh mint or
   1 tablespoon crushed dried leaf mint

1/2 cup chopped watercress, if desired
1/2 cup olive oil
1/2 cup lemon juice (5 or 6 lemons)
1 garlic clove, minced
Salt and freshly ground pepper to taste

Place pocket bread on broiler rack 4 inches from heat source. Broil until toasted. Turn and toast other side. Toast should be very crisp but not charred. Break into bite-size pieces or cut into triangles. Place in a large salad bowl. Break lettuce into bowl. Add cucumber, tomatoes, onions, parsley and mint. Add watercress, if desired. Toss. Combine remaining ingredients in a small bowl or jar. Stir or shake to mix well. Pour over salad. Toss to mix well. Serve immediately. Makes 6 servings.

Tomato & Cilantro Salad

Salatat Banadoura Yemenia (Yemen)

Refreshing and colorful.

6 medium tomatoes
1 cup chopped cilantro
Juice of 1/2 lemon (1-1/2 tablespoons)

1/4 cup vegetable oil
1 teaspoon chili powder
Salt and freshly ground pepper to taste

Slice or dice tomatoes into a large, shallow salad bowl. Sprinkle with cilantro. Add remaining ingredients. Toss gently. Makes 6 servings.

Beet Salad

Salatat Shamandar (Morocco)

Beet salad is often arranged with other colorful salads around Moroccan Couscous.

2 (1-lb.) cans julienne-cut beets
Juice of 1 lemon
1 teaspoon orange-blossom water
1 teaspoon sugar

Pinch of ground cinnamon
Pinch of ground cumin
1/2 teaspoon paprika
Salt and freshly ground pepper to taste

Drain beets, reserving 1/2 cup liquid. Place beets and reserved liquid in a deep salad bowl. Add remaining ingredients. Toss gently. Refrigerate to chill. Makes 6 servings.

Greek Village Salad

Choriatiki Salata (Greece)

Almost any vegetable may be added to this beautiful mixed salad.

4 or 5 medium tomatoes, cut in wedges
1 medium cucumber, sliced diagonally
1 small green pepper, thinly sliced
5 green onions, sliced
5 radishes, sliced
1/2 small head romaine lettuce
2 tablespoons chopped fresh dill or
   2 teaspoons dill weed
15 green or black Marinated Greek Olives,
   page 181

Salt and freshly ground black pepper to taste
1/2 cup olive oil
1/4 cup vinegar
1 large garlic clove, minced
2 tablespoons chopped fresh parsley
Pinch of crushed dried leaf oregano
1/4 lb. feta cheese, diced (about 1/2 cup)

Combine tomatoes, cucumber, green pepper, green onions, radishes, lettuce, dill and olives in a large, shallow salad bowl. Add salt and black pepper. Toss to mix well. Combine remaining ingredients except cheese in a small bowl or jar. Stir or shake to mix well. Pour over salad. Toss gently but thoroughly. Garnish with feta cheese. Makes 6 to 8 servings.

Tomato-Chutney Salad

Banadoura Ma' Anba (Iraq)

Iraqis love chutney, which was probably introduced from India during British Colonial rule.

1 cup mango chutney or chopped or
   sliced mango pickles

4 medium tomatoes, cut in wedges
1/4 cup chopped cilantro

Combine all ingredients in a large salad bowl. Toss to mix well. Makes 6 servings.

Arabic Chopped Salad   Photo on cover.

Salata Arabieh (Arabic)

Tossed garden vegetables are flavored with mint, garlic and lemon juice.

4 medium tomatoes, diced
1 medium cucumber, peeled, diced
1 medium, green pepper, diced
4 green onions, chopped
1/2 cup chopped fresh parsley
1 tablespoon chopped fresh mint or
   1 teaspoon crushed dried leaf mint

1 garlic clove, minced
Juice of 2 lemons (6 tablespoons)
1/4 cup olive oil
Salt and freshly ground black pepper to taste

In a large, shallow salad bowl, combine tomatoes, cucumber, green pepper, green onions, parsley and mint. Add garlic, lemon juice, olive oil, salt and black pepper. Toss to mix well. Refrigerate to chill. Makes 6 servings.

Potato-Pickle Salad

Salad-e Khiar Shur (Iran)

For the holidays, add whole cooked cranberries to this mixed-vegetable salad.

2 large potatoes, cooked
5 small dill pickles, sliced or diced
4 medium carrots, cooked, sliced
1 (1-lb.) can red kidney beans, drained
10 radishes, sliced
5 green onions, chopped,
2 cups shredded cabbage (1/2 head)
1/4 cup chopped fresh mint or
   2 tablespoons crushed dried leaf mint

1 teaspoon dried leaf tarragon
3/4 cup olive oil
1/2 cup lemon juice or red-wine vinegar
1 garlic clove, minced
1/2 cup plain yogurt
1 tablespoon Dijon-style mustard
Salt and freshly ground pepper to taste

Dice or slice potatoes into a large salad bowl. Add pickles, carrots, beans, radishes, green onions, cabbage, mint and tarragon. In a small bowl, combine olive oil, lemon juice or vinegar and garlic. Blend in yogurt and mustard. Pour over salad. Toss. Sprinkle with salt and pepper. Refrigerate to chill. Toss before serving. Makes 8 to 12 servings.

Chilled Bean Salad

Salatat Fasouliya (Arabic)

Bean salad is often served as an appetizer.

1 (1-lb. 4-oz.) can garbanzo, fava,
   Great Northern or kidney beans
Juice of 1/2 lemon (1-1/2 tablespoons)
2 tablespoons olive oil

1 garlic clove, minced
Salt and freshly ground pepper to taste
Chopped fresh parsley for garnish

Drain beans and rinse in cold water. Place beans in a medium bowl. Add lemon juice, olive oil, garlic, salt and pepper. Toss gently. Refrigerate to chill. Sprinkle with chopped fresh parsley. Makes 6 servings.

Cucumber-Yogurt Salad

Khiyar bi-Laban (Arabic)

A refreshing addition to a soup or sandwich lunch.

2 garlic cloves
1 teaspoon salt
2 cups plain yogurt

4 medium cucumbers, peeled, sliced
1 teaspoon crushed dried leaf mint

Place garlic and salt in a mortar. Crush. Add 1 tablespoon yogurt to garlic mixture and blend. Place remaining yogurt in a large bowl. Stir in garlic mixture. Add cucumbers. Mix well. Garnish with mint. Makes 6 servings.

Bedouin Potato Salad

Salatat Batata (Arabic)

Arabs use hearts of romaine lettuce to sandwich the potato mixture.

1-1/2 lbs. potatoes (4 or 5)	**2 tablespoons olive oil**
Lightly salted water	**1/4 teaspoon freshly ground pepper**
1/4 cup chopped green onion	**Salt to taste**
1/2 cup chopped fresh parsley	**4 or 5 romaine lettuce leaves**
1 or 2 garlic cloves, minced	**6 tomato wedges**
Juice of 1 lemon (3 tablespoons)	

Place potatoes in a large saucepan. Add lightly salted water to cover. Bring to a boil. Reduce heat and cover. Cook over medium heat until potatoes are tender but not soft, 30 to 40 minutes. Drain and cool. Peel and dice cooled potatoes. Place in a large bowl. Add green onion, parsley, garlic, lemon juice, olive oil, pepper and salt. Toss gently. Refrigerate to chill. Arrange lettuce leaves on a large platter. Top with potato salad. Garnish with tomato wedges. Makes 6 to 8 servings.

Oil & Vinegar Dressing

A typical marinade or dressing for make-ahead Middle Eastern salads.

1 cup vegetable oil	**Salt to taste**
1/2 cup vinegar	**Pinch of sugar, if desired**

Combine all ingredients in a medium bowl or jar. Stir or shake to mix well. Makes 1-1/2 cups.

Variation

Oil & Lemon Dressing (Ladolemono): Substitute lemon juice (about 3 lemons) for vinegar.

Egg & Lemon Sauce

Avgolemono (Greece)

A special flavoring for chicken soup or a topping for meatballs, savory pastry, fish or vegetables.

Juice of 2 lemons (6 tablespoons)	**1 cup hot Chicken Broth, page 36**
2 eggs or egg yolks	**Salt and freshly ground pepper to taste**

Combine lemon juice and eggs or egg yolks in blender. With blender still running, gradually add hot broth. Add salt and pepper. Process until frothy. Makes about 2 cups.

TIP

To blend Egg & Lemon Sauce into hot soup, beat a small amount of hot soup into sauce. Pour sauce into remaining hot soup. Reheat over low heat. If heat is too high, sauce will curdle.

Yogurt Sauce
Laban (Arabic)

Basic sauce tops everything—meats, fish, poultry, pasta, rice, vegetables and even sandwiches.

2 garlic cloves, crushed　　　　　　　　**1 cup plain yogurt**
Salt and freshly ground white pepper to taste

Combine all ingredients in a small bowl. Mix well. Refrigerate to chill. Makes 1 cup.

Variations
Mint-Yogurt Sauce: Add 1 teaspoon crushed dried leaf mint.
Tomato-Yogurt Sauce: Add 1 tablespoon tomato puree or 1 teaspoon tomato paste. Serve on seafood salads.
Yogurt Dressing: Add 1 teaspoon vegetable oil and 1 teaspoon lemon juice or vinegar. Serve as a topping on fried vegetables or as a dressing in salads.

Mixed-Spice Marinade
Baharat (Arabic)

Zesty marinade perks up the flavor of grilled chicken or meat.

1 cup red-wine vinegar or cider vinegar　　　　**1 teaspoon Mixed Spice, page 188**
1 garlic clove, minced

Combine all ingredients in a small bowl. Mix well. Makes about 1 cup or enough to marinate 1-1/2 pounds of meat or poultry.

Sesame-Seed Sauce
Tahini (Arabic)

Prepared sesame-seed sauce, or tahini, is available from most Middle Eastern food shops.

1 cup sesame-seed paste (tahini paste)　　　**About 1/2 cup water**
4 garlic cloves, minced　　　　　　　　　　**1 tablespoon chopped fresh parsley**
Juice of 2 lemons (6 tablespoons)　　　　　　**1 tablespoon olive oil, if desired**
Salt to taste

Combine sesame-seed paste, garlic, lemon juice and salt in blender. Process until smooth. Gradually blend in water for desired consistency. Mixture should be thick for a dip and thin for a topping. Turn into a small bowl. Stir in parsley. For dips, press your finger in center of dip, making an indentation. Fill indentation with olive oil. If sauce is to be used as a topping, leave plain. Makes 2 cups.

TIP

Thick tahini is used as a dip or coating. Thin tahini tops sandwiches, salads, vegetables or fish.

Turkish Salad

S'chug b'Ketchoff (Israel)

Created as a substitute for ketchup, this is actually a dressing for fillings in Arabic pocket bread.

1 (6-oz.) can tomato paste	**1 cup chopped fresh parsley**
1 tablespoon Hot Sauce, below, or harissa	**1 medium tomato, finely chopped**
1/4 teaspoon ground fenugreek	**About 1/4 cup cold water**

Place tomato paste in a medium bowl. Stir in Hot Sauce or harissa, fenugreek, parsley and tomato. Mix well. Thin with water to a smooth paste. Refrigerate to chill. Makes 1-1/2 cups.

Garlic Sauce

Skordalia (Greece)

Bread or potatoes give body to a versatile sauce that can be a dip or a topping for fish and vegetables.

4 garlic cloves	**Salt to taste**
Juice of 2 lemons (6 tablespoons)	**8 to 10 slices white bread, crusts removed**
1/2 cup olive oil	**Water**

In blender, combine garlic, lemon juice, olive oil and salt. Process until smooth. Soak bread in water and squeeze dry. Add moistened bread to garlic mixture. Process until smooth and creamy. Refrigerate sauce in a covered container. Use within 2 or 3 days. Makes about 2 cups.

Variations
Garlic Sauce with Mashed Potato: Substitute 2 cups cold mashed potatoes for moistened bread. If sauce is too thick, add more water. Sauce will thicken when chilled.
Garlic Sauce with Almonds: Add 1/4 cup ground unblanched almonds to mixture. Process until blended. If sauce is too thick, add more water.

Hot Sauce

Shug (Yemen)

A dipping sauce for bread and a seasoning for meats and sauces.

1 lb. hot yellow peppers	**3 teaspoons freshly ground black pepper**
1 garlic head, peeled	**3 teaspoons ground cumin**
2 teaspoons salt	

Remove stems from yellow peppers and discard. Place yellow peppers in food processor with garlic. Process until coarsely ground. Add remaining ingredients. Process until barely smooth. Makes about 2 cups.

Breads

Arabic pocket bread, or *Khubz Arabi,* is probably the most inventive form of bread known. This ancient and incredibly versatile bread is known as *pita* in Greek, *peda* in Persian, *pide* in Turkish and *pocket bread* or *pita* in the United States. Its built-in pocket can be filled with vegetables, salads, meat, cheese or omlets to make a complete meal-in-hand. Or the bread can be used as a utensil for scooping up foods. Arabs have eaten this way for thousands of years. The deftness and elegance with which pieces of bread are dipped or used to enclose foods is awesome to a Westerner accustomed to utensils. The bread is soft enough to dunk into soup and sauces and hard enough to make chewing pleasurable. Many dishes use pocket bread as an edible basket for stews or as a tray for whole barbecued lamb. Crunchy, toasted Arab bread is often broken into pieces and tossed with herbs and vegetables to make Pocket-Bread Salad.

One of the most fascinating variations on the pocket-bread theme is the large Soft Bread Sheets called *nan-e lavash* by Persians, *tonir lavash* by Armenians, and *mar'ook* by Lebanese. This is the same bread East Indians call *tandoor,* after the oven on which it is baked. I have discovered a utensil found in many modern kitchens which works just as well—an inverted wok. A pillow is used to rest the stretched dough to prevent tearing. Baking it requires some practice.

When this bread is baked until it is crisp and crackly, it becomes *lavash,* the large Cracker Bread baked chiefly by Armenians. Cracker Bread is a delightful snack or a salad bread. Armenians also stack wet sheets of lavash between cheese for a breakfast snack, called *surrum.*

Pita bread is the base for a category of pies known as *fatayer.* These pies are filled and formed into turnovers, triangles and open-faced sandwiches. Thyme Bread is a favorite. It's an open-faced sandwich spread with an oily paste called *za'tar,* a mixed spice including sumac, thyme and sesame seeds.

Persian breads are delightfully chewy. They are excellent with cheese, jam and butter for breakfast or for dunking in sauces. They tend to dry quickly, so wrap them carefully in plastic wrap as soon as they are out of the oven.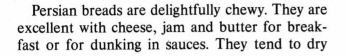

To Toast Nuts & Seeds

Oven Method—Spread nuts or seeds in a single layer on a baking sheet. Toast in a preheated 375F (190C) oven, shaking pan occasionally, until nuts or seeds are golden.
Skillet Method—Spread nuts or seeds in a single layer in a skillet. Toast over low heat, shaking skillet frequently, until nuts or seeds are golden.

Menu

Israeli Picnic

Garbanzo-Bean Patties, page 24
Arabic Pocket Bread, page 74
Garbanzo-Bean Dip, page 19
Eggplant Dip, page 26
Sesame-Seed Sauce, page 64
Parsley-Wheat Salad, page 58
Plate of Tomato Wedges, Feta Cheese
and Olives
Hot Sauce, page 65
Fresh Fruit
Israeli Cigars, page 164
Turkish Coffee, page 32

Moroccan Bread   Photo on page 147.

Khubz (Morocco)

Moroccans use the crust of this delicious bread to scoop up saucy foods.

2-1/2 cups warm water (110F, 45C)
1 (1/4-oz.) pkg. active dry yeast
   (1 tablespoon)

1 tablespoon salt
About 6 cups all-purpose flour

Pour warm water into a large bowl. Sprinkle yeast over water. Stir until dissolved. Add salt. Gradually stir in about 6 cups flour until dough pulls away from side of bowl. Turn out onto a floured surface. Knead, adding more flour if necessary, until dough is smooth and elastic. Shape dough into a 12-inch roll. Cut roll into three 4-inch portions. Shape each portion into a ball, then into a dome-shaped loaf tapering from 1 inch high in center to 1/4 inch around edges. Place loaves on ungreased baking sheets. Cover with a dry cloth towel and let rise until doubled in bulk, about 1 hour. Preheat oven to 350F (175C). Make slashes in each loaf on 4 sides, crisscrossing at corners, if desired. Bake 20 to 30 minutes or until loaves are golden brown. Remove from baking sheets and cool on a rack. Bread keeps well for several days. Serve warm or wrap cooled bread in plastic wrap and refrigerate. Bread may be stored for several days. Makes 3 loaves.

Egg Braid

Challah (Israel)

For Rosh Hashanah, the Hebrew New Year, braided Sabbath bread is shaped into a round loaf.

1-3/4 cups warm water (110F, 45C)
1/4 cup vegetable oil
2 tablespoons honey
2 tablespoons sugar
2 teaspoons salt
1 (1/4-oz.) pkg. active dry yeast
   (1 tablespoon)

1 whole egg
3 egg yolks
About 7-1/2 cups all-purpose flour
1 whole egg, beaten
1/4 cup sesame seeds

Combine warm water, oil, honey, sugar and salt in a large bowl. Sprinkle yeast over mixture. Stir to blend. Beat in 1 whole egg and egg yolks. Gradually stir in about 7-1/2 cups flour until dough pulls away from side of bowl. Cover with a dry cloth towel and let rest 15 minutes. Lightly oil a baking sheet and set aside. Turn out dough onto a floured surface. Knead, adding more flour if necessary, until dough is smooth and elastic. Divide into 3 equal portions. Roll each portion between your hands to a 12- to 14-inch rope. Place on prepared baking sheet. Press ends together and braid ropes. Tuck ends under. Cover with a dry cloth towel and let rise until doubled in bulk. Preheat oven to 350F (175C). Brush braid with beaten egg. Sprinkle with sesame seeds. Bake 45 minutes or until loaf is browned and sounds hollow when tapped. Remove from baking sheet and cool on a rack. Serve warm or wrap cooled bread in plastic wrap and refrigerate. Makes 1 large loaf.

How to Make Moroccan Bread

1/Shape dough into dome-shaped loaves tapering from 1 inch high in center to 1/4 inch around edges.

2/If desired, make slashes in each risen loaf on 4 sides, crisscrossing at corners.

Cracker Bread

Lavash (Armenia)

Crisp matzo-like cracker bread is perfect with soups and salads.

1-1/2 cups warm water (110F, 45C)
1 (1/4-oz.) pkg. active dry yeast
   (1 tablespoon)
1 teaspoon salt

2 cups all-purpose flour
About 2 cups whole-wheat flour
1/2 cup toasted sesame seeds, page 67

Pour warm water into a large bowl. Sprinkle yeast over water. Stir until dissolved. Add salt. Combine all-purpose flour and 2 cups whole-wheat flour in a large bowl. Stir flour mixture into yeast mixture until dough pulls away from side of bowl. Turn out onto a floured surface. Knead, adding more whole-wheat flour if necessary, until dough is smooth and elastic. Shape into a ball. Place ball in a large greased bowl. Turn dough to grease all sides. Cover with a dry cloth towel. Let rise in a warm place until doubled in bulk, about 1-1/2 hours. Punch down and let rise again until doubled in bulk, about 30 minutes. Preheat oven to 400F (205C). Lightly grease 2 baking sheets. Set aside. Pinch off a piece of dough about 2 inches in diameter. On a lightly floured surface, roll out each piece of dough to a paper-thin circle, about 9 inches in diameter. Place 1 or 2 on each baking sheet. Sprinkle each circle with 1 tablespoon sesame seeds. Bake 5 to 6 minutes or until bread is blistered and lightly browned. Place pale-side up under broiler a few seconds to brown lightly. Cool. Wrap in plastic wrap and store in a dry place. Makes 8 crackers.

Persian Flat Bread   Photo on page 75.

Nan-e Barbari (Iran)

Ridges in the bread are typically Iranian. Change the pattern as directed below for Armenian Peda Bread.

1/4 cup warm water (110F, 45C)
1 (1/4-oz.) pkg. active dry yeast
  (1 tablespoon)
About 5 cups all-purpose flour
1-1/2 teaspoons salt

3 tablespoons sugar
3 tablespoons butter or margarine, melted
2 cups warm water (110F, 45C)
Milk
1/4 cup sesame seeds

Pour 1/4 cup warm water into a large bowl. Sprinkle yeast over water. Stir until dissolved. Place 5 cups flour in a large bowl. Make a well in center. Add yeast mixture, salt, sugar, butter or margarine and 2 cups warm water. Gradually stir flour into liquid mixture in well until dough is thoroughly mixed. Dough will be sticky. Turn out onto a floured surface. Knead, adding more flour if necessary, until dough is smooth and elastic. Place in a large greased bowl. Turn dough to grease all sides. Cover with a dry cloth towel. Let stand until doubled in bulk, about 1 hour. Preheat oven to 350F (175C). Punch down dough. Divide into 4 equal portions. Shape each portion into a ball. Place on a floured surface and sprinkle with flour. Cover with a dry cloth towel. Let rest 20 minutes. Roll out each portion of dough to a 12'' x 6'' oval. Place on ungreased baking sheets. Use the side of your thumb to make ridges 1 inch apart lengthwise on each oval. Brush with milk. Sprinkle each oval with 1 tablespoon sesame seeds. Let rest 15 minutes. Bake 20 to 30 minutes or until golden brown. Remove from baking sheets and cool on racks. Serve warm or wrap cooled bread in plastic wrap and refrigerate. Makes 4 flat breads.

Variations

Armenian Peda Bread: After making ridges in dough, press with fingers all over surface of dough to make the traditional surface pattern. Continue with recipe.
Batons: Cut each oval into 12'' x 1/2'' strips. Brush with milk and sprinkle with sesame seeds. Bake 15 minutes or until golden brown. Makes 12 batons.
Bread Rings: Shape each ball into a log. Cut log into 4 equal pieces. Roll each piece into a 7-inch rope. Shape into a ring, pinching ends to seal. Place on baking sheets. Brush with milk and sprinkle with sesame seeds. Bake 15 minutes or until golden. Remove from baking sheets. Makes about 16 rings.

Greek Pita Bread

Pita (Greece)

Wrap this soft bread around a meat filling to make Souvlaki, below.

1 cup all-purpose flour
1 cup whole-wheat flour
1 teaspoon salt

About 1-1/4 cups water
Vegetable oil

In a large bowl, combine all-purpose flour and whole-wheat flour. Mix well. Stir in just enough water to allow dough to pull away from side of bowl. If necessary, add a few drops more water to make dough pliable. Turn out onto a floured surface. Knead with your floured hands until dough is soft and smooth. Pinch off pieces of dough about 1-1/2 inches in diameter. Shape into balls. Cover with a dry cloth towel and let rest 10 minutes. Roll out to a circle about 6 inches in diameter. Heat griddle over medium-high heat. Lighly grease griddle. Begin cooking when a drop of water sizzles on hot griddle. Cook each dough circle until browned underneath. Turn and brown other side. Bread will puff slightly when cooked. Serve warm or place immediately in plastic bags to keep soft. Makes 6 or 7 pita breads.

Greek Pita Sandwiches

Souvlaki (Greece)

A tavern in the Athens flea market served these delicious sandwiches with beer.

1 lb. ground beef or lamb
1 teaspoon crushed dried leaf oregano
Salt and freshly ground pepper to taste
1 small onion
2 cups shredded cabbage
1 large tomato, chopped

2 tablespoons lemon juice
2 tablespoons olive oil
Salt to taste
6 Greek Pita Breads, above, or
**   small flour tortillas**
Paprika

Combine ground meat, oregano, salt and pepper to taste in a medium bowl. Mix thoroughly. Pinch off pieces of mixture about 1 inch in diameter. Form into small sausage shapes or mold around a skewer in a sausage shape. Preheat oven to broil or prepare barbecue grill with medium-hot coals. Place meat under broiler or on grill 4 inches from source of heat. Cook, turning as necessary, until browned on all sides, about 5 minutes. Cut onion in half lengthwise, then slice to make long, thin strips. Combine cabbage, onion strips, tomato, lemon juice, olive oil and salt to taste in a medium bowl. Toss to mix well. Place 2 or 4 cooked sausage shapes on each pita bread or tortilla. Top with cabbage mixture. Sprinkle with paprika. Serve immediately. Makes 6 sandwiches.

Variation

Greek-Style Hamburgers: Shape meat mixture into hamburger patties. Serve on hamburger buns with desired toppings.

Soft Bread Sheets

Khubz Mar'ook (Lebanon)

A wok supplies the dome-shape required for cooking this oversized bread.

Arabic Pocket-Bread dough, page 74   **Oil for wok**
All-purpose flour

If using a new wok, season it according to manufacturer's directions. Be sure to scour the outside of your wok well during the seasoning process. Prepare dough up to the point of shaping into balls. Pinch off pieces of dough 3 inches in diameter. Place on a floured surface. Sprinkle with flour. Roll out each piece to a circle 12 inches in diameter. Place backs of your hands under dough and stretch circle by rotating it over both hands. Pull and stretch carefully to increase diameter of circle to about 20 inches. Let rest 10 minutes on a pillow or cushion covered with a clean cloth. Invert a well-cleaned wok with handles over medium-high heat. Lightly oil outside of wok. Heat until a drop of water sizzles on bottom of inverted wok. Place an enlarged dough circle on hot wok. Cook until dough is browned underneath. Turn and brown lightly on other side. Bread will be soft and floppy. Fold hot bread and place in a plastic bag. Serve warm. Or cool in bag and refrigerate. If baking is preferred, preheat oven to 450F (230C). Place dough circle on a lightly floured board. Slide circle off board onto oven floor. Bake 5 minutes or until set. Place pale-side up under broiler to brown, if desired. Makes 8 to 10 bread sheets.

Bread Sticks

Ka'ak (Syria/Lebanon)

Excellent with soup, salad and even cocktails.

2 cups warm water (110F, 45C)   **2 tablespoons ground anise seeds**
2 (1/4-oz.) pkgs. active dry yeast   **1 teaspoon caraway seeds**
  (2 tablespoons)   **1 teaspoon ground black-cherry kernels**
1/2 teaspoon salt   **(mahlab)**
1/2 cup shortening   **About 6 cups all-purpose flour**
1/2 cup butter or margarine   **1/4 cup sesame seeds, if desired**
1/4 cup vegetable oil

Pour warm water into a large bowl. Sprinkle yeast over water. Stir until dissolved. Add salt, shortening, butter or margarine, oil, anise seeds, caraway seeds and ground cherry kernels. Mix well. Gradually stir about 6 cups flour into yeast mixture until dough pulls away from side of bowl. Dough will be sticky. Turn out onto a floured surface. Knead, adding more flour if necessary, until dough is smooth and elastic. Shape into a ball. Place in a greased bowl. Turn to grease all sides. Cover with a dry cloth towel and let rise until doubled in bulk, about 1-1/2 hours. Preheat oven to 350F (175C). Pinch off pieces of dough 1 inch in diameter. Roll each piece into an 8-inch rope. Fold in half, hold one end in each hand and twist. Place twists on baking sheets. Sprinkle with sesame seeds, if desired. Bake 10 to 15 minutes or until crisp. Makes 36 sticks.

TIP ◇◇◇◇◇◇◇◇◇◇◇◇◇◇◇◇◇◇◇◇◇◇◇◇◇◇

Pinches of ground black-cherry kernels add a fragrant fruity flavor to breads, cakes and cookies. Use sparingly.

How to Make Soft Bread Sheets

1/ Place backs of your hands under dough circle and stretch by rotating it over both hands. Let stretched dough rest on a pillow covered with a clean cloth.

2/Place dough circle over inverted hot wok. Cook until dough is browned underneath. Turn and brown lightly on other side. Fold hot bread and place in a plastic bag. Serve warm. Or cool in bag and refrigerate.

Thyme Bread

Fatayer Za'tar (Syria/Lebanon)

Za'tar is a blend of thyme and sumac. Look for it in Middle Eastern grocery stores.

Arabic Pocket-Bread dough, page 74   **2 tablespoons olive oil**
1/4 cup za'tar

Prepare dough up to the point of shaping. Preheat oven to 350F (175C). Mix za'tar with olive oil in a small bowl. Divide dough into 24 equal portions. Shape each portion into a ball. Roll out each ball to a 7-inch circle. Spread za'tar mixture thinly over each circle to within 1/2 inch of edge. Bake 15 minutes. Place under broiler 1 minute, if desired. Serve immediately or cool, stack, wrap in plastic and refrigerate. Makes 24 servings.

Arabic Pocket Bread   Photo on cover.

Khubz Arabi (Arabic)

As the bread cooks, it puffs, forming a pocket for stuffing.

2-1/2 cups warm water (110F, 45C)   1 tablespoon salt
2 (1/4-oz.) pkgs. active dry yeast   About 6 cups all-purpose flour, sifted
  (2 tablespoons)   2 tablespoons vegetable oil

Pour warm water into a large bowl. Sprinkle yeast over water. Stir until dissolved. Add salt. Grad-ually add 6 cups flour and oil, kneading constantly, until dough is smooth and elastic. If dough sticks to your hands, add more flour. Place in a large greased bowl. Turn dough to grease all sides. Cover with a dry cloth towel and let rise in a warm place until doubled in bulk, about 1-1/2 hours. Punch down gently. Preheat oven to 375F (190C). Divide dough into 24 equal portions. If large pocket breads are preferred, divide into 12 portions. Shape each portion into a smooth ball. Place on a floured surface. Sprinkle tops lightly with flour and cover with a dry cloth towel. Let rest 15 minutes. Grease baking sheets. Roll out each portion of dough to a 6-inch circle for small pocket breads or a 14-inch circle for large. Place on prepared baking sheets. Bake 10 to 12 minutes for small pocket breads, 12 to 15 minutes for large pocket breads or until bread puffs. If desired, place pale-side up under broiler to brown slightly. Place hot bread immediately in a plastic bag. Serve warm. Or cool in bag and refrigerate. Makes 12 or 24 pocket breads.

Pocket-Bread Sandwiches

Pocket bread lends itself to numerous sandwich combinations. Sample some of these popular pita fill-ings with their appropriate sauces and relishes.

Eggplant-Salad Sandwich
Fried Eggplant Slices, page 84
Arabic Chopped Salad, page 60
Sesame-Seed Sauce, page 64

Ground-Meat-Kebab Sandwich
Chopped lettuce
Diced tomato
Ground-Meat Kebabs, page 126
Sliced dill pickle
Hot Sauce, page 65, or harissa
Chopped green onion

Egg Sandwich
Chopped lettuce
Herb Omlets (individual) page 51
Diced tomato
Sliced dill pickle
Sesame-Seed Sauce, page 64
Chopped green onion

Souvlaki Sandwich
Marinated Kebabs, page 138
Chopped lettuce
Diced tomatoes
Diced green onion
Garlic Sauce, page 65

Zucchini-Patty Sandwich
Zucchini Patties, page 89
Arabic Chopped Salad, page 60
Sliced dill pickle
Turkish Salad, page 65

Roast-Beef Sandwich
Chopped lettuce
Roast-Beef Slices
Zucchini-Relish Salad, page 57
Garlic Sauce, page 65
Chopped green onion

Clockwise from the top: Persian Flat Bread, page 70; Arabic Pocket Bread;
Sesame Baguettes, page 76; and Sesame Bread Rings, page 76.

Arabic Lamb Pies

Sfeeha (Arabic)

Basic Arabic Pocket-Bread dough is used to make pies of many shapes and with a variety of fillings.

Arabic Pocket-Bread dough, page 74
2 lbs. coarsely ground lean lamb
1 large onion, grated
Juice of 2 lemons (6 tablespoons)

1/2 cup plain yogurt
Salt and freshly ground pepper to taste
1/2 cup pine nuts
2 tablespoons olive oil

Prepare dough up to the point of shaping. Preheat oven to 375F (190C). Lightly grease rimmed baking sheets. Combine lamb, onion, lemon juice, yogurt, salt, pepper and pine nuts in a large bowl. Divide dough into 24 equal portions. Roll out each portion to a 6-inch circle. Place about 1/4 cup meat mixture in center of each circle. Fold 3 sides of circle over filling to make a triangle. Pinch seams together to seal. Arrange meat pies on prepared baking sheets. Bake 20 to 25 minutes or until golden. Remove from oven and brush with olive oil. Pies become darker brown after brushing with olive oil. Immediately remove pies from baking sheets. Makes 24 pies.

Sesame Bread Rings   Photo on page 75.

Cheoreg (Armenia)

Chewy bread rings, or baguettes, are a close cousin to the bagel.

1 cup warm milk (110F, 45C)
1 (1/4-oz.) pkg. active dry yeast
  (1 tablespoon)
1/2 cup butter or margarine, melted
3 eggs, beaten
1 teaspoon salt
1 teaspoon sugar

1 teaspoon ground black-cherry kernels
  (mahlab), if desired
About 5 cups all-purpose flour
1 egg
1 tablespoon water
1/2 cup sesame seeds
1/4 cup water

Pour warm milk into a large bowl. Sprinkle yeast over milk. Stir until dissolved. Add butter or margarine, 3 beaten eggs, salt, sugar and ground cherry kernels. Mix well. Add about 5 cups flour or enough to make a soft dough that does not stick to your hands. Turn out onto a floured surface. Knead until dough is smooth and elastic. Place in a large greased bowl. Turn dough to grease all sides. Cover with a dry cloth towel. Let rise until doubled in bulk, about 1 hour. Preheat oven to 350F (175C). Lightly grease 2 large baking sheets. Pinch off pieces of dough about 2 inches in diameter. Roll into 10-inch ropes. Shape each rope into a ring slightly overlapping at ends. Pinch ends together. Place on prepared baking sheets. Mix 1 egg with 1 tablespoon water. Brush over rings. Sprinkle each ring with about 1 teaspoon sesame seeds. Bake 15 to 20 minutes or until golden brown, brushing occasionally with some of the 1/4 cup water to crisp top. Remove from baking sheets and cool on racks. Serve warm or wrap cooled bread in plastic wrap and refrigerate. Makes about 25 rings.

Variation

Sesame Baguettes: Instead of shaping ropes into rings, taper ropes at each end. Place on baking sheet. Brush with egg wash and sprinkle with sesame seeds. Bake as directed for rings.

How to Make Arabic Lamb Pies

1/Roll out each portion of dough to a 6-inch circle. Place about 1/4 cup meat mixture in center of each circle.

2/Fold 3 sides of circle over filling to make a triangle. Pinch seams together to seal.

Cheese Pies

Fatayer Ma' Jebneh (Syria/Lebanon)

When you're expecting a crowd, make and fill these pies a few hours ahead of time.

Arabic Pocket-Bread dough, page 74
1 egg
2 cups ricotta cheese or Yogurt Cheese,
 page 178

1 medium onion, chopped
1 teaspoon crushed dried leaf mint or
 1 tablespoon chopped fresh mint

Prepare dough up to the point of shaping. Preheat oven to 350F (175C). Beat egg in a medium bowl. Blend in cheese, onion and mint. Divide dough into 24 equal portions. Shape each portion into a ball. Roll out each ball to a 6-inch circle. Place 1 tablespoon cheese mixture in center of a circle. Fold 3 sides of circle over filling to make a triangle. Pinch seams together. Place on ungreased baking sheets. Bake 15 minutes or until golden brown. Serve immediately. Makes 24 pies.

Variation

Substitute 3 packages of refrigerator rolls or biscuits or 3 loaves frozen bread dough. If using frozen bread dough, thaw and cut each loaf into 8 pieces.

Biscuit Bread

Bogatsa (Greece)

This easy loaf is marvelous with a salad or soup.

About 4 cups all-purpose flour	2 eggs
4 teaspoons baking powder	1 cup milk
1/2 cup sugar	1 egg, beaten
1/2 cup butter or margarine, room temperature	2 tablespoons sesame seeds

Preheat oven to 350F (175C). Grease two 14" x 8" loaf pans or round 8-inch cake pans. Combine 4 cups flour, baking powder and sugar in a large bowl. Cut in butter or margarine with a pastry blender or 2 knives. Stir in 2 eggs and milk. Mix until a sticky dough is formed. Turn out onto a floured surface. Knead, adding more flour if necessary, until dough is smooth. Shape into 2 smooth loaves to fit in pans. Place in prepared pans. Brush with beaten egg. Sprinkle with sesame seeds. Bake 20 to 30 minutes or until golden. Remove from pans and cool on racks. Serve warm or wrap cooled bread in plastic wrap and refrigerate. Makes 2 loaves.

New Year's Bread

Vasilopita (Greece)

A coin is hidden in the bread. Whoever finds it will have good luck in the New Year.

1/2 cup water	3/4 cup warm milk (110F, 45C)
1 whole nutmeg	1/2 teaspoon salt
1 cinnamon stick	1/2 cup butter or margarine, melted and cooled to warm
1/2 teaspoon whole cloves	
Pinch of anise seeds	3 eggs, room temperature
1 tablespoon grated orange peel	1 cup sugar
2 (1/4-oz.) pkgs. active dry yeast (2 tablespoons)	About 5 cups all-purpose flour

Pour 1/2 cup water into a small saucepan. Add nutmeg, cinnamon, cloves, anise seeds and orange peel. Bring to a boil. Boil 5 minutes to blend flavors. Strain 1/4 cup into a large bowl. Discard remaining water. Cool spiced water to warm. Sprinkle yeast into warm spiced water. Add warm milk, salt and butter or margarine. Beat eggs in a small bowl. Beat in sugar. Add to milk mixture. Gradually add about 5 cups flour until dough pulls away from side of bowl. Turn out onto floured board. Knead with floured hands, adding more flour if necessary, until dough is smooth and elastic. Shape dough into a ball. Place in a large greased bowl. Turn dough to grease all sides. Cover and let rise until doubled in bulk, about 1-1/2 hours. Punch down and let rise 2 more times. Preheat oven to 350F (175C). Grease 2 round 8-inch pans. Divide dough into 2 equal portions. Shape each portion into a ball. If desired, wrap 2 coins in 2 small pieces of foil; insert a wrapped coin into each ball. Place each ball in a prepared pan. Pat down. Brush with beaten egg and sprinkle with sesame seeds. Let rest 30 minutes. Bake 30 minutes or until golden brown. Remove from pans and cool on racks. Serve warm or wrap cooled bread in plastic wrap and refrigerate. Makes 2 loaves.

Greek Holiday Bread

Tsourekia (Greece)

Mary Deamos of Pasadena shared her excellent recipe for a festive bread.

1 cup warm water (110F, 45C)	**1-1/2 cups sugar**
2 (1/4-oz.) pkgs. active dry yeast	**2 large eggs**
(2 tablespoons)	**1/2 cup orange juice**
Pinch of sugar	**About 9 cups all-purpose flour**
2 cups milk	**1 egg, beaten**
1/4 cup butter or margarine	**1/4 cup sesame seeds**

Pour warm water into a large bowl. Sprinkle yeast over water. Add pinch of sugar. Stir until yeast is dissolved. Combine milk, butter or margarine and 1-1/2 cups sugar in a medium saucepan. Scald by heating mixture until bubbles appear around edges. Beat eggs in a small bowl. Stir in orange juice. Add about 1/2 cup milk mixture to egg mixture. Stir into milk mixture in saucepan until blended. Cool to warm. Add to yeast mixture. Stir until blended. Stir about 9 cups flour into yeast mixture until dough pulls away from side of bowl. Turn out onto a floured surface. Knead, adding more flour if necessary, until dough is smooth and elastic. Shape into a ball. Place in a greased bowl. Turn to grease all sides. Cover with a dry cloth towel and let rise until doubled in bulk, about 1 hour. Preheat oven to 350F (175C). Grease baking sheets. Set aside. For large rolls, divide dough into 16 equal pieces and shape as desired. For small rolls, divide dough into 32 equal pieces and shape as desired. For braids, divide dough into 2 equal portions. Divide each portion into 3 equal pieces. Shape each piece into a 12- to 14-inch rope. Pinch ropes together at one end. Braid and pinch ends together. Place on prepared baking sheets. Brush with beaten egg. Sprinkle with sesame seeds. Let rest 30 minutes. Bake large rolls 20 to 30 minutes. Bake small rolls 15 to 20 minutes. Bake braids 30 to 40 minutes. Bread should be golden. Remove from baking sheets and cool on racks. Serve warm. Or wrap cooled bread in plastic wrap and refrigerate. Makes 16 large rolls, 32 small rolls or 2 braids.

Variation

Greek Easter Braid: Shape ropes and braid as directed. Insert colored hard-cooked eggs in braid indentations. Bake as directed.

G reek and Turkish cooks have foolproof methods for perking up ordinary vegetables. Greeks cook their vegetables in oil without water over low heat. The secret is to keep the heat low enough to prevent scorching. The drawback, if you prefer your vegetables on the crisp side, is that vegetables prepared the Greek way are usually slightly overcooked and rather soft. But you can adjust the cooking time so the vegetables are done to the crispness you desire. Turkish cooks fry vegetables in oil and butter, or just in olive oil. They season them simply with salt and pepper and stir in a little yogurt. Whichever basic method you choose for cooking vegetables, you'll find the flavor is superb.

Yogurt plays an important role in Middle Eastern vegetable cookery. Any plain or garlic-flavored yogurt can be served with sautéed, fried or baked vegetables.

Stuffing vegetables is one way to expand the function of simple vegetables from side dish to main dish. Recipes for both meatless and meat-filled stuffed vegetables are given in this section. Stuffed vegetables may be served hot or cold and usually are made in quantities that will supplement lunch the next day or that can be served to unexpected guests. For vegetarians, cabbage stuffed with bulgur makes a delightfully nourishing main dish.

There is no cuisine in the world that plays up eggplant as much as that of the Middle East. That's because eggplant is native to southeastern Asia—probably India—where it is said to have been cultivated over 4,000 years ago. Arabs were the first to import eggplant to the Middle East and from there to Spain. The Moors of Andulusia in Spain introduced eggplant to the Mediterranean region. A particularly interesting and satisfying eggplant casserole is *Mousakas* from Greece.

Because meat is a rare commodity for many Middle Easterners, vegetarian dishes flourish. Plant proteins are classified as *incomplete proteins* because they are deficient in one or more of the essential amino acids. Combining different protein foods, such as legumes with nuts, cereals with beans, and grains with legumes, boosts the protein value of each meal. In Egypt, the national bean dish called *Fool* has been a mainstay of the diet since the days of the pharoahs. It is a bean pot with plenty of juices to sop up with flat bread. Even today, an Egyptian begins his day at a local shop with a bowl of fava beans. The beans have cooked slowly overnight in huge narrow-necked vats. By morning they are ready to ladle into plates to eat as Egyptians like best—dressed with oil and lemon juice and some green onion.

Some people lack an enzyme which is necessary for the digestion of fava beans. They may suffer mild discomfort or an extreme toxic reaction from eating this type of bean. If you suspect—through heredity or from your own experience—that you have this problem, avoid eating fava beans.

Falafels which are bean patties or balls have replaced meat in the Middle Eastern diet for thousands of years. Today, in Israel, falafels have almost reached the status of a national dish. They can be patted into large or small patties for a nutritious main dish, or shaped into tiny balls to serve with cocktails or to fill pocket bread. You can find the recipe on page 24. ✄

Menu

Vegetarian Dinner	Baghdad Supper
Yogurt Drink, page 28 Vegetarian Skillet, page 87 Greek Village Salad, page 60 Moroccan Bread, page 68 Bananas Wrapped in Filo, page 166 Floral Tea, page 30	Plate of Olives and Cucumber Sticks Tomato-Chutney Salad, page 60 Spiced Meat Skillet, page 125 Saffron Rice, page 100 Arabic Pocket Bread, page 74, or French Bread Fresh Fruit Iraqi Tea, page 30

Mixed-Vegetable Casserole

Türlü (Turkey)

Any seasonal vegetables may be used for this casserole.

2 large potatoes, peeled, thickly sliced
2 medium zucchini, thickly sliced
1 lb. green beans, cleaned, trimmed, or
   1 (10-oz.) pkg. frozen cut green beans,
   thawed
1 lb. okra, trimmed, or
   1 (10-oz.) pkg. frozen okra, thawed
2 onions, thinly sliced

Salt and freshly ground pepper to taste
1/2 cup chopped fresh parsley
1/4 cup chopped fresh dill or
   2 tablespoons dill weed
4 medium tomatoes, diced
1 cup Chicken Broth, page 36, or water
1/3 cup olive oil

Preheat oven to 350F (175C). Arrange layers of potatoes, zucchini, green beans, okra and onions in a large baking pan. Sprinkle with salt and pepper, parsley and dill. Top with tomatoes. Carefully pour broth or water into casserole. Sprinkle with olive oil. Cover. Bake 1-1/4 to 1-1/2 hours or until vegetables are tender. Serve hot. Makes 10 to 12 servings.

Variations

Vegetable Casserole with Eggplant: Substitute 1 small unpeeled eggplant, sliced, for green beans or okra. If desired, sauté eggplant slices in oil before adding to casserole.
Vegetable Casserole with Green Peppers: Substitute 2 large green peppers, sliced, for okra or green beans. If desired, sauté pepper slices in oil before adding to casserole.

Vegetarian Stuffed Cabbage

Siyami (Arabic)

Bulgur and garbanzo beans add protein to this meatless dish.

1 cup medium-grade bulgur
Water
1 medium cabbage
1 cup water
1 (1-lb.) can garbanzo beans, drained
1 medium tomato, chopped
1/2 cup chopped fresh parsley

1 medium onion, chopped
1/4 teaspoon ground cinnamon
1/4 teaspoon ground cumin
Salt and freshly ground pepper to taste
2 tablespoons olive oil
1 (10-oz.) can tomato juice

Place bulgur in a large bowl. Cover with water. Let stand 30 minutes. Place cabbage in a large saucepan. Add 1 cup water. Cover. Simmer over low heat 10 minutes or until outer leaves are barely softened. Drain in a colander. Cool. Puree garbanzo beans in blender or food processor. Set aside. Drain bulgur if necessary, squeezing out excess moisture. In a large bowl, combine drained bulgur, pureed garbanzo beans, tomato, parsley, onion, cinnamon, cumin, salt and pepper. Add olive oil. Mix well. Preheat oven to 350F (175C). Grease a 13" x 9" baking pan. Separate leaves from cabbage. Trim off bulky stem ends. Place about 1 tablespoon filling in center of each leaf; use more filling if leaves are large. Fold in sides. Roll up jelly-roll fashion. Place cabbage rolls seam-sides down in prepared baking pan in a single layer. Pour tomato juice over rolls. Cover. Bake 45 minutes to 1 hour or until filling is tender. Makes 6 to 8 servings.

Eggplant Casserole

Mousakas (Greece)

A delicious and inexpensive Greek classic!

Meat Sauce, see below
Cream Sauce, see below
2 large eggplants, unpeeled

Salt
Oil for frying
1/4 cup grated Parmesan cheese (3/4 oz.)

Meat Sauce:
2 tablespoons butter or margarine
1 onion, chopped
1-1/2 lbs. ground lean beef
1/2 teaspoon ground cinnamon

Pinch of sugar
1/2 cup chopped fresh parsley
Salt and freshly ground pepper to taste
2 tablespoons tomato paste

Cream Sauce:
2-1/2 cups milk
6 tablespoons butter or margarine
1/2 cup all-purpose flour
6 egg yolks

Pinch of ground nutmeg
1/4 cup grated Parmesan cheese (3/4 oz.)
Salt and freshly ground white pepper to taste

Prepare Meat Sauce and Cream Sauce. Set aside. Cut eggplants crosswise into 1/2-inch slices. Sprinkle lightly with salt. Let stand 15 minutes to leach out bitter flavor. Drain and pat dry with paper towels. Pour oil 1/2 inch deep into a large skillet. Heat to 365F (185C) on a deep-fry thermometer. At this temperature, a 1-inch cube of bread will turn golden brown in 60 seconds. Fry 3 or 4 eggplant slices at a time, turning once, until golden on both sides. Add more oil as needed. Drain on paper towels. Preheat oven to 350F (175C). Arrange a third of the fried egg-plant slices in a single layer in a 13" x 9" baking pan. Sprinkle with 2 tablespoons Parmesan cheese. Pour half the Meat Sauce over eggplant layer. Place another third of the eggplant slices over Meat Sauce. Top with remaining Meat Sauce and eggplant slices. Spread Cream Sauce evenly over eggplant slices. Sprinkle with remaining Parmesan cheese. Bake 1 hour or until top is golden brown and bubbly. Serve hot. Makes 8 to 12 servings.

Meat Sauce:
Melt butter or margarine in a large saucepan or skillet. Add onion. Sauté until tender. Add beef, cinnamon, sugar, parsley, salt and pepper. Cook until meat is browned and crumbly. Stir in tomato paste. Cook 5 minutes to blend flavors. Makes about 3 cups.

Cream Sauce:
In a 1-quart saucepan, heat milk until bubbles appear around edges. Melt butter or margarine in a large saucepan. Stir in flour until smooth. Stir over low heat until mixture is golden. Gradually Stir in hot milk. Cook, stirring constantly, until thickened. Remove from heat. Beat egg yolks in a small bowl. Stir a small amount of milk mixture into beaten egg yolks. Add egg mixture to hot milk mixture in saucepan. Stir in nutmeg, Parmesan cheese, salt and pepper. Return to heat. Cook and stir until sauce is smooth and thickened. Makes about 3 cups.

TIP

Eggplant slices may be broiled instead of fried. Brush each slice with oil. Place on broiler rack 3 inches from source of heat. Broil until golden. Turn and broil other side until golden.

Fainting Imam

Patlican Imam Bayıldı (Turkey)

According to legend, the Imam, or Moslem priest, was so enchanted by this stuffed eggplant, he swooned.

8 Japanese eggplants
3 medium onions
1/2 cup vegetable oil
2 medium tomatoes, diced
2 medium, green or red bell peppers,
   cut in 3" x 1/4" strips
1 small red or yellow hot pepper,
   seeded, minced

2 tablespoons chopped fresh parsley
5 garlic cloves, minced
Salt and freshly ground black pepper to taste
2 tablespoons olive oil
1-1/2 cups Beef Broth, page 36, or
   Chicken Broth, page 36
Juice of 1/2 lemon (1-1/2 tablespoons)
1 teaspoon sugar

Rinse eggplants and pat dry. Slit each eggplant lengthwise from end to end almost all the way through. Cut onions in half lengthwise, then slice to make long, thin strips. Heat vegetable oil in a large skillet. Add eggplants. Cook over medium-high heat, turning frequently to blister on all sides, about 2 minutes. Drain on paper towels. Add onion strips, half the tomatoes, bell peppers, hot pepper, parsley, garlic, salt and black pepper. Sauté until onions are barely tender. Set aside. Preheat oven to 350F (175C). Grease a large baking pan. Place eggplants in prepared baking pan slit-side up. Spoon onion mixture into each slit, pressing with spoon to pack tightly. Sprinkle stuffing with olive oil. Top with remaining tomatoes. Pour broth into pan. Sprinkle eggplants with lemon juice and sugar. Cover. Bake 40 minutes to 1 hour or until eggplants and stuffing are very soft. Makes 8 servings.

Fried Eggplant Slices

Dabgevadz Sempug (Armenia)

Excellent as a side dish or as a filling for Arabic pocket bread.

1 small eggplant, unpeeled
Salt and freshly ground black pepper
2 eggs
1/4 cup all-purpose flour

Oil for frying
1 medium tomato, sliced
1 medium, green bell pepper,
   cut in thin strips

Cut eggplant crosswise into 1/4-inch slices. Sprinkle lightly with salt and black pepper. Let stand 15 minutes to leach out bitter flavor. Drain and pat dry on paper towels. Beat eggs in a shallow bowl. Stir in flour until smooth. Pour oil 1/2 inch deep into a large skillet. Heat to 375F (190C) on a deep-fry thermometer. At this temperature, a 1-inch cube of bread will turn golden brown in 50 seconds. Dip each eggplant slice in egg mixture, shaking off excess. Carefully add 1 dipped eggplant slice at a time to hot oil. Fry, turning once, until golden on both sides, about 3 minutes. Drain on paper towels. Arrange on a platter. Garnish with tomato slices and strips of green pepper. Serve immediately. Makes 6 servings.

Variation

Fried Cauliflowerets: Break 1 cauliflower into flowerets. Dip each floweret into egg mixture. Fry in hot oil until golden. Drain on paper towels. Sprinkle with salt and pepper to taste. If desired, sprinkle with lemon juice or top with plain yogurt. Serve as an appetizer or side dish.

How to Make Fainting Imam

1/Cook eggplants about 2 minutes, turning frequently to blister on all sides. Drain on paper towels.

2/Spoon onion mixture into slit in each eggplant. Press with spoon to pack tightly.

Eggplant Puree

Hünkar Beğendi (Turkey)

This excellent puree, called Sultan's Delight, is usually served as a bed for stews or roast chicken.

1 large eggplant
1/4 cup butter or margarine
1/4 cup all-purpose flour

1 cup milk or half and half
1/2 cup grated Parmesan cheese (1-1/2 oz.)
Salt and freshly ground white pepper to taste

Pierce eggplant in several places. Preheat oven to 400F (205C). Place pierced eggplant on oven rack and bake 1 hour or until soft. If using microwave oven, pierce eggplant and microwave at full power (HIGH) 5 to 7 minutes, depending on size. Peel softened eggplant. Place pulp in a bowl and mash. Set aside. Melt butter or margarine in a medium saucepan over low heat. Stir in flour until smooth. Gradually add milk or half and half. Cook, stirring constantly, until mixture is thickened and smooth, about 5 minutes. Stir in cheese, salt and pepper. Fold in mashed eggplant. Cook, stirring constantly, until thickened, about 3 minutes. Do not scorch. Serve immediately. Makes 6 to 8 servings.

Vegetarian Lentils, Pasta & Rice

Koushari (Egypt)

A salad and crusty bread will complete this vegetarian meal-in-a-dish.

1/4 cup olive oil
1 large onion, chopped
2 garlic cloves, minced
1 cup lentils, rinsed
1 (8-oz.) can tomato sauce
4 cups Chicken Broth, page 36, or water

2 cups cooked elbow or tube macaroni
2 cups cooked long-grain rice
Salt and freshly ground pepper to taste
1 tablespoon chopped fresh parsley
Lemon wedges for garnish

Heat olive oil in a large saucepan. Add onion and garlic. Sauté until onion is tender. Add lentils. Sauté 1 minute. Stir in tomato sauce. Cook 1 minute to blend flavors. Add broth or water. Bring to a boil. Reduce heat and cover. Cook over medium-low heat 40 minutes or until lentils are tender. Fold in cooked macaroni, rice, salt and pepper. Heat through, stirring frequently. Garnish with parsley and lemon wedges. Makes 6 to 8 servings.

Variation

Baked Lentil, Pasta & Rice Casserole: In a small skillet, sauté onion and garlic in olive oil. Add lentils. Sauté 1 minute. Add tomato sauce. Place lentil mixture in a large baking pan. Add 4 cups broth or water. Cover. Bake at 350F (175C) until lentils are tender, about 1 hour. Add cooked macaroni, rice, salt and pepper. Cover and bake 15 minutes longer or until heated through. Garnish as desired.

Greens with Sesame-Seed Sauce

Tahini ma'Khoudra (Arabic)

Arab cooks top seasonal greens with Sesame-Seed Sauce.

Sesame-Seed Sauce, see below
1 lb. Swiss chard or other cooking greens

Water
Salt and freshly ground pepper to taste

Sesame-Seed Sauce:
1/2 cup sesame-seed paste (tahini paste)
Juice of 2 lemons (6 tablespoons)
2 garlic cloves, crushed

Salt to taste
Water for thinning

Prepare Sesame-Seed Sauce. Set aside. Trim and rinse greens. Cut into 1-inch lengths. Pour water 1 inch deep into a large saucepan. Bring to a boil. Add cut greens, salt and pepper. Reduce heat. Cook over medium heat 5 minutes. Drain. Cool. Pour Sesame-Seed Sauce over greens before serving. Makes 4 to 6 servings.

Sesame-Seed Sauce:
Combine sesame-seed paste, lemon juice, garlic and salt in a small bowl. Mix until blended. Add water for desired consistency. Use about 2 tablespoons water for a medium sauce or 1/4 cup water for a thin sauce. Makes about 2/3 cup.

Vegetarian Skillet

Shakchoukah (Israel)

From North Africa to Jerusalem, vegetables and eggs are served on toast, rice or in Arabic pocket bread.

1/2 cup olive oil
1 garlic clove
2 medium onions, thinly sliced
1/2 cup Chicken Broth, page 36, or water
2 medium, green bell peppers, diced
2 large potatoes, cubed
4 medium tomatoes, diced

2 medium zucchini, diced
Salt and freshly ground black pepper to taste
1/2 small eggplant, if desired,
   unpeeled, diced
6 to 8 eggs
Freshly ground black pepper
   to taste

Heat olive oil in a large skillet. Add garlic. Cook until golden. Discard garlic. Add onions to hot oil. Sauté until tender. Add broth or water, green peppers, potatoes, tomatoes, zucchini, salt and black pepper. Add eggplant, if desired. Mix well. Cover. Cook over medium-low heat, stirring occasionally, until vegetables are almost tender, 30 to 40 minutes. Break eggs over vegetables, spacing them evenly around skillet. Cover. Simmer over low heat until eggs are poached as desired, about 4 minutes. For each serving, use a spatula to serve vegetable mixture with an egg on top. Sprinkle with black pepper to taste. Makes 6 to 8 servings.

Green-Bean Stew

Fasoulakia (Greece)

A simple and tasty dish to make with green beans, zucchini or green peas.

1 lb. fresh green beans, cleaned, trimmed
1 large onion, thinly sliced
1 (8-oz.) can whole tomatoes, undrained,
   crushed, or 2 large tomatoes, diced

Salt and freshly ground pepper to taste
1/2 cup vegetable oil

Snap large green beans in half. Place in a large saucepan. Add onion, tomatoes, salt and pepper. Mix lightly. Pour oil over vegetables. Cover. Simmer over very low heat, stirring occasionally to prevent scorching, 40 to 50 minutes or until beans are very tender. Serve hot. Makes 6 servings.

Variations

Zucchini Stew: Substitute 1 pound zucchini, cut into 1/2-inch slices, for the green beans.
Green-Pea Stew: Substitute 3 pounds green peas, shelled, for the green beans.

Stuffed Potatoes

Batata Charp (Iraq)

Potato patties filled with meat are served as appetizers or as a main dish.

Meat Filling, see below	**Salt to taste**
2-1/2 lbs. potatoes (7 medium), cooked	**Oil for frying**
1 egg	**Melted butter or margarine for baking**
1 tablespoon cornstarch	

Meat Filling:

2 tablespoons olive oil	**3/4 lb. ground lean beef**
1 medium onion, chopped	**Salt and freshly ground pepper to taste**

Prepare Meat Filling. Set aside. Peel potatoes. Place in a large bowl and mash; do not use food processor. Add egg, cornstarch and salt. Mix well. Moisten your hands and pinch off 2-inch pieces of potato mixture. Shape each piece into a ball and then into a cup. Place about 1 tablespoon Meat Filling in potato cup. Pinch seams together to enclose filling completely. Shape into 2-1/2-inch rounded patties, balls or torpedo shapes. Refrigerate to chill. Potatoes may be fried or baked. To fry, pour oil about 1-1/2 inches deep into a large skillet. Heat to 350F (175C) on a deep-fry thermometer. At this temperature, a 1-inch cube of bread will turn golden brown in 65 seconds. Carefully lower potatoes into hot oil. Do not crowd in skillet. Fry, turning frequently to brown evenly, until golden on all sides, 5 to 8 minutes. To bake, preheat oven to 350F (175C). Arrange stuffed potatoes on a greased baking sheet. Brush with melted butter or margarine. Bake 30 to 35 minutes or until golden. Makes about 20 patties.

Meat Filling:

Heat olive oil in a large saucepan. Add onion. Sauté until tender. Add beef, salt and pepper. Cook until beef is browned and crumbly. Set aside.

Variation

Potato-Beef Casserole (Kibbe Batata): Spread half the potato mixture in a greased 13" x 9" baking pan. Spread Meat Filling over potato layer. Top with remaining potato mixture. Sprinkle with cinnamon, if desired. Dot with 2 tablespoons butter or margarine. Bake at 350F (175C) 30 to 40 minutes or until golden. Cut into squares to serve.

Fried Potatoes

Patates Kızartması (Turkey)

Serve these as you would French fries with steak, chops or eggs.

4 or 5 large baking or boiling potatoes, or	**1/4 cup butter or margarine**
10 small boiling potatoes	**2 tablespoons crushed dried leaf oregano**
1/2 cup olive oil	**Salt and freshly ground pepper to taste**

Peel potatoes. Cut large potatoes crosswise into 1/4-inch slices. Cut small potatoes lengthwise into quarters. Heat olive oil and butter or margarine in a large skillet until butter or margarine melts. Add potatoes. Fry, tossing occasionally, until golden brown on all sides, 4 to 5 minutes. Drain on paper towels. Sprinkle with oregano, salt and pepper. Makes 6 servings.

How to Make Stuffed Potatoes

1/With moistened hands, shape each 2-inch piece of potato mixture into a ball and then a cup. Place about 1 tablespoon filling in potato cup.

2/Pinch seams together to enclose filling completely. Shape into 2-1/2-inch rounded patties, balls or torpedo shapes.

Zucchini Patties

Kussa Falafel (Arabic)

Serve them as hors d'oeuvres or as a side dish.

**2 cups shredded zucchini
    (about 5 medium zucchini)
1 cup all-purpose flour
1 cup buttermilk or milk
2 eggs
1 tablespoon chopped fresh parsley**

**1 tablespoon chopped fresh mint or
    1 teaspoon crushed dried leaf mint
2 garlic cloves, minced
1 small onion, grated
Salt and freshly ground pepper to taste
Oil for frying**

Drain zucchini and squeeze out excess moisture. Place zucchini in a large bowl. Stir in flour. Add buttermilk or milk, eggs, parsley, mint, garlic, onion, salt and pepper. Mix well. Pour oil about 1-1/2 inches deep into a large saucepan. Heat to 375F (190C) on a deep-fry thermometer. At this temperature, a 1-inch cube of bread will turn golden brown in 50 seconds. Carefully drop zucchini mixture from a tablespoon into hot oil. Fry, turning frequently, until golden brown on all sides, about 3 minutes. Drain on paper towels. Serve hot or cold. Makes 12 patties.

Stuffed Peppers

Dolmeh-ye Felfel Sabz (Iran)

Combining dill and mint may seem unusual—but the resulting flavor is superb.

2 tablespoons butter or margarine
1 large onion, chopped
1/2 lb. ground lean beef or lamb
1 (8-oz.) can tomato sauce
Salt and freshly ground black pepper to taste
Pinch of sugar
Grated peel of 1 lemon
Juice of 1 lemon (3 tablespoons)
1 cup converted rice
1-1/2 cups Beef Broth, page 36, or
   Chicken Broth, page 36

1 cup chopped fresh parsley
1 cup chopped green onions
1/2 cup fresh dill leaves or
   2 tablespoons dill weed
1 teaspoon crushed dried leaf tarragon
1 tablespoon chopped fresh mint or
   1 teaspoon crushed dried leaf mint
6 large green or red bell peppers
1 cup Beef Broth, page 36
2 tablespoons butter or margarine

Melt 2 tablespoons butter or margarine in a large saucepan. Add onion. Sauté until tender. Add meat. Cook until browned and crumbly. Add half the tomato sauce, salt and black pepper. Cook 1 minute. Add sugar, lemon peel, lemon juice and rice. Cook and stir until rice glistens. Add 1-1/2 cups broth. Bring to a boil. Reduce heat and cover. Simmer over low heat 10 minutes or until liquid is almost absorbed. Stir in parsley, green onions, dill, tarragon and mint. Cook 5 minutes. Preheat oven to 350F (175C). Cut a thin slice from stem end of each pepper; reserve to use as lids. Remove seeds and white membranes from peppers. Place peppers in a large baking pan. Spoon meat mixture into peppers. Combine remaining ingredients, including remaining tomato sauce, in a small saucepan. Heat until butter or margarine melts. Pour over stuffed peppers. Cover with reserved lids. Cover baking pan with foil. Bake 1 hour or until peppers are tender and filling is done. Makes 6 servings.

Variations

Stuffed Cabbage: Cook 1 whole medium cabbage in boiling water 8 to 10 minutes, depending on size. Drain and cool. Separate leaves. Place 1 tablespoon filling on each leaf. Roll up, tucking in edges. Place cabbage rolls in a large baking pan, making a single layer. Continue with recipe.

Stuffed Tomatoes: Substitute 8 large tomatoes for the green peppers. Cut a thin slice from each stem end. Scoop out pulp. Add to meat mixture. Heat 5 minutes before stuffing tomatoes. Continue with recipe.

Stuffed Eggplant: Substitute 8 long Japanese eggplants for the green peppers. Slit each eggplant lengthwise without cutting all the way through. Heat 1/2 cup vegetable oil in a large skillet. Cook each eggplant in hot oil until blistered on all sides. Remove from skillet. Drain on paper towels and let cool. Stuff with meat mixture. Continue with recipe.

From left to right: Stuffed Cabbage; Stuffed Tomatoes; and Stuffed Peppers.

Beans with Vegetables

Plaki (Armenia)

White beans with vegetables can be served hot or cold as a side dish, soup or salad.

2 cups dried Great Northern beans, sorted,
  rinsed
8 cups water
1 large onion, chopped
3 garlic cloves, minced
4 medium carrots, cut in 1-inch pieces
1 medium, green bell pepper, diced

1 small celery stalk with leaves, diced
1/4 cup chopped fresh parsley
Salt and freshly ground black pepper to taste
2 large tomatoes, diced
1 tablespoon tomato paste
1/2 cup olive oil

Place beans in a large saucepan. Add water. Bring to a boil. Reduce heat and cover. Cook over medium-low heat 1-1/2 hours. Add onion, garlic, carrots, green pepper, celery, parsley, salt and black pepper. Cover and cook 30 minutes. Add tomatoes. Stir in tomato paste. Cover. Cook 15 minutes longer. Stir in olive oil. Cook, uncovered, 15 minutes. Makes 6 servings.

Spinach with Yogurt

Borani-e Esfenaj (Iran)

Yogurt and vegetable dishes are often served with roasts.

2 lbs. fresh spinach or
  2 (10-oz.) pkgs. frozen chopped spinach,
  thawed
1/4 cup butter or margarine

1 medium onion, chopped
Salt and freshly ground pepper to taste
2 cups plain yogurt

Rinse fresh spinach thoroughly several times. Drain. Remove and discard stems. Chop leaves. If using frozen spinach, squeeze dry after thawing and fluff to separate. Melt butter or margarine in a large saucepan. Add onion. Sauté until onion is tender. Add spinach, salt and pepper. Cook and stir until spinach glistens. Cover. Simmer over very low heat 7 minutes. Fold in yogurt until mixed well. Serve warm or chilled. Makes 6 to 8 servings.

Spiced Green Beans

Loubia (Algeria)

Delicious but easy vegetable stew is especially good with roast lamb.

1 lb. green beans, cleaned, trimmed
2 cups lightly salted water
2 tablespoons olive oil
2 garlic cloves, minced
1/4 teaspoon ground cumin

1/8 teaspoon paprika
Pinch of ground cloves
Pinch of red (cayenne) pepper
Salt to taste

Place green beans in a large saucepan. Add lightly salted water. Bring to a boil. Reduce heat and cover. Cook over medium-low heat 30 to 40 minutes or until green beans are done as desired. Drain. Place green beans in a bowl. Set aside. Heat olive oil in the same saucepan. Add remaining ingredients. Cook over medium-high heat, stirring constantly to blend flavors, about 2 minutes. Add cooked green beans. Toss to coat well. Makes 4 to 6 servings.

Cauliflower Casserole

Karnabitt (Egypt)

The typical method for preparing seasonal vegetables in Egypt.

1 large cauliflower
Water
1/4 cup butter or margarine
1 large onion, chopped

2 garlic cloves, minced
1 (8-oz.) can tomato sauce, stewed tomatoes
** or 1 cup tomato juice**
Salt and freshly ground pepper to taste

Place cauliflower in a large saucepan. Add water to come halfway up cauliflower. Bring to a boil. Reduce heat and cover. Simmer over medium heat 10 minutes. Drain. Cool slightly and separate into flowerets. Melt butter or margarine in a large skillet. Add onion and garlic. Sauté until onion is tender. Add tomato sauce, stewed tomatoes or juice, salt and pepper. Bring to a boil. Add flowerets. Reduce heat and cover. Simmer over medium-low heat until cauliflower is fork-tender, 15 to 20 minutes. Makes 6 servings.

Egyptian Beans

Fool Medames (Egypt)

The Egyptian national dish is eaten for breakfast or any time of day with green onions and bread.

1 lb. dried small fava beans or pink beans,
** sorted, rinsed**
Lightly salted water
1/2 cup red lentils
Juice of 1 lemon (3 tablespoons)

1/4 cup olive oil
1/2 teaspoon ground cumin
Salt and freshly ground pepper to taste
1/2 cup chopped green onions

Place beans in a large saucepan. Add lightly salted water to cover. Bring to a boil. Reduce heat and cover. Simmer over low heat 2-1/2 hours. If necessary, add more water to keep beans covered. Add lentils. Cover. Simmer 30 minutes longer or until lentils and beans are tender and mixture is thick but not soupy. Stir in lemon juice, olive oil, cumin, salt and pepper. Serve hot. Sprinkle each serving with green onions. Makes 8 to 10 servings.

TIP

Egyptian brown beans, or small fava beans, and red lentils are available in most Middle Eastern grocery stores. Or substitute pink beans for the brown beans and brown lentils for the red lentils.

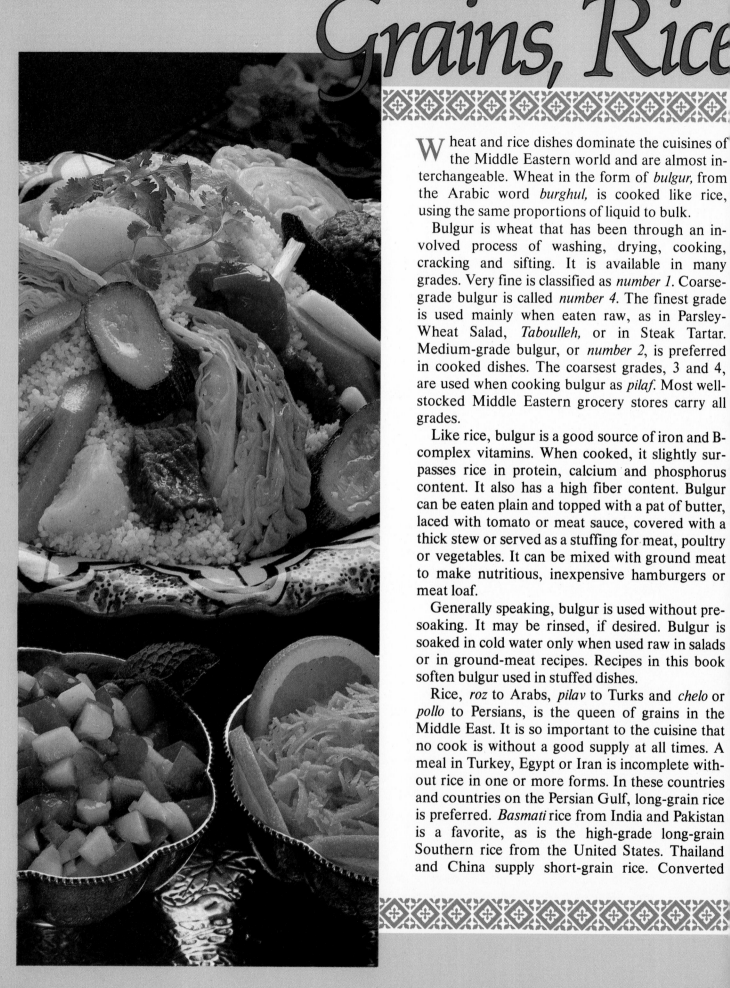

W heat and rice dishes dominate the cuisines of the Middle Eastern world and are almost interchangeable. Wheat in the form of *bulgur,* from the Arabic word *burghul,* is cooked like rice, using the same proportions of liquid to bulk.

Bulgur is wheat that has been through an involved process of washing, drying, cooking, cracking and sifting. It is available in many grades. Very fine is classified as *number 1.* Coarse-grade bulgur is called *number 4.* The finest grade is used mainly when eaten raw, as in Parsley-Wheat Salad, *Taboulleh,* or in Steak Tartar. Medium-grade bulgur, or *number 2,* is preferred in cooked dishes. The coarsest grades, 3 and 4, are used when cooking bulgur as *pilaf.* Most well-stocked Middle Eastern grocery stores carry all grades.

Like rice, bulgur is a good source of iron and B-complex vitamins. When cooked, it slightly surpasses rice in protein, calcium and phosphorus content. It also has a high fiber content. Bulgur can be eaten plain and topped with a pat of butter, laced with tomato or meat sauce, covered with a thick stew or served as a stuffing for meat, poultry or vegetables. It can be mixed with ground meat to make nutritious, inexpensive hamburgers or meat loaf.

Generally speaking, bulgur is used without presoaking. It may be rinsed, if desired. Bulgur is soaked in cold water only when used raw in salads or in ground-meat recipes. Recipes in this book soften bulgur used in stuffed dishes.

Rice, *roz* to Arabs, *pilav* to Turks and *chelo* or *pollo* to Persians, is the queen of grains in the Middle East. It is so important to the cuisine that no cook is without a good supply at all times. A meal in Turkey, Egypt or Iran is incomplete without rice in one or more forms. In these countries and countries on the Persian Gulf, long-grain rice is preferred. *Basmati* rice from India and Pakistan is a favorite, as is the high-grade long-grain Southern rice from the United States. Thailand and China supply short-grain rice. Converted

& Pasta

rice, a product of modern technology, is gaining in popularity in countries such as Iraq where taste for modern processed foods is growing. Converted rice is steamed before milling to enable it to retain much of the natural vitamin and mineral content normally lost in processing. It requires a longer cooking time than regular rice and takes 2-1/2 parts liquid to 1 part rice, compared with the 2-to-1 ratio for regular rice.

Every Middle Eastern cook has a favorite method for cooking rice. The steaming method used by Iranian cooks is the most effective and foolproof. The saucepan is covered with a cloth and a lid. The rice then steams over low heat until the liquid is absorbed. The cloth absorbs excess moisture, creating fluffy and somewhat dry rice with well-separated grains—the Middle Eastern cook's goal in rice cookery. Rice should be moist but dry enough to discern every grain. The basic Iranian recipe is Persian Steamed Rice. If you want to try something different, use one of the steamed-rice variations. Iranian rice dishes are served plain and eaten with meat or other foods. *Pollo* is usually cooked with or mixed into other foods. These recipes are only a few samplings of the scores of rice dishes in Iranian cooking. Other rice specialties include steamed, molded, caked and spiced rice dishes. Basic rice stuffing often glamorizes lamb, turkey and vegetables.

Couscous, the preferred grain of North Africa, is actually semolina, a byproduct in the manufacture of flour. Made of coarsely crushed heart of durum wheat, it is used mainly in pasta-making and in place of farina in puddings. When making puddings with semolina, use the finest grade which can be purchased in bulk.

Couscous, like bulgur, goes through a steaming and drying process. It, too, comes in several grades from fine to pellet-size. The most popular grade for the dish called *couscous* is found in package form at Middle Eastern grocery stores. It is labeled *couscous mix*. Softened couscous mix is steamed in a *couscousiere*, a special double boiler fitted with a steaming unit. The pot is often available at gourmet cookware or Middle Eastern grocery stores.

Although pasta is generally regarded as a rarity in Middle Eastern cooking, some countries such as Greece and Turkey make inspired use of it. Greece, which has always faced both East and West, boasts a layered Macaroni Casserole called *Pastitsio*. In Lybia, pasta dishes emerged during Italian colonization and are still enjoyed. ✤

Menu

Tunisian Couscous Party

Plate of Olives and Pistachio Nuts	Mixed Salad, page 57
Tunisian Couscous, page 98	Harissa, page 15
Carrot & Orange Salad, page 56	French Cigarettes, page 164
Zucchini-Relish Salad, page 57	Tunisian Coffee, page 32
	Fruit Tray Decorated with Leaves and Blossoms

The couscous is placed in the center of a large, low, round table with salads all around. Harissa, a hot sauce, is passed to use sparingly. Guests sitting on cushions around the table, spoon some of the couscous on plates and top it with an assortment of vegetables and meat. Some of the broth is ladled into the individual dishes, as each diner desires.

Bulgur Stuffing

Hashwet Burghul (Arabic)

Stuff lamb, game or vegetables with this basic stuffing or one of the variations below.

1/4 cup butter or margarine
1 large onion, chopped
Gizzards from 1 chicken, chopped
2 cups fine-grade bulgur

1 tablespoon chopped fresh mint or
   1 teaspoon crushed dried leaf mint
Salt and freshly ground pepper to taste
4 cups Chicken Broth, page 36

Melt butter or margarine in a large skillet. Add onion and gizzards. Sauté until onion is tender and gizzards are browned. Stir in bulgur, mint, salt and pepper. Add broth. Bring to a boil. Reduce heat and cover. Cook over medium-low heat 30 minutes or until bulgur is soft and liquid is absorbed. Makes enough stuffing for 2 chickens, 1 small turkey or 12 large vegetables.

Variations

Raisin-Bulgur Stuffing: Sauté 1/2 cup raisins with onion-and-gizzard mixture.
Orange-Bulgur Stuffing: Substitute juice of 1 orange (1/3 cup) for 1/3 cup broth.
Pignolia-Bulgur Stuffing: Sauté 1/2 cup pine nuts with onion-and-gizzard mixture.

Bulgur with Chicken

Keshkeg (Armenia)

Stir any chopped or shredded poultry or meat into the bulgur.

1/4 cup butter or margarine
1 small onion, chopped
1 cup coarse-grade bulgur
2-1/2 to 3 cups Chicken Broth, page 36
Pinch of paprika

Salt and freshly ground pepper to taste
2 cups diced or shredded cooked chicken
2 tablespoons butter or margarine
1/2 teaspoon paprika

Melt 1/4 cup butter or margarine in a large saucepan. Add onion. Sauté until onion is tender. Add bulgur. Sauté 1 minute. Add 2-1/2 cups broth, pinch of paprika, salt and pepper. Bring to a boil. Reduce heat and cover. Simmer over low heat 20 to 30 minutes or until bulgur is soft and liquid is almost absorbed, adding more broth for a mushy consistency. Fold in chicken. Heat 5 minutes. Melt 2 tablespoons butter or margarine in a small skillet. Add 1/2 teaspoon paprika. Pour over bulgur mixture. Makes 6 servings.

Bulgur Pudding

Burbara (Arabic)

Although sweet, this pudding may be served as a side dish with roast lamb, pork or poultry.

Nut Topping, see below
1 cup coarse-grade bulgur
3 cups water
1 cinnamon stick

3/4 cup sugar
1/2 cup raisins
1 teaspoon ground anise seeds
Salt to taste

Nut Topping:
1 cup chopped toasted almonds or walnuts,
   page 67

2 teaspoons ground cinnamon
1/2 teaspoon ground nutmeg

Prepare Nut Topping. Set aside. Combine bulgur, water and cinnamon stick in a large saucepan. Bring to a boil. Reduce heat and cover. Simmer over low heat until bulgur is soft and liquid is almost absorbed. Mixture should have a pudding consistency. Add sugar, raisins, anise and salt. Simmer, uncovered, 5 minutes longer, stirring often. Fluff bulgur with a fork. Turn into a serving bowl. Sprinkle with Nut Topping. Makes 6 servings.

Nut Topping:
Combine all ingredients in a small bowl.

Bulgur Pilaf

Burghul Mfalfal (Arabic)

This basic method for cooking bulgur is similar to cooking rice.

3 tablespoons butter or margarine
2 cups coarse-grade bulgur
4 cups Chicken Broth, page 36

Salt and freshly ground pepper to taste
2 teaspoons grated lemon peel

Melt butter or margarine in a large saucepan. Add bulgur. Sauté 5 minutes. Add broth, salt and pepper. Bring to a boil. Reduce heat and cover. Simmer over low heat, stirring occasionally, 20 minutes or until bulgur is soft and liquid is absorbed. Stir in lemon peel. Makes 6 servings.

Variations

Bulgur with Tomato Sauce: Sauté 1 chopped onion in 2 tablespoons butter or margarine until onion is tender. Stir in bulgur. Sauté 2 minutes. Stir in 2 tablespoons tomato paste, 1/2 cup tomato sauce, and broth. Cook as directed above.

Bulgur with Currants & Pine Nuts: Sauté 1 chopped onion, 1/4 cup currants and 2 tablespoons pine nuts in 2 tablespoons butter or margarine until onion is golden. Stir in bulgur. Sauté 2 minutes. Stir in broth. Cook as directed above.

Tunisian Couscous   Photo on pages 10 and 11.

Couscous Complet Tunisien (Tunisia)

An exquisite party meal made in a special utensil called a couscousiere.

Stuffed Meatballs, page 124
Carrot & Orange Salad, page 56
Zucchini-Relish Salad, page 57
Mixed Salad, page 57
2 cups packaged couscous
3 tablespoons vegetable oil
2 cups water
1 tablespoon salt
Water
2 lbs. boneless chuck beef, cubed
1 medium onion, quartered
1/4 cup vegetable oil

1 medium tomato, cut in wedges
1 medium turnip, peeled, cut in pieces
4 medium carrots, peeled
2 medium potatoes, peeled, cut in wedges
Salt to taste
1 small cabbage, cut in wedges
2 medium zucchini, cut in
    1-inch diagonal slices
6 green onions, sliced
Few sprigs cilantro
Few sprigs parsley
Harissa

Prepare Stuffed Meatballs. Set aside. Prepare Carrot & Orange Salad, Zucchini-Relish Salad and Mixed Salad. Refrigerate. Place couscous in a large bowl. Sprinkle with 3 tablespoons oil. Gradually stir in 2 cups water and 1 tablespoon salt. Rub mixture between palms of your hands to separate grains. Let stand 30 minutes or longer. Fill bottom section of couscousière with water. Add beef, onion, 1/4 cup oil, tomato, turnip, carrots, potatoes and salt to taste. If needed, add more water to cover. Bring to a boil. Reduce heat and cover. Cook over medium heat 45 minutes. Add cabbage, zucchini, green onions, cilantro and parsley. Cover and cook over medium-low heat 10 minutes. Place couscous mixture in top section of couscousière. Make a well in center of mixture so steam will circulate while cooking. Fit top section of couscousière over bottom section where soup is cooking. Be sure liquid in bottom section does not touch couscous through perforated base of top section; couscous should cook by steaming. Cover and simmer over low heat 30 minutes. Turn steamed couscous into a large, shallow platter. Cool slightly. Toss to break up any lumps. If necessary, use your fingers to separate grains. Arrange couscous in a mound on platter. Pour some soup liquid over couscous, if desired. Top with Stuffed Meatballs and meat and vegetables from soup. Pour soup liquid into individual bowls. Place Carrot & Orange Salad, Zucchini-Relish Salad and Mixed Salad in small bowls around platter. To eat, spoon couscous on your plate. Top with meats and vegetables. Ladle soup liquid over couscous on your plate. Season sparingly with harissa. Eat with small servings of each salad. Makes 6 to 8 servings.

Variation

Tunisian Couscous with Barbecued Meats: Grilled or barbecued sausages and baby lamb rib chops may be added to couscous platter.

TIP

Packaged couscous is a granulated pasta (semolina) made from the heart of durum wheat. Harissa is a paste made from hot peppers. They are both often available at Middle Eastern grocery stores. Harissa is also available at some gourmet shops. Bottled hot-pepper sauce may be substituted.

How to Make Tunisian Couscous

1/Use your fingers to break up lumps in soaked couscous.

2/Prepare meat and vegetables to be cooked and served with couscous.

Egyptian Rice

Roz (Egypt)

This is the rice used at almost every Egyptian meal.

1/4 cup butter or margarine
1 cup long-grain rice

2 cups water
Salt to taste

Melt butter or margarine in a medium saucepan. Add half the rice. Sauté until rice is transparent. Add remaining rice, water and salt. Bring to a boil. Reduce heat and cover. Simmer over medium heat about 20 minutes or until liquid is absorbed. Makes 4 servings.

Moroccan Couscous

Couscous à la Marocaine (Morocco)

You don't need a couscousière for this version of couscous.

2 cups packaged couscous	**1/4 cup olive oil**
Water	**10 cups water (2-1/2 qts.)**
2 tablespoons olive oil	**Salt and freshly ground pepper to taste**
1-1/2 lbs. lamb shanks or shoulder of lamb, cut in serving pieces	**Pinch of saffron threads or powder, if desired**
4 chicken drumsticks	**1 small cabbage, cut in eighths**
1 small turnip, peeled, quartered	**2 medium zucchini, cut in pieces**
4 medium carrots, cut in pieces	**2 medium tomatoes, cut up**
2 onions, quartered	**2 parsley sprigs**
1/2 cup dried garbanzo beans, sorted, rinsed, or 1 (1-lb.) can garbanzo beans, drained	**4 or 5 cilantro sprigs**
	2 tablespoons butter or margarine
	1/4 cup raisins

Place couscous in a large bowl. Add water to cover. Let stand 1 hour or until water is absorbed. Add 2 tablespoons olive oil. Toss to coat well. If necessary, use your fingers to break up lumps. Set aside. In a large pot, combine lamb, chicken, turnip, carrots, onions, garbanzo beans, 1/4 cup olive oil, 10 cups water, salt and pepper. Add saffron, if desired. Bring to a boil. Reduce heat and cover. Simmer over low heat 1 hour 15 minutes. Remove 2 cups hot broth from soup. Set aside. Add cabbage, zucchini, tomatoes, parsley and cilantro to soup. Simmer 20 to 30 minutes or until vegetables are tender. Place reserved broth in a large saucepan. Bring to a boil. Add soaked couscous and butter or margarine. Mix well. Remove from heat. Place a clean cloth towel over saucepan. Place lid on towel. Bring corners of towel up and over top of lid. Fasten securely with a rubber band. Simmer over low heat 20 minutes. Remove lid and towel. Fluff couscous with a fork. Turn out into a large, shallow platter. Top with meat and vegetables from soup. Sprinkle with raisins. Pour liquid from soup into a separate bowl or tureen. To eat, place some couscous on your plate. Top with meat and vegetables. Ladle soup liquid over couscous. Makes 8 to 12 servings.

Saffron Rice

Timen Za'afaran (Iraq)

Stews, roast meats or vegetables are often served on fragrant Saffron Rice.

1 teaspoon or less saffron threads or powder	**Salt and freshly ground white pepper to taste**
1 teaspoon rose water	**2 cups long-grain rice**
4 cups water	

Place saffron in a small cup. Add rose water. Let stand 5 minutes. Place water in a large saucepan. Strain saffron water into saucepan. Discard saffron. Add salt and pepper. Bring to a boil. Add rice. Reduce heat and cover. Cook over medium heat 20 to 30 minutes or until rice is tender and liquid is absorbed. Makes 6 to 8 servings.

Stuffed Rice Balls

Kibbe bi-Maraqa (Arabic)

Mrs. Moussa Al-Moussawi of Iraq showed me how to shape these rice balls.

2 cups cooked short-grain rice
1/4 teaspoon turmeric
1/4 teaspoon ground cumin
Grated peel of 1 lime
Salt and freshly ground pepper to taste
2 tablespoons butter or margarine
1 small onion, chopped

1/2 lb. ground lean beef or lamb
1 tablespoon chopped fresh parsley
Salt and freshly ground pepper to taste
1 (8-oz.) can tomato sauce
1 cup Chicken Broth, page 36, or
   Beef Broth, page 36

In a medium bowl, combine cooked rice, turmeric, cumin, lime peel, salt and pepper to taste. Knead until mixture becomes a paste. Or process to a paste in food processor or blender. Set aside. Melt butter or margarine in a large skillet. Add onion. Sauté until onion is tender. Add meat. Sauté until meat is browned and crumbly. Add parsley, salt and pepper. Sauté 1 minute to blend flavors. Moisten your hands, pinch off pieces of rice mixture 2 inches in diameter and shape into balls. Shape each ball into a cup. Place 1 tablespoon meat mixture in each rice cup. Pinch edges of cup together to enclose filling completely. Shape into smooth balls. Combine tomato sauce and broth in a shallow saucepan or skillet. Add rice balls. Bring to a boil. Reduce heat and cover. Simmer over low heat 20 minutes or until rice balls are heated through. Makes 6 servings.

Herb Rice

Sabzi Pollo (Iran)

Here is a prized dish among the literally hundreds of Persian rice dishes.

About 4 cups lightly salted water
2 cups long-grain rice
1 bunch green onions, green part only,
   chopped (about 1 cup)

1 bunch parsley, chopped (1 cup)
2 bunches cilantro, chopped (2 cups)
1/4 cup butter or margarine

Bring about 4 cups lightly salted water to a boil in a large saucepan. Add rice. Water should cover rice by about 1 inch. Cook, uncovered, over medium heat 10 minutes. Drain. Rinse rice with cold water. Drain again. Combine chopped green onions, parsley and cilantro in a medium bowl. Mix well. Melt butter or margarine in a large saucepan. Add a fourth of the rice. Sprinkle with a third of the herbs. Alternate layers of rice and herbs, ending with rice. Remove from heat. Place a clean cloth towel over saucepan. Place lid on towel. Bring corners of towel up and over top of lid. Fasten securely with a rubber band. Simmer over very low heat 25 to 30 minutes or until rice is soft and fluffy. Makes 6 servings.

Basic Dry Pilaf

Draining cooked rice in a colander produces a slightly dry rice preferred by Middle Eastern cooks.

8 cups water (2 qts.)
2 teaspoons salt
2 cups converted rice

1/2 cup butter or margarine
Freshly ground pepper to taste

In a medium saucepan, bring water to a boil. Add salt and rice. Reduce heat and cover. Simmer over medium-low heat 20 to 30 minutes or until rice is just tender but not too soft. Drain well in a colander. In the same saucepan, melt butter or margarine over medium heat until golden. Add rice. Toss to coat well. Turn out onto a platter. Sprinkle generously with pepper. Makes 6 to 8 servings.

Variations

Pilaf with Yogurt: Top each serving with 1 or 2 tablespoons yogurt.
Pilaf with Almonds & Raisins: Prepare pilaf, omitting butter or margarine and pepper. In a small skillet, melt 1/2 cup butter or margarine. Add 2 tablespoons sliced almonds, 2 tablespoons seedless raisins and 1 tablespoon shredded orange peel. Sauté until raisins are plumped, about 3 minutes. For a sweet pilaf, add 1/2 teaspoon cinnamon and 1 tablespoon sugar. Fold into pilaf.

Basic Soft Pilaf

Middle Eastern cooks usually stir in another ingredient for increased flavor and texture.

1/4 cup butter or margarine
1 cup converted rice

1 teaspoon salt
2 cups water or Chicken Broth, page 36

In a medium saucepan, melt butter or margarine over medium heat. Add rice. Stir and cook 1 minute. Add salt and water or broth. Bring to a boil and cover. Simmer over medium-low heat 20 to 30 minutes or until liquid is absorbed. Makes 4 servings.

Variations

Pilaf with Almonds: Fold 1/4 cup toasted slivered or sliced blanched almonds into hot cooked rice.
Pilaf with Raisins: Fold 1/4 to 1/2 cup seedless raisins into hot cooked rice. Cover and let stand about 10 minutes to plump raisins.
Pilaf with Orange Peel: Stir 2 tablespoons grated orange peel into hot cooked rice.

Lentils & Rice

Mujadarah (Arabic)

This vegetarian dish needs only a salad and Arabic pocket bread to be a complete meal.

1/4 cup butter or margarine	1 cup long-grain rice
1 medium onion, sliced	1 teaspoon ground cumin
1 cup lentils, sorted, rinsed	Salt and freshly ground pepper to taste
4 cups Chicken Broth, page 36, or water	6 lemon wedges

Melt butter or margarine in a large saucepan. Add onion. Sauté until onion is tender but not browned. Add lentils. Sauté 1 minute. Add broth or water. Bring to a boil. Reduce heat and cover. Simmer over low heat 20 minutes. Add rice, cumin, salt and pepper. Simmer 30 to 40 minutes or until rice and lentils are tender and liquid is absorbed. Mixture will be mushy. Serve with lemon wedges. Makes 4 to 6 servings.

Variation

Lentils & Rice with Meat or Chicken: Add 2 cups diced, cubed or shredded cooked beef, lamb, veal or chicken to lentil and rice mixture 10 minutes before end of cooking time.

Rice Stuffing for Turkey or Lamb

Roz Mfalfal (Arabic)

Arab cooks often stuff a whole small lamb with rice stuffing.

1/4 cup butter or margarine	1/2 cup pine nuts
2 medium onions, chopped	1 teaspoon ground cinnamon
2 celery-heart stalks with leaves, diced	1/4 teaspoon ground allspice
1/4 cup chopped fresh parsley	Salt and freshly ground pepper to taste
3 cups short-grain rice	3-1/2 to 7 cups Chicken Broth,
1/2 cup dried currants	page 36, or water

Melt butter or margarine in a large saucepan. Add onions, celery and parsley. Sauté until onions are tender. Add rice, currants, pine nuts, cinnamon, allspice, salt and pepper. Sauté until rice is glazed. Add 3-1/2 cups broth or water. Cover and cook 10 minutes or until liquid is absorbed. Set aside to cool before stuffing lamb or turkey. To bake separately, preheat oven to 350F (175C). Grease a shallow 4-quart baking pan or casserole. Place sautéed rice mixture in prepared pan or casserole. Add remaining 3-1/2 cups broth or water. Cover with foil. Bake 45 minutes or until liquid is absorbed. Makes about 12 servings or stuffing for one 15-pound turkey or lamb.

Persian Steamed Rice

Chelo (Iran)

An unusual steaming method makes this rice light and fluffy.

About 4 cups lightly salted water	**2 tablespoons butter or margarine**
2 cups long-grain rice	**Salt and freshly ground pepper to taste**

Bring about 4 cups lightly salted water to a boil in a large saucepan. Add rice. Water should cover rice by 2 inches or more. Add more boiling water, if necessary. Cook, uncovered, over medium heat 10 minutes. Drain. Rinse rice with cold water. Drain again. Melt butter or margarine in a large saucepan. Add drained rice. Stir lightly to coat well. Place saucepan lid on a clean cloth towel. Bring corners of towel up and over top of lid. Fasten securely with a rubber band. Place lid firmly on saucepan. Cook over medium-low heat 25 to 30 minutes or until rice is fluffy and water is absorbed. Keep covered until ready to serve. Makes 6 servings.

Variations

Steamed Crusty Rice: Attach towel and lid as directed above. Steam rice a total of 40 to 45 minutes over very low heat or until rice in bottom of saucepan is golden and crusty. Serve rice with pieces of crust lifted from bottom of saucepan.

Steamed Rice with Fruits & Nuts: Sauté 1/4 cup chopped mixed dried fruit, 1/4 cup slivered almonds and 1/4 cup raisins in 1/4 cup butter or margarine. Add drained rice. Sauté 1 minute. Continue with recipe.

Savory Steamed Rice: Sauté 1 chopped onion, 2 tablespoons chopped fresh parsley, 2 tablespoons chopped cilantro, 1/4 tablespoon chopped fresh dill or 1 teaspoon dill weed in 1/4 cup butter or margarine. Add drained rice. Sauté 1 minute. Continue with recipe.

Rice with Sour Cherries (Alo-baloo Pollo): Fold about 6 tablespoons sour-cherry jam into 4 cups steamed rice.

TIP

Sour-cherry jam is imported from Greece and Yugoslavia and is available at Middle Eastern grocery stores. Cherry jam may be substituted.

Noodles with Feta Cheese

Fithe me Djath (Albania)

Here's a quick and easy noodle dish to accompany roasts.

1 lb. broad egg noodles	**Salt and freshly ground pepper to taste**
1/2 cup butter or margarine	**1/2 lb. feta cheese, crumbled (1-1/2 cups)**
1 teaspoon dill weed	**Additional freshly ground pepper**

Cook noodles according to package directions. Drain. Place in a warmed large bowl. Melt butter or margarine in a small skillet. Add dill, salt and pepper to taste. Pour over noodles. Toss. Add cheese. Toss again. Sprinkle with additional pepper. Makes 6 to 8 servings.

How to Make Steamed Crusty Rice

1/Add drained rice to melted butter or margarine in a large saucepan. Stir lightly to coat well.

2/Place saucepan lid on a clean cloth towel. Bring corners of towel up and over top of lid. Fasten securely.

3/Place towel-covered lid firmly on saucepan.

4/Steam rice until bottom is golden and crusty.

Steamed Rice Mold

Pilav (Turkey)

Some of the numerous variations for this molded rice are given below.

2 tablespoons butter or margarine	Salt and freshly ground pepper to taste
2 cups long-grain rice	Parsley sprigs for garnish
3-1/2 cups strong Chicken Broth, page 36	

Melt butter or margarine in a large saucepan. Add rice. Sauté 2 minutes or until rice is glazed. Add broth, salt and pepper. Bring to a boil. Reduce heat and cover. Cook over medium heat 25 minutes or until rice is tender and liquid is absorbed. Oil an 8-inch ring mold. Turn cooked rice into mold. Smooth top with the back of a spoon. Cover with a double thickness of waxed paper. Place lid on top. Let stand 10 to 20 minutes to set. Run a metal spatula around inside of mold. Place a platter upside-down over mold. Invert mold and platter. Remove mold. Garnish with parsley sprigs. Makes 6 to 8 servings.

Variations

Rice & Carrot Mold: Sauté 4 grated carrots in 1/4 cup butter or margarine. Sprinkle with 1 teaspoon sugar. Add rice. Sauté 2 minutes to glaze. Continue with recipe.

Rice & Spinach Mold: Omit butter or margarine. Sauté 2 bunches chopped spinach or 1 (10-ounce) package frozen spinach, thawed and squeezed dry, in 1/4 cup olive oil. Add rice. Sauté 2 minutes to glaze. Continue with recipe.

Jeweled Rice Mold: Alternate layers of cooked rice, 1/4 cup chopped mixed dried fruit, 1/4 cup slivered almonds, 1/4 cup raisins or currants in mold. Continue with recipe.

Spinach & Rice

Burani (Albania)

A favorite rice dish to serve with roasted meat.

2 bunches fresh spinach or	1 tablespoon chopped fresh dill or
2 (10-oz.) pkgs. frozen chopped spinach,	1 teaspoon dill weed
thawed	2 cups long-grain rice
1/2 cup olive oil	4 cups Chicken Broth, page 36, or water
1 medium onion, chopped	Salt and freshly ground white pepper to taste

Rinse fresh spinach. Remove and discard stems. Chop leaves. If using thawed frozen spinach, squeeze dry. Heat olive oil in a large saucepan. Add onion and dill. Sauté until onion is tender. Add spinach. Sauté until fresh spinach wilts or thawed frozen spinach is hot. Add rice. Sauté 2 minutes to glaze. Add broth or water, salt and pepper. Bring to a boil. Reduce heat and cover. Cook over medium heat 30 minutes or until rice is tender and liquid is absorbed. Makes 6 servings.

Macaroni Casserole

Pastitsio (Greece)

Thick, Greek-style spaghetti or ziti may be used in this freezer-to-oven party casserole.

Meat Sauce, see below
Cream Sauce, see below
1 lb. large elbow macaroni or spaghetti
1/4 cup butter or margarine, melted
1/2 cup grated Parmesan cheese

1/4 teaspoon ground nutmeg or cinnamon
Pinch of sugar
Salt and freshly ground pepper to taste
3 eggs, beaten
1/4 cup grated Parmesan cheese

Meat Sauce:
2 tablespoons butter or margarine
1 medium onion, chopped
1 garlic clove, minced
1-1/2 lbs. ground lean beef
2 tablespoons tomato paste

1 cup Beef Broth, page 36
2 tablespoons chopped fresh parsley
1/2 teaspoon ground cinnamon, if desired
Pinch of sugar
Salt and freshly ground pepper to taste

Cream Sauce:
3 cups milk
6 tablespoons butter or margarine
1/4 cup all-purpose flour

Pinch of nutmeg
Salt and freshly ground white pepper to taste
6 egg yolks, beaten

Prepare Meat Sauce and Cream Sauce. Cook macaroni or spaghetti as directed on package. Drain. Return drained pasta to pan. Add butter or margarine, 1/2 cup Parmesan cheese, nutmeg or cinnamon, sugar, salt and pepper. Toss gently. Add eggs. Toss to coat pasta well. Set aside. Preheat oven to 350F (175C). Grease a 13'' x 9'' baking pan. Spread half the pasta mixture evenly in baking pan. Spoon Meat Sauce over pasta. Top with remaining pasta mixture. Pour Cream Sauce evenly over pasta layer. Sprinkle with 1/4 cup Parmesan cheese. Bake 50 to 55 minutes or until golden. Cut into 3-inch squares and serve immediately. Makes 12 servings.

Meat Sauce:
Melt butter or margarine in a large skillet. Add onion and garlic. Sauté until onion is tender. Add beef. Cook until browned and crumbly. Stir in tomato paste. Add remaining ingredients. Cover and simmer over low heat 20 minutes. Makes about 3 cups.

Cream Sauce:
Scald milk by heating in a medium saucepan over medium heat until bubbles appear around edge. Melt butter or margarine in another medium saucepan over low heat. Stir in flour. Cook and stir 2 minutes. Gradually add scalded milk. Stir over low heat until mixture comes to a boil. Boil 1 minute, stirring constantly. Stir in nutmeg, salt and pepper. Cool slightly. Gradually stir in egg yolks until sauce is smooth. Makes about 4 cups.

Variation
Greek-Style Lasagna: Substitute 1 pound lasagna noodles for elbow macaroni or spaghetti. Cook as directed on package. Continue with recipe, layering noodles lengthwise in casserole.

Baked Stuffed Dumplings

Mante (Armenia)

Using wonton wrappers to make stuffed dumplings is easier than making your own pasta dough.

1-1/2 lbs. ground lean beef or lamb
1 medium onion, minced
1 garlic clove, minced
1/4 cup chopped fresh parsley
1 (12-oz.) pkg. wonton wrappers
  (3-1/2-inch square)

1/4 cup butter or margarine, melted
6 cups Chicken Broth, page 36
2 cups plain yogurt
Minced garlic to taste, if desired
Sumac to taste, if desired

Combine meat, onion, 1 garlic clove and parsley in a large bowl. Mix well. Set aside. Preheat oven to 350F (175C). Grease a large, deep baking pan. Set aside. Cut each wonton wrapper into 4 squares. Use your finger dipped in water to moisten the edges of each square. Place about 1/2 teaspoon beef mixture in center of 1 square. Pinch opposite corners together to form a canoe, pushing up filling slightly. Repeat with remaining squares and filling. Place dumplings in prepared pan in a single layer. Brush with butter or margarine. Bake about 45 minutes or until golden brown but not dry. Let stand until 30 minutes before serving. Heat broth in a medium saucepan. Bring to a boil. Pour over dumplings. Place pan in 350F (175C) oven or over low heat. Bake or simmer 30 to 40 minutes or until dumplings are tender. Spoon yogurt into a medium bowl. Place garlic and sumac, if desired, in separate small dishes. Serve dumplings in soup bowls with some of the broth. Top with yogurt. Garnish with garlic and sumac, if desired. Makes 6 to 8 servings.

Rice with Orzo

Pilafi me Orzo (Greece)

Orzo is the popular name for tiny rice-shaped noodles sold at Middle Eastern grocery stores.

1/4 cup butter or margarine
2 cups long-grain rice
4 cups Chicken Broth, page 36

2 tablespoons orzo
Salt and freshly ground pepper to taste

Melt butter or margarine in a large saucepan. Add rice. Sauté until golden. Add broth. Bring to a boil. Add orzo. Reduce heat and cover. Cook over medium heat 25 to 30 minutes or until rice is tender and liquid is almost absorbed. Makes 6 servings.

Variation

Rice with Orzo & Peas: Add 1 cup fresh peas (1 pound in pods) or thawed frozen peas 15 minutes before end of cooking time.

The dough that is so fine you can see your hand through it is commonly called *filo* from *phyllo*, the Greek word for leaf. No one seems to know the origins of filo. It is impossible to trace this evolutionary process of several thousand years to a single source. Some authorities theorize that the Byzantines, who were innovative bakers, refined the thin dough they used to enclose food. Others speculate that Middle Eastern and Oriental spice traders sparked the adaptation of a thin dough similar to Chinese wonton wrappers and egg-roll skins.

Filo has travelled far and wide over the centuries. Marching Byzantine, Islamic and Ottoman armies spread filo to Europe and North Africa. In France, the invention of puff pastry was an attempt to copy flaky filo pastry. Or so some say.

Filo pastry is known by many names: *ouarka* in Morocco, *yufka* or *baklava hamaru* in Turkey, *peta* in the Balkan Peninsula and *strudel* in Central Europe. Pastries are called *breik* in Tunisia, *bourek* in Algeria, *borekia* in Turkey, *bourekia* in Greece and *sambousik* or *mutabbaq* in Arabic countries.

The method for preparing filo pastry has not changed since ancient times. The basic recipe of flour, water and perhaps an egg, remains the same. The dowel for rolling out the dough is always no more than 3/4 inch in diameter and about 36 inches long. Instead of rolling out the dough, the cook may chose to stretch it on a long table. Although in some areas of the world modern machinery methods have lessened the work, many Middle Eastern cooks continue to roll out or stretch their filo dough by hand.

If you are an average cook, I do not recommend making your own filo dough. If you are an experienced pastry cook, try the recipe for Homemade Filo Dough. The rolling out requires skill that only experience of many years can bring. Young girls in countries where filo pastry is an art, start rolling out filo dough when they are five years old. Even with continuing practice, they are not expected to be experts until they reach marital age. Those who do not make the grade are ridiculed.

Happily, filo sheets can be purchased at any Middle Eastern grocery store and many gourmet shops. Most packages contain 18 to 20 sheets. Depending on the individual manufacturer, the sheets vary in thickness. A single thick sheet can often take the place of two thin sheets.

Although working with filo is really easy, there are some ground rules to observe. Avoid using dough that has become dry or it will crumble and flake. Filo can be stored up to one month in the refrigerator. It can be used as needed, provided the sheets are wrapped airtight and are fresh to begin with. If your newly purchased filo is too dry or moldy, return it to the store.

Despite its fragile appearance, filo is a hardy material with a high tolerance for abuse. Tears may be patched with a small piece of moistened filo. Crinkles can be patted or smoothed down. Somewhat dry sheets can be revived by misting them lightly with water from a spray bottle used for plants. Filo can be molded against almost any shape. Chicken & Rice Turban is an example. Filo can be layered like a pie, folded like a flag and rolled like cigarettes or cigars.

Any filling can be used with filo. A list of suggested fillings is on page 115.

When using filo, either butter or oil is recommended for brushing to keep it from drying and flaking. Oil is usually preferred for dishes using vegetables. But butter or margarine can be used as well. Clarifying the butter not only removes the milky, rather gritty residue, but enhances the flavor. If clarifying butter poses a problem, use melted butter or margarine. Directions for clarifying butter are on page 157. ✄

Menu

Moroccan Bastela Supper	Turkish Wedding Supper
North African Lentil Soup, page 38	Plate of Feta Cheese and Black Olives
Beet Salad, page 59	Whiskeyed Chicken Livers, page 19
Carrot & Orange Salad, page 56	Wedding Soup, page 45
Chicken Pastry, page 116	Chicken & Rice Turban, page 118
Moroccan Bread, page 68	Tomato & Cucumber Salad, page 56
Fruit Tray Decorated with Leaves and Blossoms	Wedding Cakes, page 164
Mint Tea, page 30	Turkish Coffee, page 32
Coins, page 171	

Layered Cheese Pie

Boureki (Adapted Greek)

Cutting pastry before baking prevents excessive puffing and flaking.

1 (1-lb.) carton large-curd cottage cheese, drained
1 (3-oz.) pkg. cream cheese
1/2 lb. feta cheese, crumbled
1/2 cup grated Parmesan cheese (1-1/2 oz.)
6 eggs, beaten
2 tablespoons butter or margarine

1 small onion, minced
1 teaspoon dill weed or
    1 tablespoon chopped fresh dill
Freshly ground white pepper to taste
24 filo pastry sheets
1/2 cup butter, clarified, page 157,
    or margarine, melted

Combine cottage cheese, cream cheese, feta cheese, Parmesan cheese and eggs in a large bowl. Melt 2 tablespoons butter or margarine in a small skillet. Add onion. Sauté until golden brown. Add dill and pepper. Add to cheese mixture. Mix well. Butter a 13'' x 9'' baking pan. Stack filo pastry sheets. Trim to fit pan. Cut in half if sheets are large. Cover with plastic wrap to prevent drying out. Place half the filo sheets in prepared pan, brushing each with clarified butter or melted margarine. Pour cheese mixture over filo layers. Top with remaining filo sheets, brushing each with butter or margarine. Brush top sheet with butter or margarine. Freeze 1 hour to solidify slightly. Preheat oven to 350F (175C). Cut pastry into 2-inch diamond or square shapes. Bake 35 to 45 minutes or until golden brown. Makes about 24 pieces.

Wrapped Cheese Pie

Tyropita (Greece)

My sister, Mary Thomas, uses this method of wrapping the pastry around the filling.

6 eggs
1 cup milk or plain yogurt
2 lbs. feta cheese, crumbled
1/4 cup chopped fresh dill or
    1 tablespoon dill weed

Freshly ground white pepper to taste
1 lb. filo pastry sheets
1/2 cup butter, clarified, page 157, or
    margarine, melted

Beat eggs in a large bowl. Blend in milk or yogurt. Stir in feta cheese, dill and pepper. Mix well. Preheat oven to 350F (175C). Butter a 13'' x 9'' baking pan. Brush 1 filo pastry sheet with clarified butter or melted margarine. Place in baking pan, allowing overhang all around. Set aside 2 filo sheets and cover with plastic wrap to prevent drying out. Place remaining filo sheets over first sheet, brushing each with butter or margarine. Spread cheese filling over filo layers. Bring overhanging ends of filo over filling. Smooth creases. Brush with butter or margarine. Top with remaining 2 filo sheets. Trim edges. Brush with butter or margarine. Bake 40 to 50 minutes or until golden brown. Let stand 20 minutes to set before cutting. Cut into 3-inch diamond or square shapes. Makes 12 pieces.

Variation

Cheese Triangles (Tyrotrigona): Cut stacked filo sheets lengthwise in halves, making strips. Use 1 strip for each triangle. Brush strip with clarified butter or melted margarine. Fold lengthwise in half or in thirds to make a long, 2-inch-wide strip. Place 1 teaspoon filling in corner of strip. Fold flag-fashion, page 121, to make a triangle. Brush with butter or margarine. Place on lightly greased baking sheets. Bake at 350F (175C) 10 to 15 minutes or until golden brown. Makes 40 pastries.

How to Make Layered Cheese Pie

1/Trim filo to fit pan. Cut sheets in half if they are large. Cover with plastic wrap to prevent drying out.

2/Place half the filo sheets in pan, brushing each with clarified butter or melted margarine.

3/Filo pastry is so fragile it often tears. When this happens, cover the tear with a small piece of moistened pastry and continue layering sheets.

4/Freeze layered pie 1 hour to solidify slightly. Cut pastry into 2-inch diamond or square shapes before baking.

Pumpkin Custard Pie

Burek me Kungull (Albania)

During pumpkin season, my mother often served this as a snack or as a side dish with roasts.

2 lbs. pumpkin
2 cups milk
6 eggs
1/2 cup all-purpose flour
1 tablespoon sugar
Pinch of salt

2 tablespoons butter or margarine, melted
1 lb. filo pastry sheets
1/2 cup butter, clarified, page 157, or
    margarine, melted
2 tablespoons cold water

Peel pumpkin. Shred into a large bowl. Combine milk and eggs in a medium bowl. Beat to blend. Stir in flour until smooth. Add sugar, salt and 2 tablespoons melted butter or margarine. Stir into pumpkin. Mix well. Set aside. Preheat oven to 350F (175C). Butter a 13" x 9" baking pan. Set aside. Stack filo pastry sheets. Trim to fit pan. Cut in half if sheets are large. Cover with plastic wrap to prevent drying out. Layer half the filo sheets in prepared pan, brushing each with clarified butter or melted margarine. Pour pumpkin mixture over filo layers. Top with remaining filo sheets, brushing each with butter or margarine. Brush top sheet with butter or margarine. Sprinkle with cold water. Bake 40 to 50 minutes or until a knife inserted near center comes out clean. Let stand 20 minutes to set before cutting. Cut into 3-inch diamond or square shapes. Makes 12 pieces.

Homemade Filo Dough

You will need a 36-inch dowel, a deft hand and much patience.

4 cups all-purpose flour
2 egg yolks

1-1/2 cups water
Cornstarch

Place flour in a large bowl. Make a well in center. Beat egg yolks in a medium bowl. Beat in water. Pour into well in flour. Mix until a stiff dough is formed. Knead 5 minutes until smooth and pliable. Divide dough into 12 equal portions. Shape into balls. Sprinkle generously with cornstarch. Cover with plastic wrap to prevent drying out. Work with 1 ball at a time. Generously sprinkle a flat surface with cornstarch. Place 1 ball on cornstarch and sprinkle with more cornstarch. Flatten with the palm of your hand. Roll out to a 10-inch circle using a dowel 36 inches long and 3/4 inches in diameter. Place dowel at bottom of circle. Fold bottom of circle over dowel. Roll out lightly, rolling up dough and moving your hands from center of dowel to edges in a continuous motion. Unroll dowel from dough and repeat process, stretching dough slightly. Sprinkle dough frequently with cornstarch to aid stretching and prevent sticking, until dough is about 30 inches in diameter. Completely wind dough around dowel. Unwind and place on a clean surface. Cover with a clean cloth towel while working with other pieces of dough. Stack until ready to use. When all dough is rolled out, use immediately. Makes 12 filo pastry sheets.

Spinach Pie

Spanakopita (Greece)

Most greens and any cheese may be used as a filling for this famous pie.

2 lbs. fresh spinach or	**2 medium onions, chopped**
2 (10-oz.) pkgs. frozen chopped spinach,	**1/4 cup chopped fresh dill or**
thawed	**1 tablespoon dill weed**
6 eggs	**Salt and freshly ground pepper to taste**
1 cup milk	**1 lb. filo pastry sheets**
1/2 lb. feta cheese, crumbled	**1/2 cup olive oil**
1/4 cup olive oil	**2 tablespoons cold water**

Rinse fresh spinach thoroughly several times. Trim stems and discard. Chop leaves and drain well. If using frozen spinach, squeeze dry after thawing and fluff to separate. Beat eggs in a large bowl. Blend in milk. Stir in feta cheese. Heat 1/4 cup olive oil in a large skillet. Add spinach and onions. Sauté until spinach wilts, about 2 minutes. Add dill, salt and pepper. Sauté 1 minute to blend flavors. Add to cheese mixture. Mix well. Set aside. Preheat oven to 350F (175C). Oil a 13" x 9" baking pan. Stack filo pastry sheets. Trim to fit pan. Cut in half if sheets are large. Cover with plastic wrap to prevent drying out. Heat 1 cup olive oil in a small skillet. Place half the filo sheets in prepared pan, brushing each with hot oil. Pour spinach mixture over filo layers. Top with remaining filo sheets, brushing each with hot oil. Brush top sheet with hot oil. Sprinkle with cold water. Bake 40 to 50 minutes or until golden brown. Let stand 20 minutes to set before cutting. Cut into 3-inch diamond or square shapes. Makes 12 pieces.

Variations

Spinach Triangles: Use 1 filo pastry sheet for each triangle. Brush with hot oil. Fold in thirds to make a rectangle 4 inches wide. Brush again with hot oil. Place 1 mounded tablespoon spinach mixture in corner of rectangle. Fold flag-fashion, page 121, to make a triangle. Brush top with oil. Place on baking sheet. Bake at 350F (175C) 15 to 20 minutes or until golden brown. Makes about 20 triangles.

Spinach Wontons: May be baked or fried. Substitute 1 (12-ounce) package wonton wrappers for filo pastry sheets. Place about 2 teaspoons spinach mixture in center of each wrapper. Fold sides over filling, making rectangles. Moisten edges to seal seams. Place on greased baking sheets. Brush with hot oil. Bake at 350F (175C) 20 to 25 minutes or until golden. To fry, do not brush with oil; heat oil for frying to 275F (135C) on a deep-fry thermometer. Fry wontons until golden on all sides. Drain on paper towels. Makes 50 wontons.

Filo pastry is a glamorous cover-up for leftovers. Here is a list of filling suggestions using everyday foods. Instructions for shaping filo into triangles, rectangles, or layered pies are in this chapter. Place triangles or rectangles on an ungreased baking sheet. Brush the pastry generously with clarified butter, page 157, or melted margarine, making sure all surfaces are covered. Bake the pastries in a preheated 350F (175C) oven for 10 to 20 minutes, depending on size, or until golden brown. Bake a layered pie in a large baking pan for 45 minutes to 1 hour.

Chicken salad	Meatballs
Egg salad	Meat mixture for Sloppy Joes
Lobster, shrimp, crab or tuna salad	Salisbury Steak
Chili with or without beans	Swiss Steak
Meat stew	Meat loaf, sliced
Cooked vegetables, chopped and seasoned to taste	Chops, cooked only
	Broiled or baked fish, boned, cubed or whole

Chicken Pastry

Bastela (Morocco)

For your next party, serve this at a low table. Let everyone sit on high pillows.

1 (2-1/2-lb.) chicken, cut up
Salt and freshly ground black pepper
   to taste
2 tablespoons peanut oil
1 medium onion, chopped
2 cups Chicken Broth, page 36, or water
Pinch of saffron threads or powder,
   if desired
1 cinnamon stick
1/2 cup chopped fresh parsley
1/2 cup chopped cilantro

8 eggs, beaten
2 cups ground toasted almonds, page 67
1/4 cup granulated sugar
1/2 teaspoon ground cinnamon
7 filo pastry sheets
1/4 cup butter, clarified, page 157,
   or margarine, melted
1/4 cup powdered sugar
Ground cinnamon for garnish
Kumquats for garnish, if desired

Place chicken in a large skillet. Sprinkle with salt and pepper. Pour peanut oil over chicken. Add onion and broth or water. Stir in saffron, if desired. Bring to a boil. Add cinnamon stick. Reduce heat and cover. Simmer over low heat 1 hour or until chicken is very tender. Remove chicken from skillet. Reserve liquid. Cool chicken. Remove meat from bones. Shred chicken into a bowl. Set aside. Remove cinnamon stick from skillet and discard. Measure 1 cup liquid and return to skillet. Bring to a boil. Add parsley and cilantro. Simmer, uncovered, over low heat 3 minutes. Add beaten eggs. Cook and stir until scrambled and liquid is absorbed. Set aside. Combine almonds, granulated sugar and 1/2 teaspoon cinnamon in a small bowl. Set aside. Preheat oven to 350F (175C). Butter a 10-inch ovenproof skillet with rounded sides. Stack filo pastry sheets. Cover with plastic wrap to prevent drying out. Place 4 filo sheets in bottom of skillet, brushing each with clarified butter or melted margarine. Allow a 5- to 6-inch overhang. Sprinkle a third of the almond mixture over filo sheets. Top with half the shredded chicken. Top with another third of the almond mixture. Drain egg mixture, if necessary. Place half the egg mixture over almond mixture. Repeat until all ingredients are used, ending with almond mixture. Fold overhang over filling. Smooth down creases. Brush with butter or margarine. Top with remaining 3 filo sheets, brushing each with butter or margarine and folding overhang under. Bake 25 to 35 minutes or until golden brown. Cool slightly. Invert onto a platter. Sprinkle with powdered sugar. Make a decorative crisscross design with remaining cinnamon. Garnish with kumquats, if desired. Cut in wedges and serve hot. Makes about 6 servings.

Chicken & Rice Turban

(Adapted Albanian)

My mother's chicken and rice pastry was often transformed into a turban shape for an elegant luncheon.

Egg & Lemon Sauce, page 63
1 (3-lb.) chicken
Water
1 medium onion, halved
1 carrot
Few parsley sprigs
Salt and freshly ground black pepper
   to taste
2 tablespoons butter or margarine

1 medium onion, chopped
1 cup long-grain rice
3 eggs, beaten
1 cup milk
1 teaspoon crushed dried leaf mint
Salt and freshly ground black pepper to taste
6 filo pastry sheets
1/2 cup butter, clarified, page 157,
   or margarine, melted

Prepare Egg & Lemon Sauce. Set aside. Place chicken in a large saucepan. Add water to cover. Add onion halves, carrot, parsley, salt and pepper. Bring to a boil. Reduce heat and cover. Cook over medium-low heat 40 minutes or until chicken is tender. Drain, reserving 2-1/2 cups broth. Remove chicken. Cool. Remove meat from bones. Shred chicken finely into a large bowl. Set aside. Melt 2 tablespoons butter or margarine in a medium saucepan. Add chopped onion. Sauté until tender. Add rice. Sauté 2 minutes. Add reserved broth. Bring to a boil. Reduce heat and cover. Cook over medium heat 20 minutes or until liquid is absorbed. Add rice to chicken. Add eggs, milk, mint, salt and pepper. Mix well. Set aside. Preheat oven to 350F (175C). Grease a 10-inch Bundt pan. Brush 1 filo pastry sheet with melted butter or margarine. Carefully place in pan, molding creases diagonally against bottom, side and around center tube. Brush another filo sheet with butter or margarine. Carefully place over first sheet, molding against pan. Add 2 more filo sheets, brushing each with butter or margarine. Fill pastry-lined pan with chicken mixture. Fold any filo overhang over mixture. Place 2 filo sheets over chicken mixture, brushing each with butter or margarine. Trim edges and discard. Bake 40 to 50 minutes or until golden brown. Let stand 15 minutes to set before serving. Heat Egg & Lemon Sauce. Turn into a sauce boat. Invert pastry onto a serving plate. Cut into slices. Serve with Egg & Lemon Sauce. Makes 8 to 12 servings.

Variation

Beef & Rice Turban: Substitute 1-1/2 pounds ground lean beef or 1 pound beef cubes for chicken. Cook in 2 tablespoons butter or margarine until browned. Add water to cover. Season with salt and pepper. Bring to a boil. Reduce heat and cover. Simmer over low heat 1-1/2 hours or until meat is tender. Shred meat. Use as directed for chicken.

How to Make Chicken & Rice Turban

1/Carefully place filo in Bundt pan, molding creases di-agonally against bottom, side and around center tube. Repeat with 3 more filo sheets.

2/Let baked pastry stand 15 minutes to set before serving. To serve, invert pastry onto a serving plate. Cut into slices.

Onion Pie

Burek me Qjep (Albania)

Here's a Balkan version of French quiche.

1/4 cup olive oil
6 medium onions, thinly sliced
1 tablespoon crushed dried leaf mint
Salt and freshly ground pepper to taste

6 eggs
1 cup milk
20 filo pastry sheets
1/3 cup olive oil

Heat 1/4 cup olive oil in a large skillet. Add onions. Sauté until golden but not browned. Add mint, salt and pepper. Beat eggs in a large bowl. Beat in milk. Add onion mixture. Preheat oven to 350F (175C). Butter a 13" x 9" baking pan. Stack filo pastry sheets. Trim to fit pan. Cut in half if sheets are large. Cover with plastic wrap to prevent drying out. Heat 1/3 cup olive oil in a small skillet. Layer 11 filo pastry sheets in prepared pan, brushing each with hot oil. Pour onion mixture over filo layers. Top with remaining 9 filo sheets, brushing each sheet with oil. Brush top sheet with oil. Bake 35 to 40 minutes or until golden and firm. Cut into 3-inch diamond or square shapes. Makes 12 pieces.

Filo Triangles
Sambousik (Arabic)

Prepare one of the fillings suggested for these Arabic-style triangles.

Cheese Filling, see below
Meat Filling, see below
Spinach Filling, see below

20 filo pastry sheets
1/3 cup butter, clarified, page 157,
   or margarine, melted

Cheese Filling:
1 cup crumbled feta cheese, ricotta cheese,
   Syrian cheese or soft Mexican cheese
   (about 4 oz.)

1/2 cup chopped fresh parsley
1 small onion, grated
Salt and freshly ground white pepper to taste

Meat Filling:
1 tablespoon butter or margarine
1 small onion, chopped
1/2 lb. ground lean beef or lamb
2 tablespoons pine nuts

1/4 teaspoon ground allspice
Pinch of cinnamon
Salt and freshly ground pepper to taste
2 teaspoons lemon juice

Spinach Filling:
1 lb. fresh spinach or 1 (10-oz.) pkg.
   frozen chopped spinach, thawed
1/4 cup olive oil
1 small onion, chopped
1/4 cup crumbled feta cheese, cottage cheese
   or soft Mexican cheese (1 oz.)

Juice of 1 lemon (3 tablespoons)
1/4 teaspoon sumac
Salt and freshly ground black pepper to taste

Prepare desired filling. Set aside. Preheat oven to 350F (175C). Stack filo pastry sheets and cut lengthwise into thirds, making long, thin strips. Stack strips. Cover with plastic wrap to prevent drying. Use 3 strips of filo for each triangle. Stack 3 strips, brushing each with clarified butter or melted margarine. Place 1 heaping tablespoon filling in corner of strip. Fold flag-fashion, opposite, to make a triangle. Place seam-side down on baking sheets. Brush tops with butter or margarine. Bake 15 to 20 minutes or until golden. Makes 20 triangles.

Cheese Filling:
Combine all ingredients in a medium bowl. Mix well.

Meat Filling:
Melt butter or margarine in a small saucepan. Add onion. Sauté until tender. Add meat. Cook until just browned. Add remaining ingredients. Cook and stir 2 minutes.

Spinach Filling:
Rinse fresh spinach thoroughly several times. Trim off stems and discard. Chop leaves and drain well. If using frozen spinach, squeeze dry after thawing and fluff to separate. Place spinach in a large bowl. Heat olive oil in a small skillet. Add onion. Sauté 1 minute. Add to spinach. Add remaining ingredients. Toss gently to mix well.

Filling & Folding Filo Pastry Sheets

To fill and fold filo flag-fashion for Filo Triangles, cut stacked pastry sheets into long, thin strips. Stack 3 strips, brushing each with clarified butter or melted margarine. Place 1 heaping tablespoon filling in corner of strip. Fold corner over filling, making a triangle. Continue folding strip as in a flag fold, maintaining triangle shape.

To fill and fold filo pastry flag-fashion for Filo Triangles, cut stacked pastry sheets into long, thin strips. Stack 3 strips, brushing each with butter or margarine. Place 1 heaping tablespoon filling in corner of strip. Fold corner over filling, making a triangle. Continue folding strip as in a flag fold, maintaining triangle shape.

Potato-Stuffed Filo Pastry

Rghaif Del Ferran (Morocco)

Potato-filled pastries make wonderful snacks or a quick lunch.

2 medium potatoes, cooked, mashed
1 medium onion, chopped
1 cup chopped fresh parsley
1/2 cup chopped cilantro
1 egg
1 garlic clove, minced
1 tablespoon vegetable oil

1 tablespoon vinegar
1 tablespoon paprika
1 teaspoon ground cumin
Salt and freshly ground pepper to taste
10 filo pastry sheets
1/4 cup vegetable oil

Combine potatoes, onion, parsley, cilantro, egg, garlic, oil, vinegar, paprika, cumin, salt and pepper in a large bowl. Mix well. Preheat oven to 350F (175C). Grease a baking sheet. Stack filo sheets and cut into twenty 8- or 9-inch squares. Cover with plastic wrap to prevent drying out. Brush 1 square with oil. Top with another square and brush with oil. Place 2 tablespoons potato mixture near bottom of square. Fold 2 opposite sides of square over filling. Fold top and bottom over filling, making a neat 3-inch-square packet. Place seam-side down on prepared baking sheet. Brush with oil. Repeat with remaining squares and potato mixture. Bake 20 to 30 minutes or until golden brown. Makes 10 pastries.

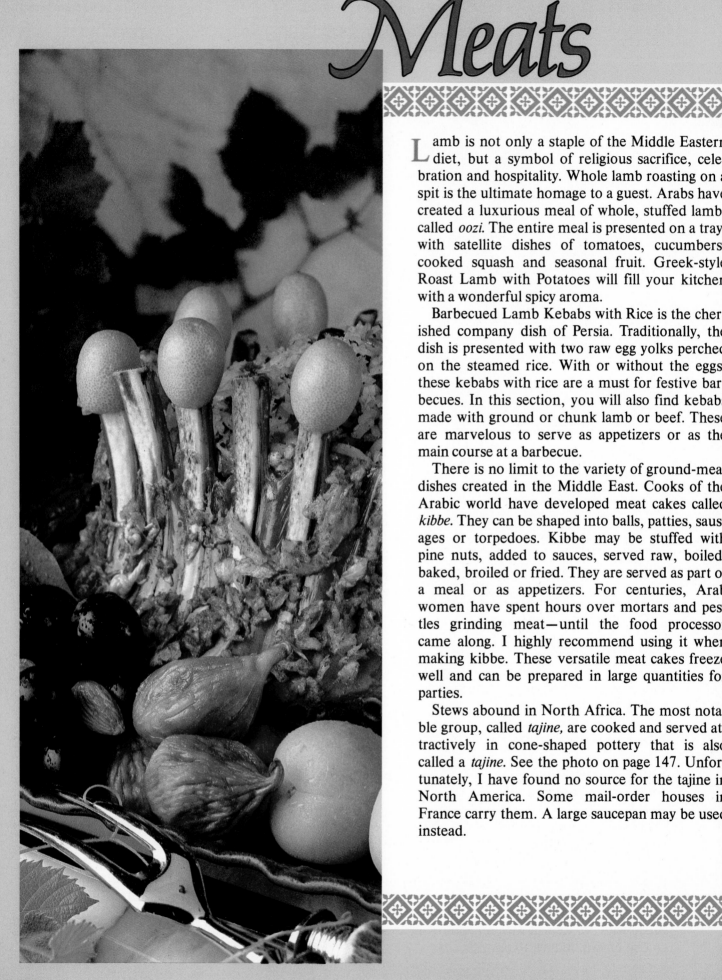

Meats

Lamb is not only a staple of the Middle Eastern diet, but a symbol of religious sacrifice, celebration and hospitality. Whole lamb roasting on a spit is the ultimate homage to a guest. Arabs have created a luxurious meal of whole, stuffed lamb, called *oozi*. The entire meal is presented on a tray, with satellite dishes of tomatoes, cucumbers, cooked squash and seasonal fruit. Greek-style Roast Lamb with Potatoes will fill your kitchen with a wonderful spicy aroma.

Barbecued Lamb Kebabs with Rice is the cherished company dish of Persia. Traditionally, the dish is presented with two raw egg yolks perched on the steamed rice. With or without the eggs, these kebabs with rice are a must for festive barbecues. In this section, you will also find kebabs made with ground or chunk lamb or beef. These are marvelous to serve as appetizers or as the main course at a barbecue.

There is no limit to the variety of ground-meat dishes created in the Middle East. Cooks of the Arabic world have developed meat cakes called *kibbe*. They can be shaped into balls, patties, sausages or torpedoes. Kibbe may be stuffed with pine nuts, added to sauces, served raw, boiled, baked, broiled or fried. They are served as part of a meal or as appetizers. For centuries, Arab women have spent hours over mortars and pestles grinding meat—until the food processor came along. I highly recommend using it when making kibbe. These versatile meat cakes freeze well and can be prepared in large quantities for parties.

Stews abound in North Africa. The most notable group, called *tajine,* are cooked and served attractively in cone-shaped pottery that is also called a *tajine.* See the photo on page 147. Unfortunately, I have found no source for the tajine in North America. Some mail-order houses in France carry them. A large saucepan may be used instead.

Greece boasts some wonderfully fragrant stews prepared *plaki*-style, meaning filled with herbs and vegetables. Greeks cook Beef & Onion Stew, called *Stifado,* over low heat for hours. It will remind you of Germany's *Sauerbraten.* The recipe in this book uses standard cooking methods, but you may use a crockpot if the stew cooks eight hours or longer.

Organ meats such as liver, tripe, heart, lung, kidney, brains and sweetbreads are widely used in Middle Eastern cookery. Every scrap of a lamb or camel is utilized. It is considered sacrilegious to waste any portion of an animal which provides food, clothing and labor to man.

When lamb is called for in this section, beef may be substituted. It may be more easily available and less expensive. In dishes where lamb is preferred, it is mentioned first and beef is mentioned second. Middle Easterners prefer lamb cooked well, not pinkish.

You will enjoy Crown Roast of Lamb with Rice Stuffing. It is an adaptation of a Bedouin recipe. Holiday cooks will find this recipe a welcome change from turkey or ham. �֎

Menu

Desert Feast

Cucumber Sticks, Platter of Olives, Pistachio Nuts, Romaine Leaves, Mint Sprigs, Radishes Arabic Chopped Salad, page 60 Cucumber-Yogurt Salad, page 62 Arabic Pocket Bread, page 74	Crown Roast of Lamb with Rice Stuffing, page 130 Fresh Fruit, Nuts and Dates Arabic Cheese-Filled Pastry, page 160 Arabic Coffee, page 32

The Crown Roast of Lamb with Rice Stuffing replaces the whole stuffed lamb traditionally served over rice at feasts. The lamb roast is placed in the center of the table, carpet-covered floor or tray table, and surrounded with fruits and nuts for a self-contained meal. The condiments, salad and bread are placed around the table. Diners sit around the table and help themselves to the dishes as desired. Coffee and dessert are served after the meal.

Stuffed Meatballs

Kubbe (Iraq)

These stuffed meat patties are always part of an Iraqi buffet.

Kubbe Filling, page 129
1-1/2 lbs. ground extra-lean beef
1 cup medium-grade bulgur
1/2 cup fine-grade semolina or farina

1-1/2 teaspoons baking soda
l cup water
Salt to taste
Oil for frying

Prepare Kubbe Filling. Set aside. Place ground beef, bulgur, semolina or farina, baking soda, water and salt in food processor. Process until smooth. Pinch off pieces of mixture 2 inches in diameter. Shape into balls. Moisten your hands and mold each ball into a cup 1-1/2 inches deep. Place 1 tablespoon Kubbe Filling in each cup. Shape meat mixture around filling, pinching seams together to enclose filling completely. Shape into rounded patties about 2-1/2 inches in diameter. Pour oil about 1 inch deep into a large skillet. Heat to 350F (175C) on a deep-fry thermometer. At this temperature, a 1-inch cube of bread will turn golden brown in 65 seconds. Fry a few meat patties at a time until golden on both sides, about 10 minutes. Drain on paper towels. Serve hot. Makes about 20 patties.

Sabbath Stew

Cholent (Israel)

Popular in Israel and Eastern Europe where it originated as a poorman's meatless stew.

3 tablespoons chicken fat
3 lbs. lean short ribs, beef chuck,
    cut up, or stew meat
3 medium onions, diced
3 garlic cloves, minced
Salt and freshly ground pepper to taste
1/2 cup dried lima beans, sorted, rinsed
1/2 cup dried kidney beans, sorted, rinsed

1/2 cup dried Great Northern beans,
    sorted, rinsed
1/2 cup dried black beans, sorted, rinsed
1 cup barley
2 tablespoons all-purpose flour
2 teaspoons paprika
Chicken Broth, page 36, or water

Melt chicken fat in a large saucepan or Dutch oven. Add meat. Sauté until browned on all sides. Add onions, garlic, salt and pepper. Sauté until onion is tender. Add all beans and barley. Sprinkle with flour and paprika. Add broth or water to come 1/2 inch or more above surface of meat. Bring to a boil. Reduce heat and cover. Simmer over very low heat 4 to 5 hours or until meat is very tender. Remove meat from bones. Discard bones. Leave ribs whole, if desired. Place on a platter. Serve with barley and beans. Makes 6 servings.

TIP ◈◈◈◈◈◈◈◈◈◈◈◈◈◈◈◈◈◈◈◈

The traditional method of cooking Cholent is to start it 24 hours in advance to avoid cooking on the Sabbath. An electric crockpot set on Low may be used. Traditionalists also add derma which are beef intestines stuffed with cooked, seasoned buckwheat groats, bulgur, semolina, flour or bread. Derma, purchased at Jewish delicatessens, may be added to the stew at the end of cooking time to heat through.

Tunisian Meatballs

Boulettes de Viande (Tunisia)

Meatballs are part of Tunisian Couscous but may be served by themselves.

1 lb. ground lean veal, lamb or beef
3 green onions, chopped
1/4 cup chopped fresh parsley
1 slice French bread or white bread
Water
2 garlic cloves, minced
1 egg, beaten
Pinch of ground cinnamon
Salt and freshly ground pepper to taste

1 (6-inch) celery-heart stalk,
   cut in 1-inch pieces
1 small potato, peeled, cut in 6 cubes
1 egg
All-purpose flour
Oil for frying
1 (8-oz.) can tomato sauce
1/4 cup dry red wine
Salt and freshly ground pepper to taste

Combine meat, green onions and parsley in a large bowl. Moisten bread in water. Squeeze dry. Add to meat mixture. Add garlic, 1 beaten egg, cinnamon, salt and pepper. Mix well. Divide into 6 equal portions. Shape into balls. Insert pieces of celery and potato into center of meatballs. Celery and potato should be completely covered with meat. Beat 1 egg in a shallow bowl. Dip meatballs in beaten egg. Roll in flour. Pour oil 1/2 inch deep into a large skillet. Heat to 350F (175C) on a deep-fry thermometer. At this temperature, a 1-inch cube of bread will turn golden brown in 65 seconds. Fry meatballs until browned on all sides, about 4 minutes. Remove from skillet and set aside. Drain all but 2 tablespoons oil from skillet. Stir in remaining ingredients. Bring to a simmer. Reduce heat. Add meatballs. Cover and cook over medium heat 30 minutes or until meatballs are firm. Serve hot. Spoon sauce over meatballs. Makes 6 meatballs.

Spiced Meat Skillet

Timen Ajami (Iraq)

Serve this quick and easy skillet dish over Saffron Rice.

2 tablespoons vegetable oil
1 large onion, chopped
1-1/2 lbs. ground lean beef or lamb
1/4 teaspoon ground allspice
1/4 teaspoon curry powder

Salt and freshly ground pepper to taste
2 tablespoons rose water
1/2 cup dried currants
1/2 cup chopped almonds

Heat oil in a large skillet. Add onion. Sauté until onion is tender. Add meat. Cook until browned and crumbly. Drain off fat, if necessary. Add allspice, curry powder, salt and pepper to cooked meat. Cook 3 minutes to blend flavors. Add remaining ingredients. Reduce heat and cover. Simmer over low heat 15 minutes, stirring occasionally to prevent sticking. Serve hot. Makes 6 to 8 servings.

Ground-Meat Kebabs

Kefta Kabab (Morocco)

I watched Moroccans in Marrakech prepare delicious sausage-like burgers over a portable brazier.

1 lb. ground lean beef or lamb	1 teaspoon ground cumin
1/4 cup chopped fresh parsley	1 teaspoon paprika
1/4 cup chopped cilantro	1 teaspoon freshly ground pepper
1 medium onion, grated	Salt to taste

Combine all ingredients in a large bowl. Mix well. Let stand 1 hour to blend flavors. Preheat oven to broil. Or prepare hot coals on barbecue grill. Using about 1/4 cup mixture for each kebab, mold into a sausage shape around flat metal skewers. Moistening your hands will help mold the meat mixture onto skewers. Taper ends of sausage shapes to prevent meat from slipping off skewers during cooking. Place skewers on broiler rack 4 inches from heat source on grill or over hot coals. Turn frequently to brown evenly until meat is done as desired, 10 to 15 minutes. Makes 8 to 10 servings.

Picnic Meatballs

Kufteh Tabrizi (Iran)

Stuffed meatballs are festive fare for a picnic held on the 13th day of the Persian New Year.

2 tablespoons butter or margarine	1/2 cup coarsely chopped walnuts
1 medium onion, chopped	2 large hard-cooked eggs, coarsely chopped
2 lbs. ground lean beef	10 pitted prunes
4 eggs	1/2 cup raisins or dried currants
1-1/2 cups garbanzo-bean flour	4 cups Beef Broth, page 36, or water
1 cup water	Salt and freshly ground pepper to taste
Salt and freshly ground pepper to taste	Pinch of saffron threads or powder
Pinch of saffron threads or powder	

Melt butter or margarine in a small skillet. Add onion. Sauté until onion is tender and golden brown. Set aside. Combine beef, eggs, bean flour, 1 cup water, salt, pepper and saffron in a large bowl. Mix well. Knead until meat mixture is dough-like. Pinch off pieces of meat mixture about 3 inches in diameter. Shape into large patties. Place 1 teaspoon walnuts, 1 teaspoon sautéed onion, 1 teaspoon chopped egg, 1 prune and 1 teaspoon raisins or currants in center of each patty. Mold patty around filling, pinching seams to enclose filling completely. Shape into meatballs. Place meatballs in a large shallow saucepan. Pour 4 cups broth or water over meatballs. Sprinkle with salt, pepper and saffron. Bring to a boil. Reduce heat and cover. Simmer over low heat 40 minutes or until meatballs are done as desired. Serve hot. Makes 10 large meatballs.

TIP

Garbanzo-bean flour, a high-protein flour, may be purchased at Middle Eastern grocery stores and some health-food stores. See page 14 for substitution information.

How to Make Ground-Meat Kebabs

1/Using about 1/4 cup mixture for each kebab, mold into a sausage shape around flat metal skewers.

2/Taper ends of sausage shapes to prevent meat from slipping off skewers during cooking.

Fried Meatballs

Keftedes Tiganites (Greece)

Basic meatballs to serve on wooden picks as appetizers or with your favorite sauce over pasta or rice.

1 lb. ground lean lamb or beef	**1 tablespoon chopped fresh mint or**
1 medium onion, finely chopped	**1 teaspoon crushed dried leaf mint**
1 garlic clove, minced	**2 or 3 tablespoons dry red wine or water**
2 slices white bread, crusts removed	**Pinch of ground allspice**
Water	**Salt and freshly ground pepper to taste**
1 egg, beaten	**All-purpose flour**
3 tablespoons chopped fresh parsley	**Oil for frying**

Combine meat, onion and garlic in a large bowl. Moisten bread in water. Squeeze dry. Add to meat mixture. Add egg, parsley, mint, wine or water, allspice, salt and pepper. Mix well. Refrigerate 1 hour to blend flavors. Pinch off pieces of meat mixture 1 inch in diameter. Shape into balls. Roll in flour. Pour oil 1/2 inch deep into a large skillet. Heat to 350F (175C) on a deep-fry thermometer. At this temperature, a 1-inch cube of bread will turn golden brown in 65 seconds. Carefully lower a few meatballs at a time into hot oil. Do not crowd in skillet. Fry until browned on all sides and done as desired. Drain on paper towels. Serve hot. Makes 18 to 20 meatballs.

Beef & Onion Stew

Stifado (Greece)

If you like sauerbraten, you'll enjoy this sweet-and-sour stew.

1/4 cup olive oil	**1 cinnamon stick**
2 lbs. lean boneless beef chuck, cubed	**4 whole cloves**
1 lb. small white onions, peeled	**1/2 cup vinegar**
5 garlic cloves, minced	**1 (1-lb.) can whole tomatoes, drained**
1 teaspoon pickling spice,	**1/2 cup Beef Broth, page 36, or water**
** tied in cheesecloth**	**Salt and freshly ground pepper to taste**

Heat olive oil in a large saucepan. Add beef. Cook until browned on all sides. Add onions and garlic. Cook until onions are golden. Add pickling spice in cheesecloth, cinnamon stick, cloves, vinegar, tomatoes, broth or water, salt and pepper. Bring to a boil. Reduce heat and cover. Simmer over low heat 1-1/2 to 2 hours or until meat is very tender. Remove pickling spice in cheesecloth. Serve stew hot. Makes 6 to 8 servings.

Beef Curry

Kari (Iraq)

Curry probably came to Iraq from India while the British ruled both countries.

1/4 cup butter or margarine	**2 cups water**
4 large onions, chopped	**2 lbs. lean beef or lamb,**
4 garlic cloves, minced	** cut into 1-inch cubes**
1/4 cup Madras curry powder or	**Salt and freshly ground pepper to taste**
** other Indian curry powder**	**4 medium potatoes, diced**
6 medium tomatoes, diced	**Hot cooked rice, if desired**
3 tablespoons tomato paste	

Melt butter or margarine in a large saucepan. Add onions and garlic. Sauté until golden but not browned. Stir in curry powder. Reduce heat. Cook over low heat 10 minutes to blend flavors. Add tomatoes. Sauté 3 minutes. Mix tomato paste with water. Stir into onion mixture. Add meat, salt and pepper. Bring to a boil. Reduce heat and cover. Simmer over low heat 1 hour. Add potatoes. Cook, covered, 40 minutes longer or until meat is tender. Serve over hot cooked rice, if desired. Makes 6 servings.

Variations

Chicken Curry: Omit meat. Substitute 3 pounds chicken pieces. Cook 20 minutes before adding potatoes.

Vegetarian Curry: Omit meat. Add potatoes after adding tomato-paste mixture and bringing to a boil. Cook 15 minutes. Add 2 pounds sliced summer squash, zucchini or green beans, or 1 medium, cubed eggplant, 2 cups green peas or 2 (10-ounce) packages drained, thawed, frozen okra. Other vegetables may be substituted.

Barbecued Butterflied Lamb

Psito Skhara (Greece)

The longer the lamb marinates, the better the flavor.

1 (3-1/2- to 4-lb.) leg of lamb,	**4 or 5 garlic cloves, slivered**
boned, butterflied	**1/2 cup olive oil**
Salt and freshly ground pepper to taste	**1/2 cup red-wine vinegar**
2 tablespoons crushed dried leaf oregano	**1 medium onion, sliced, separated in rings**
1 teaspoon crushed dried leaf mint	**Few dried oregano sprigs, if desired**

Place leg of lamb flat on a clean surface. Rub on both sides with salt and pepper, oregano and mint. Make deep slits in several places in meat. Insert garlic slivers into slits. Combine olive oil and vinegar in a large shallow bowl. Scatter half the onion slices over vinegar mixture. Place lamb in marinade. Turn to coat other side with marinade. Scatter remaining onion slices over lamb. Top with oregano sprigs, if desired. Cover. Marinate 2 to 24 hours in refrigerator. Prepare hot coals on barbecue grill. Place meat cut-side up on grill. Cook, turning and basting frequently with marinade, until browned and done as desired, 20 to 30 minutes. Cut into slices to serve. Makes 6 to 8 servings.

Variation

Barbecued Rack of Lamb: Substitute 4 baby racks of lamb for leg of lamb. French-cut tips of ribs by cutting 1 inch of the meaty portion from each rib tip. Cover rib tips with foil to prevent charring. Continue with recipe.

TIP

Packaged sprigs of dried oregano are often available at Middle Eastern grocery stores.

Kubbe Filling

Use this tasty filling to make Stuffed Meatballs.

2 tablespoons olive oil	**1/2 teaspoon Mixed Spice, page 188, or**
2 small onions, finely chopped	**salt and freshly ground pepper to taste**
3/4 lb. coarsely ground lean beef	

Heat olive oil in a medium skillet. Add onions. Sauté until tender. Add beef. Cook until beef is browned and crumbly. Add Mixed Spice or salt and pepper. Cook 1 minute longer to blend flavors. Makes enough filling for Stuffed Meatballs.

Crown Roast of Lamb with Rice Stuffing

(Adapted Arabic)

I've substituted a crown roast of lamb for a whole baby lamb—the traditional Arabic lamb feast.

1 (5- to 6-lb.) lean crown roast of lamb	1-1/2 cups short-grain rice
2 tablespoons butter or margarine	1/4 cup dried currants
1 medium onion, chopped	1/4 cup pine nuts
1 teaspoon ground cinnamon	1/2 teaspoon ground cinnamon
1/4 teaspoon ground cloves	1/8 teaspoon ground allspice
1/4 teaspoon ground cardamom	Salt and freshly ground pepper to taste
2 tablespoons butter or margarine	2 cups Chicken Broth, page 36, or water
1 medium onion, chopped	Grapes, almonds, apricots, kumquats,
1 celery-heart stalk with leaves, diced	pomegranate wedges, dates and figs
2 tablespoons chopped fresh parsley	for garnish, as desired

Preheat oven to 350F (175C). Have butcher prepare crown of 3 or 4 racks of lamb. Wipe meat with damp cloth. Melt 2 tablespoons butter or margarine. Add 1 chopped onion, 1 teaspoon cinnamon, cloves and cardamom. Sauté until onion is tender. Rub roast all over with onion mixture. Place rib-end up in a roasting pan. Wrap rib tips with foil to prevent charring. Roast 2 to 2-1/2 hours or until meat thermometer inserted in thickest part of roast registers 155F to 160F (85C) for rare, 175F to 180F (80C) for well-done. About 40 minutes before roast is done, melt 2 tablespoons butter or margarine in a large skillet. Add 1 chopped onion, celery and parsley. Sauté until vegetables are tender. Add rice, currants, pine nuts, 1/2 teaspoon cinnamon, allspice, salt and pepper. Sauté until rice is glazed. Add broth or water. Bring to a boil. Reduce heat and cover. Boil 10 minutes or until liquid is absorbed. Fill center of roast with stuffing. Cover loosely with foil. Continue roasting until meat is done. Place on a platter. Let stand 15 minutes before carving. Keep rice covered with foil until ready to serve. To serve, remove foil from rib tips and rice. Fluff rice with a fork. Garnish roast as desired. Carve roast, allowing 2 chops per person. Makes 6 to 8 servings.

Variation

Crown Roast of Pork with Rice Stuffing: Substitute crown roast of pork for lamb. Have butcher prepare crown of 2 loins of pork. Place roast rib-end up on rack in roasting pan. Wrap rib tips with foil. Roast at 350F (175C) 3 to 3-1/2 hours or until meat thermometer inserted in thickest part of roast registers 185F (80C). Continue with recipe. Allow 3 chops per person. If gravy is desired, strain pan juices into a small saucepan. Skim off fat with a large spoon. Stir 1 tablespoon flour into 1/4 cup water to make a paste. Gradually add paste to strained pan juices. Heat and stir until slightly thickened. Pour into gravy boat and serve with roast.

Shish Kebab   Photo on cover.

Şiş Kebabı (Turkey)

Vary your kebabs by adding small whole onions and sliced zucchini.

1 large onion	**1 large eggplant, cubed**
1/4 cup olive oil	**4 medium tomatoes, quartered, or**
1/2 cup red-wine vinegar	**16 cherry tomatoes**
2 garlic cloves, minced	**4 green bell peppers, halved or quartered**
Salt and freshly ground black pepper	**2 tablespoons butter or margarine, melted**
to taste	
1 (3-1/2- to 4-1/2-lb.) leg of lamb,	
boned, cut in 1-1/2-inch cubes	

Cut onion in half lengthwise, then slice to make long, thin strips. Combine olive oil, vinegar, onion strips, garlic, salt and black pepper in a large shallow bowl. Mix well. Add meat. Toss to coat well. Cover and marinate in refrigerator 2 to 24 hours. Preheat oven to broil. Or prepare hot coals on barbecue grill. Alternately thread marinated lamb, eggplant, tomatoes and green pepper on long metal skewers. Brush with butter or margarine. Place skewers on broiler rack 4 inches from heat source or on grill over hot coals. Cook, turning and basting frequently with marinade, until meat is done as desired, 15 to 20 minutes. Makes 8 servings.

Barbecued Lamb Kebabs with Rice

Chelo Kabab (Iran)

For an authentic touch, top rice with two egg yolks and serve sumac spice in tiny saucers for sprinkling.

2 lbs. leg of lamb, cut in	**1/2 cup lemon juice (3 medium lemons)**
4" x 5" x 1/4" slices	**3 tablespoons vegetable oil**
Salt and freshly ground pepper to taste	**Persian Steamed Rice, page 104**
1 medium onion	

Place meat slices in a shallow bowl or dish. Sprinkle with salt and pepper. Cut onion in half lengthwise, then slice to make long, thin strips. Cover meat with onion strips. Sprinkle with lemon juice and oil. Cover and marinate in refrigerator several hours or overnight, turning meat occasionally. Prepare Persian Steamed Rice. Keep warm. Preheat oven to broil. Or prepare hot coals on barbecue grill. Thread meat by weaving strips on metal skewers. Place skewers on broiler rack 4 inches from heat source or on grill over hot coals. Cook, turning frequently to brown evenly, until done as desired, 5 to 10 minutes. Serve hot with Persian Steamed Rice. Makes 6 to 8 servings.

Variations

Kebabs Marinated in Yogurt: Omit marinade. Mix 1 cup yogurt with 1 grated onion in a large bowl. Marinate meat strips in yogurt mixture several hours. Thread meat on skewers and cook as directed.

Kebabs with Cherry Tomatoes: Cut meat into 1-inch cubes. Marinate as directed above. Thread on metal skewers alternately with cherry tomatoes.

Lamb & Potato Stew

Maraka (Iraq)

Plates of Lamb & Potato Stew over rice were served to us at a roadside mountain cafe in Northern Iraq.

3 to 4 lbs. shoulder of lamb or
  beef short ribs
2 cups water
1 teaspoon ground cardamom
1/2 teaspoon ground cloves

Salt and freshly ground pepper to taste
1 tablespoon tomato paste
2 cups Beef Broth, page 36, or water
4 medium, new potatoes, peeled, quartered

Place lamb or beef in a large saucepan. Add 2 cups water, cardamom, cloves, salt and pepper. Bring to a boil. Reduce heat and cover. Cook over medium-high heat until pan is almost dry, 20 to 30 minutes. Stir in tomato paste. Cook and stir 1 minute to blend flavors. Add broth or water and potatoes. Bring to a boil. Reduce heat and cover. Simmer over low heat, stirring occasionally, 1 hour or until meat and potatoes are tender. Skim off fat. Serve stew hot. Makes 6 to 8 servings.

Greek Stew

Yahni (Greece)

A hearty basic stew with many seasonal variations.

1/4 cup olive oil
2 medium onions, chopped
2 garlic cloves, minced
2 lbs. lean boneless lamb,
  cut in 1-inch cubes
1 lb. medium tomatoes, chopped, or
  1 (1-lb.) can whole tomatoes,
  drained, crushed

1 tablespoon chopped fresh parsley
Salt and freshly ground pepper to taste
2 cups Beef Broth, page 36, or water
Juice of 1/2 lemon (1-1/2 tablespoons),
  if desired

Heat olive oil in a large saucepan. Add onions and garlic. Sauté until onions are tender. Add lamb. Cook until lamb is browned on all sides. Add tomatoes, parsley, salt and pepper. Cook 1 minute. Add broth or water. Bring to a boil. Reduce heat and cover. Simmer over low heat 1-1/2 to 2 hours or until meat is tender. Sprinkle with lemon juice before serving, if desired. Makes 6 servings.

Variations

Lamb & Green-Bean Stew: Add 1 pound trimmed green beans, broken in 1-inch pieces, to stew 40 minutes before end of cooking time. Cover and cook as directed.

Lamb & Artichoke Stew: Add 6 small artichokes, outer leaves and fuzzy chokes removed, to stew 30 minutes before end of cooking time. Cover and cook as directed.

Lamb & Spinach Stew: Add 1 bunch spinach, trimmed, rinsed and chopped, or 1 (10-ounce) package frozen leaf spinach, thawed, to stew about 20 minutes before end of cooking time. Cover and cook as directed.

Lamb & Potato Stew: Add 2 large new potatoes, peeled and thickly sliced, to stew 40 minutes before end of cooking time. Cover and cook as directed.

Upside-Down Meat Pie
Makloubeh (Arabic)

The top rice layer ends up in the bottom of this delicately spiced stew.

1/4 cup vegetable oil
2 medium onions, chopped
1 garlic clove, minced
1/4 cup slivered almonds or pine nuts
1-1/2 lbs. boneless lean lamb,
   beef or veal, diced or coarsely chopped
1/4 teaspoon ground cumin
1/8 teaspoon ground allspice
Pinch of ground cinnamon
Pinch of ground cloves
Pinch of ground cardamom
Salt and freshly ground pepper to taste

About 1-1/2 cups Beef Broth, page 36,
   or water
1 small eggplant, unpeeled,
   cut lengthwise into 1/4-inch slices
Salt
Oil for frying
1 cup long-grain rice
Boiling water
1/4 cup warm water
1/4 teaspoon saffron threads or powder
Dash of rose water
Broth or water as needed

Heat 1/4 cup oil in a large saucepan. Add onions, garlic and almonds or pine nuts. Sauté until onions are tender. Add meat. Cook until meat is browned. Add cumin, allspice, cinnamon, cloves, cardamom, salt and pepper. Add 1-1/2 cups broth or water. Bring to a boil. Reduce heat and cover. Simmer over low heat 1 hour or until meat is tender. Sprinkle eggplant slices with salt. Let stand 5 minutes to leach out bitter flavor. Pat dry. Pour oil for frying 1/2 inch deep into a large skillet. Heat to 375F (190C) on a deep-fry thermometer. At this temperature, a 1-inch cube of bread will turn golden brown in 50 seconds. Fry eggplant slices, turning once, until golden on both sides. Drain on paper towels. Place rice in a medium bowl. Add boiling water to cover. Let stand 5 minutes. Pour 1/4 cup warm water into a small bowl. Sprinkle saffron over water. Add rose water. Drain rice. Return to medium bowl. Strain saffron mixture over rice. Discard saffron threads, if used. Toss rice mixture to mix well. Set aside. When meat is done, strain pan juices into a 2-cup measure. Add broth or water to make 1-1/2 cups. Set aside. Brush oil on bottom and side of a 10-inch skillet with rounded side. Spread meat evenly in skillet. Layer eggplant slices over meat. Spread rice over eggplant slices. Carefully pour reserved 1-1/2 cups broth mixture over rice. Cover and cook over medium heat 5 minutes. Reduce heat and cover. Simmer over low heat 30 minutes or until rice is tender and most of liquid is absorbed. Mixture should be moist but firm. Keep covered until ready to serve. Loosen edge of rice with a spatula. Place a platter upside-down on skillet. Invert skillet and platter. Remove skillet. Serve meat pie immediately. Makes 6 servings.

How to Make Upside-Down Meat Pie

1/Spread meat evenly in a skillet. Layer eggplant slices over meat. Spread rice over eggplant slices.

2/To serve pie, loosen edge of rice. Place a platter upside-down on skillet. Invert skillet and platter. Remove skillet.

Lamb Ragout

Tas Kebabı (Turkey)

Turks prepare this basic stew with whatever vegetables are seasonal.

1/4 cup olive oil
2 medium onions, chopped
2 to 2-1/2 lbs. lean boneless leg of lamb,
   cut in 1-inch cubes
2 large tomatoes, chopped
1 tablespoon tomato paste

1 hot green pepper, seeded, diced
1 teaspoon crushed dried leaf marjoram
1 bay leaf
Salt and freshly ground pepper to taste
1 cup Beef Broth, page 36, or water

Heat olive oil in a large saucepan. Add onions. Sauté until onions are tender. Add lamb. Cook until lamb is browned on all sides. Add tomatoes, tomato paste, hot pepper, marjoram, bay leaf, salt and pepper. Cook 2 minutes. Add broth or water. Bring to a boil. Reduce heat and cover. Simmer over low heat 2 hours or until meat is tender and sauce is thick. Serve hot. Makes 6 to 8 servings.

Variations

Lamb Ragout with Potatoes: Cook Lamb Ragout 1-1/2 hours. Add 4 peeled and thickly sliced potatoes. Simmer 30 minutes longer or until potatoes are tender.
Lamb Ragout with Green Beans: Cook Lamb Ragout 1 hour. Add 1 pound trimmed green beans, broken in 1-inch pieces. Simmer 40 to 50 minutes longer or until beans are very tender.

Lamb in a Bread Basket

(Adapted Arabic)

Bread becomes an edible container for ground meat laced with tahini sauce.

1 lb. frozen bread dough, thawed, or
   Arabic Pocket-Bread dough, page 74
1 tablespoon fennel seeds
1 teaspoon caraway seeds
Sesame-Seed Sauce, page 64
2 tablespoons olive oil

1 medium onion, minced
2 garlic cloves, minced
1-1/2 lbs. ground lean lamb or beef
2 tomatoes, chopped
Salt and freshly ground pepper to taste
1/4 cup chopped chives or green onions

Prepare dough to the point of rolling out. If using Arabic Pocket-Bread dough, knead in fennel seeds and caraway seeds with flour. If using thawed bread dough, knead slightly then knead in fennel and caraway seeds. Preheat oven to 350F (175C). Grease a 10-inch pie plate. On a floured surface, roll out dough to a 12-inch circle. Fit dough into prepared pie plate, making a raised edge as you would for a pie. Bake 30 to 35 minutes or until golden brown. Or, to prevent dough from puffing during baking, fill with dried beans and bake 35 to 40 minutes; remove beans before adding meat filling. Prepare Sesame-Seed Sauce. Set aside. Heat olive oil in a large saucepan. Add onion and garlic. Sauté until onion is tender, about 5 minutes. Add meat, tomatoes, salt and pepper. Cook until meat is browned and crumbly. Drain off fat, if necessary. Add chives or green onions. Cook 1 minute. Remove from heat. Cover and let stand 10 minutes. Remove baked bread from pie plate. Place on a platter. Spoon meat mixture evenly into bread shell. Pour half the Sesame-Seed Sauce over meat mixture. To serve, cut into wedges and top with remaining sauce. Makes 6 servings.

Roast Lamb with Potatoes

Arni Psito (Greece)

Greeks enjoy lamb well-done inside and crisp outside.

1 (4- to 5-lb.) leg of lamb
4 garlic cloves, slivered
3 tablespoons chopped fresh mint or
   1 tablespoon crushed dried leaf mint
Salt and freshly ground pepper to taste
1/2 cup water
6 medium potatoes, peeled, thinly sliced or
   quartered
Juice of 1/2 lemon (1-1/2 tablespoons)

Salt and freshly ground pepper to taste
2 tablespoons butter or margarine, diced
2 large onions, sliced, separated in rings
2 large tomatoes, chopped
1 bay leaf
1 cinnamon stick
About 1 cup Beef Broth, page 36, or water
1/2 cup dry red wine

Preheat oven to 350F (175C). Make slits in several places around surface of lamb. Insert slivers of garlic and mint leaves into slits or rub lamb with dried mint. Sprinkle with salt and pepper. Place lamb in roasting pan. Add 1/2 cup water to pan. Bake 1 hour. Place potatoes around lamb. Sprinkle with lemon juice, salt and pepper. Dot with butter or margarine. Scatter onion rings and tomatoes over lamb and potatoes. Place bay leaf and cinnamon stick on top of lamb. Add 1/2 cup broth or water and wine to pan. Bake, basting frequently with pan juices, 1-1/2 hours longer or until done as desired. Add remaining broth or water as needed to keep pan moist. Serve lamb with vegetables and pan juices. Makes 6 to 8 servings.

Marinated Kebabs

Souvlaki (Greece)

Greek kebabs are served with rice or in pita bread with feta cheese and olives.

Marinade, see below
1 teaspoon crushed dried leaf oregano
1 teaspoon crushed dried leaf sweet basil
1/2 teaspoon crushed dried leaf marjoram
1/4 teaspoon ground thyme
1 large onion, sliced, separated in rings

2 garlic cloves, minced
2 bay leaves, crumbled
Salt and freshly ground pepper to taste
1 (3-lb.) leg of lamb, boned,
**   cut in 1-inch cubes**

Marinade:
1 cup olive oil
1/2 cup lemon juice (3 medium lemons)
1/4 cup dry red wine

1/4 cup wine vinegar
2 garlic cloves, minced
Salt and freshly ground pepper to taste

Prepare marinade. Set aside. Combine oregano, basil, marjoram, thyme, onion rings, garlic, bay leaves, salt and pepper in a medium bowl. Place half the lamb cubes in a single layer in a shallow bowl or dish. Sprinkle with half the oregano mixture. Top with a layer of remaining lamb cubes. Sprinkle with remaining oregano mixture. Pour marinade over meat layers. Cover and marinate in refrigerator, turning meat occasionally, 2 to 24 hours. Preheat oven to broil. Or prepare hot coals on barbecue grill. Thread meat on long metal skewers. Place on broiler rack 4 inches from heat source or on grill over hot coals. Cook, turning and basting frequently with marinade, about 15 minutes or until done as desired. Remove lamb from skewers before serving. Serve hot. Makes 6 to 8 servings.

Marinade:
Combine all ingredients in a medium bowl. Makes 2 cups.

Grilled Spicy Liver

Boulfaf (Morocco)

For appetizers, use small skewers and thread one liver cube on each skewer.

1/4 cup peanut oil or olive oil
2 teaspoons ground cumin
2 teaspoons paprika

1/2 teaspoon chili powder
Salt and freshly ground pepper to taste
1 lb. calves' liver, cut in 1-inch cubes

Preheat oven to broil. Or prepare hot coals on barbecue grill. Combine oil, cumin, paprika, chili powder, salt and pepper in a large bowl. Add liver. Toss to coat well. Marinate in refrigerator 1 hour or longer, tossing occasionally. Thread 4 or 5 liver cubes on each skewer. Place skewers on broiler rack 4 inches from heat source or on grill over hot coals. Cook, turning frequently to brown evenly, until livers are browned, about 10 minutes. Makes 6 servings.

Roast Leg of Lamb with Orzo

Giouvetsi (Greece)

Use a baking dish that's pretty enough to serve from.

1 (5- to 6-lb.) leg of lamb
4 garlic cloves, slivered
1/4 cup fresh mint or
   2 tablespoons crushed dried leaf mint
1 teaspoon crushed dried leaf oregano
1 large onion, thinly sliced
Salt and freshly ground pepper to taste
1 cup water

Juice of 2 lemons (6 tablespoons)
4 cups Chicken Broth, page 36, or
   Beef Broth, page 36
2 cups orzo
1/2 cup tomato sauce
Salt and freshly ground pepper to taste
1/2 cup grated Kefalotiri or Parmesan cheese

Preheat oven to 350F (175C). Rinse lamb and pat dry. Make deep slits in lamb in several places. Insert slivered garlic and fresh mint in slits. If using dried mint, combine with oregano, salt and pepper. Rub lamb all over with oregano mixture. Spread onion slices evenly in a large baking dish. Place lamb over onion slices. Pour water into baking dish. Bake 2-1/2 hours or until a meat thermometer inserted in thickest part of roast registers 160F (70C). Place roast on a platter. Sprinkle with lemon juice. Set aside and keep warm. Scrape up brown bits from baking dish. Skim off fat with a large spoon. Set baking dish with pan juices and brown bits aside. Pour broth into a large saucepan. Bring to a boil. Add orzo, tomato sauce, salt and pepper. Reduce heat. Cook, uncovered, over medium heat 20 minutes or until orzo is tender and most of the liquid is absorbed. Add cooked orzo to pan juices. Sprinkle with cheese. Toss to mix well. Bake 15 minutes longer. Carve lamb. Arrange slices over noodles. Makes 6 servings.

Tripe with Walnuts

Paça (Albania)

Versions of this dish appear throughout the various Middle Eastern cuisines.

2 lbs. honeycomb tripe
Water
2 tablespoons butter or margarine
1 small onion, chopped
1/4 teaspoon ground red (cayenne) pepper or
   1 tablespoon tomato paste

1 egg
1 tablespoon cornstarch
2 cups Chicken Broth, page 36, or water
Salt and freshly ground black pepper to taste
1 cup coarsely chopped walnuts

Place tripe in a large saucepan. Add water to cover. Cook over medium heat until tripe is very tender, about 2 hours. Drain. Cool tripe enough to handle. Use your fingers or 2 forks to shred cooled tripe into a large bowl. Set aside. Melt butter or margarine in a large skillet. Add onion. Sauté until onion is tender. Add tripe. Sauté until golden brown. Blend in red pepper or tomato paste. Cook and stir 1 minute to blend flavors. Beat egg in a large bowl. Add cornstarch. Stir to blend. Gradually stir in broth or water until blended. Gradually add to tripe mixture in saucepan. Bring to a boil. Reduce heat. Stir constantly over medium-low heat until sauce thickens slightly. Add salt and pepper. Place tripe mixture on a platter. Sprinkle with walnuts. Serve hot. Makes 6 servings.

There was a time in most parts of the Middle Eastern world when a scrawny chicken stewing in a pot was considered sheer luxury. This is no longer so. Production of poultry in the Middle East is on the rise and exports from other countries are keeping the area supplied. In Baghdad, you will find cooks in stalls selling what Iraquis call *Kentak-ee.* I have discovered that this is the Iraqi form of the word *Kentucky* after the commercial take-out brand that originated in the United States.

The once-rare chicken has found its way into some of the most-lowly as well as the most-epicurean dishes. Persian cuisine is especially rich in poultry dishes. The sweet flesh lends itself to exotic treatment with herbs, fruits and candied fruits. Persian dishes classified as stews-served-with-rice, or *khoresht,* include the fabulous Duckling in Walnut-Pomegranate Sauce. It is adored by most Persians.

North African cooks compose some exquisite chicken dishes. Lemon Chicken is so captivating a dish that Moroccan restaurants outside Morocco often include it on their menus.

Chicken Sumac is a popular fast food in Jordan and Jerusalem. It is an exciting dish of bread covered with sautéed onions and chicken and seasoned with sumac, a favorite spice in the Arab world.

In Istanbul's Abdullah restaurant, chicken was served on a bed of snow-white Eggplant Puree which the Turks call *Sultan's Delight.* The name refers to Sultan Murat IV for whom the dish was created.

Roast Chicken with Rice & Pine-Nut Stuffing will be a fine addition to your repertoire of stuffings. And there's a variation for Rice-Stuffed Chicken Breasts which is perfect to serve at your next dinner party. Savory stuffing is rolled up in boneless chicken breasts. After cooking, the rolls can be sliced and served with a saffron sauce

& Seafood

Religious restrictions and cultural attitudes have limited the use of seafood in the Middle East. Judaic dietary laws prohibit eating any seafood without scales or fins. All crustaceans such as shrimp, lobster and crab are taboo. Islamic law allows fish and shellfish in the Moslem diet, but restrictions are often imposed by custom. A Bedouin from the inland desert of Saudi Arabia has probably never eaten fish nor observed it being served. He is likely to look askance at fish or people who eat it. Many Moslems regard shellfish as inedible and shun it.

Still, fish dishes abound in the Middle East because many countries are surrounded, patched or veined by waterways. The Tigris and Euphrates Rivers in Turkey and Iraq supply numerous varieties of fish. Large fish are sold by the foot at stalls along the Tigris River banks in Baghdad. At some stalls, you may choose your own fish to cook on stakes around an open eucalyptus-branch fire. After it is cooked, the succulent fish is served with freshly baked bread, a salad and Iraqi beer.

The Persian Gulf supplies some of the world's finest pink shrimp as well as an abundance of mackerel, porgy, grouper, stingray and many others. Waters of the Aegean Sea, the Mediterranean Sea, the Sea of Marmara, the Black Sea, the Caspian Sea and the Red Sea are filled with swordfish, turbot, mussels, shrimp and crab. The finest white fish, sturgeon and caviar in the world are from the Caspian Sea. Turkey's Bosphorus strait supplies firm-fleshed sea bass called *levrek* and a turbot known as *kalkan*. These are served at restaurants along the Galata Bridge in Istanbul. Grey mullet from the Red Sea produces the expensive roe which are dried to serve as an hors d'oeuvre on toast at Egypt's finest tables. Carp, raised in salt-water ponds in Israel, replaces pike commonly used in *gefilte* fish.

An Arabic specialty is Sesame Fish Bake topped with sesame-seed sauce, a favorite dressing of Arab cooks. One of the most dramatically fragrant fish dishes is the Fish Bake from Greece. The fish is baked *plaki*-style, meaning filled with herbs and vegetables. Turkish Swordfish Kebabs threaded on skewers with bay leaf, can marinate several hours before the party begins. And for an elegant dinner party or luncheon, wrap sea bass in filo pastry as in Sea Bass en Croûte. This same dish is served at a famous Istanbul restaurant.

Stuffed mussels are relished by Armenians, Turks and Greeks. Rice-Stuffed Mussels contain pine nuts, raisins and spices. The recipe may also be used for clams. ✖

Menu

Seafood Barbecue

Platter of Feta Cheese,
Romaine Leaves, Green Onions,
Olives, Radishes
Latin Quarter Kebabs,
page 150
Arabic Chopped Salad,
page 60
Arabic Pocket Bread, page 74
Almond Ice Cream, page 182

Gulf Supper

Shrimp Abu Dhabi, page 150
Chicken & Rice Skillet,
page 144
Pocket-Bread Salad, page 59
Dates
Fresh Fruit
Arabic Coffee, page 32

Chicken Sumac

Musakhan (Jordan)

Use only sumac purchased at Middle Eastern grocery stores. Many species are not related to the spice.

1 (2-1/2-lb.) chicken, quartered	1/4 cup olive oil
Chicken Broth, page 36, or water	4 medium onions, chopped, or
1 small celery stalk with leaves	sliced and separated in rings
1 small onion, halved	4 teaspoons sumac
Salt and freshly ground pepper to taste	1/4 cup or more toasted pine nuts, page 67
4 Arabic pocket breads	

Place chicken quarters in a large saucepan. Add broth or water barely to cover. Add celery, onion halves, salt and pepper. Bring to a boil. Reduce heat and cover. Simmer over low heat 30 minutes. Remove chicken. Reserve 1/3 cup broth. Preheat oven to 350F (175C). Place Arabic pocket breads on an ungreased baking sheet with rimmed sides. Set aside. Heat olive oil in a large skillet. Add chopped onions. Sauté until onions are browned, about 8 minutes. Spread onions equally over each pocket bread. Top each onion-covered bread with a cooked chicken quarter. Pour reserved broth over chicken quarters. Sprinkle each chicken quarter with 1 teaspoon sumac. Bake 30 minutes or until chicken quarters are golden brown. Garnish with pine nuts. Makes 4 servings.

Variations

Cut chicken into small pieces. Place on bread. Spread onions over chicken. Top with pine nuts.

Bread made with refrigerator biscuits, crescent-roll dough or thawed frozen dough may be used in place of pocket bread. Pat dough for biscuits or rolls or thawed dough into 6- to 8-inch circles. Bake at 350F (175C) 10 minutes to set. Use as directed above.

Barbecued Chicken Kebabs   Photo on cover.

Kabab-e Morgh (Iran)

Golden chicken kebabs are traditionally served with Persian Steamed Rice.

1/4 cup olive oil	2 (2-lb.) chickens, quartered
1/2 cup lemon juice (about 3 lemons)	1/4 cup butter or margarine
1 small onion, thinly sliced	1/2 teaspoon crushed saffron threads or
2 garlic cloves, crushed	powder
Salt and freshly ground pepper to taste	16 cherry tomatoes

In a large, shallow container, combine olive oil, lemon juice, onion, garlic, salt and pepper. Add chicken quarters. Turn to coat well. Cover. Marinate in refrigerator 2 to 24 hours, turning chicken occasionally. Melt butter or margarine in a small skillet. Stir in saffron until dissolved. Preheat oven to broil. Or prepare hot coals on barbecue grill. Brush chicken with saffron mixture. Thread chicken and cherry tomatoes on metal skewers. Place on broiler rack 4 inches from heat source or on grill over coals. Cook, basting frequently with marinade and turning frequently to cook on all sides, until chicken is very tender, 40 to 45 minutes. Makes 6 to 8 servings.

How to Make Chicken Sumac

1/Spread onions over pocket bread. Top with a cooked chicken quarter. Pour broth over chicken and sprinkle with sumac.

2/Bake 30 minutes or until chicken quarters are golden brown. Garnish with toasted pine nuts.

Oasis Duck

Bat el Fayyoumi (Egypt)

Ducks raised in the Oasis of Fayyoum in Egypt are prepared this way.

1 (3- to 3-1/2-lb.) duckling, cleaned
Salt and freshly ground pepper to taste
Juice of 1 lemon (3 tablespoons)
1/2 cup coarse-grade bulgur
Water
2 tablespoons butter or margarine
1 medium onion, finely chopped
1 small heart of celery with leaves,
    chopped

1 garlic clove, minced
Salt and freshly ground pepper to taste
1 small onion, chopped
1/4 cup lemon juice
1 teaspoon salt
1 tablespoon chopped fresh dill or
    1 teaspoon dill weed, if desired
1/2 cup water

Rinse duckling thoroughly. Sprinkle all over and inside cavities with salt and pepper. Rub with lemon juice. Refrigerate. Place bulgur in a medium bowl. Add water to cover. Let stand about 20 minutes or until water is absorbed. Use your hands to squeeze out any excess water. Fluff to separate grains. Preheat oven to 350F (175C). Melt butter or margarine in a large skillet. Add onion, celery and garlic. Sauté until onion is tender. Add softened bulgur, salt and pepper. Mix well. Stuff into duckling cavity, packing loosely. Close cavity opening with metal or bamboo skewers. In a small bowl, combine onion, lemon juice and salt. Mix well. Rub all over duckling. Sprinkle with dill, if desired. Bake 2 hours, basting frequently with pan juices. Makes 4 servings.

Chicken with Feta-Cheese Stuffing

Kotopoulo Yemisto me Tiri Feta (Greece)

If you like feta cheese, you'll probably like this pungent stuffing.

1 (3- to 4-lb.) roasting chicken
Salt and freshly ground pepper to taste
2 tablespoons butter or margarine
1/2 lb. chicken livers, diced
1/2 lb. feta cheese, crumbled
Juice of 1/2 lemon (1-1/2 tablespoons)
2 garlic cloves, minced

1 tablespoon fresh dill or
  1 teaspoon dill weed
Freshly ground pepper to taste
1/4 cup butter or margarine, melted
Lemon slices for garnish
Few sprigs watercress for garnish
Tomato wedges for garnish

Preheat oven to 350F (175C). Rinse chicken thoroughly. Sprinkle all over and inside cavities with salt and pepper. Melt 2 tablespoons butter or margarine in a medium saucepan. Sauté chicken livers until browned. Add feta cheese, lemon juice, garlic, dill and pepper. Mix well. Fill chicken cavity and neck opening with stuffing. Close openings with wooden picks or skewers. Place stuffed chicken in a large roasting pan. Brush with some of the 1/4 cup butter or margarine. Bake 1-1/2 hours or until chicken is tender, basting frequently with remaining butter or margarine and pan juices. Remove wooden picks or skewers. Place chicken on a platter. Garnish with lemon slices, watercress and tomato wedges. Makes 6 servings.

Chicken & Rice Skillet

Kabsa (Arab Gulf States)

This colorful party dish is probably a forerunner of paella.

1/4 cup butter or margarine
1 (2-1/2- to 3-lb.) chicken, cut up
1 large onion, chopped
5 garlic cloves, minced
1/4 cup tomato sauce or puree
2 medium tomatoes, chopped
2 medium carrots, grated
Grated peel of 1 orange
3 whole cloves

2 cardamom pods or
  1/2 teaspoon ground cardamom seeds
1 cinnamon stick
Salt and freshly ground pepper to taste
3 cups Chicken Broth, page 36
1 cup long-grain rice
1/4 cup raisins
1/4 cup toasted sliced or
  slivered almonds, page 67

Melt butter or margarine in a large skillet. Add chicken pieces. Sauté until browned on all sides. Remove from skillet. Set aside. Add onion and garlic to skillet. Sauté until onion is tender. Stir in tomato sauce or puree. Simmer over low heat 1 minute to blend flavors. Add tomatoes, carrots, orange peel, cloves, cardamom, cinnamon stick, salt and pepper. Cook 1 minute. Add broth. Return chicken pieces to skillet. Bring to a boil. Reduce heat and cover. Simmer over low heat 30 minutes. Stir rice into liquid between pieces of chicken. Or remove chicken, stir in rice, then return chicken pieces to skillet. Cover. Simmer 30 minutes longer or until rice is tender. Garnish with raisins and almonds. Makes 6 to 8 servings.

Roast Chicken with Rice & Pine-Nut Stuffing

Djaj Mahshi (Arabic)

Enjoy this spicy stuffing in your next holiday turkey.

2 tablespoons butter or margarine	1/4 teaspoon ground allspice
1 medium onion, finely chopped	Salt and freshly ground pepper to taste
1/2 lb. ground beef, lamb or veal	1 cup Chicken Broth, page 36, or water
1/2 cup long-grain rice	1 (3-lb.) roasting chicken
2 tablespoons pine nuts	Salt and freshly ground pepper to taste
1/2 teaspoon ground cinnamon	2 tablespoons butter or margarine, melted

Melt 2 tablespoons butter or margarine in a large skillet. Add onion. Sauté until onion is tender. Add ground meat. Sauté until meat is browned and crumbly. Add rice, pine nuts, cinnamon, allspice, salt and pepper. Cook 2 minutes. Add broth or water. Bring to a simmer. Continue to cook, uncovered, over medium-high heat until water is almost absorbed, about 5 minutes. Preheat oven to 350F (175C). Rinse chicken thoroughly. Sprinkle all over and inside cavities with salt and pepper. Spoon stuffing into breast cavity. Close openings with wooden picks or skewers. Brush chicken with 2 tablespoons melted butter or margarine. Place in a roasting pan. Bake 1-1/2 hours or until chicken is tender, basting frequently with pan juices. Remove wooden picks or skewers. Place chicken on a platter. Makes 6 servings.

Variation

Rice-Stuffed Chicken Breasts: Use 12 to 16 boneless chicken-breast halves. Pound breasts between sheets of waxed paper until flattened. Discard waxed paper. Place 1 heaping tablespoon rice filling on each breast half. Roll up, tucking in ends. Fasten seams with wooden picks or tie rolls with string. Sauté in 2 tablespoons butter or margarine until golden brown. Add 1-1/2 cups broth or water, salt and pepper to taste and a pinch of saffron. Bring to a boil. Reduce heat and cover. Cook over medium-low heat 40 minutes. Mix 1 tablespoon cornstarch with 1 tablespoon water. Stir into pan juices until mixture is smooth. Simmer over low heat 5 minutes until sauce is slightly thickened. Remove wooden picks or string. Serve chicken rolls topped with sauce. Or cut rolls into slices, arrange on a platter, and spoon sauce over slices. Makes 12 to 16 chicken rolls.

Barbecued Chicken

Mashwi (North Africa)

Elegant metal skewers bring exotic elegance to barbecued chicken quarters.

2 (2-lb.) chickens, quartered	1 teaspoon ground cumin
Salt and freshly ground pepper to taste	1/4 teaspoon chili powder
1 tablespoon paprika	1/4 cup melted butter or margarine

Preheat oven to broil. Or prepare low-heat coals on barbecue grill. Thread chicken quarters on skewers. Sprinkle chicken with salt and pepper. Combine remaining ingredients in a small saucepan. Heat until butter or margarine is melted. Brush spice mixture all over chicken quarters. Place skewers on broiler rack 4 inches from source of heat or on grill over hot coals. Cook until chicken is tender, 40 to 45 minutes, basting frequently with spice mixture and turning skewers frequently to brown chicken evenly. Makes 8 servings.

Lemon Chicken

Poulet au Citron (Morocco)

This dish is a favorite of Moroccans everywhere.

2 (2-lb.) chickens
2 cups Chicken Broth, page 36, or water
1/4 cup peanut oil
1 tablespoon olive oil
2 medium onions, sliced
Gizzards from 1 chicken
1 garlic clove, minced
1 teaspoon ground ginger or
   1 (1-inch) piece fresh gingerroot

Pinch of crushed saffron threads or powder
Salt and freshly ground pepper to taste
Peel of 1 Preserved Lemon, page 176, or
   1 fresh lemon, quartered
1/2 cup green olives
Lemon wedges for garnish
Parsley sprigs for garnish

Rinse chickens thoroughly. Place in a large pot. Add broth or water. Pour peanut oil and olive oil over chickens. Add onions, gizzards, garlic, ginger, saffron, salt and pepper. Bring to a boil. Reduce heat and cover. Simmer over low heat 40 minutes or until chickens are almost tender, turning once or twice to cook evenly. Discard gizzards and fresh ginger, if used. Add lemon peel or fresh lemon. Simmer 15 minutes longer or until chickens are tender. Discard lemon peel or fresh lemon. Add olives. Heat through. Garnish with lemon wedges and parsley. Makes 6 to 8 servings.

Turkey Stuffed with Couscous

(North African-Style)

Basting with honey ensures a golden-brown bird.

1 (1-lb.) pkg. couscous mix
Water
1 (6-lb.) turkey
Salt and freshly ground pepper to taste
1/4 cup butter or margarine
1 medium onion, finely chopped
1/4 teaspoon ground cinnamon

Salt and freshly ground pepper to taste
Pinch of saffron threads or powder, if desired
1/4 cup butter or margarine
1/4 cup honey
1/4 teaspoon ground cinnamon
1/4 teaspoon ground ginger
2 cups water

Place couscous mix in a large bowl. Add water barely to cover. Let stand 10 minutes or until liquid is absorbed. Set aside. Preheat oven to 350F (175C). Rinse turkey thoroughly. Sprinkle all over and inside cavities with salt and pepper. Place in a roasting pan. Melt 1/4 cup butter or margarine in a large skillet. Add onion, 1/4 teaspoon cinnamon, salt and pepper. Add saffron, if desired. Sauté until onion is tender. Add softened couscous. Cook 2 minutes, mixing well. Spoon couscous mixture into turkey cavities. Close openings with wooden picks or skewers. Tie legs together. Melt 1/4 cup butter or margarine in a small skillet. Stir in honey, 1/4 teaspoon cinnamon and ginger. Brush honey mixture all over turkey. Pour 2 cups water into roasting pan. Bake 2-1/2 to 3 hours, basting frequently with honey mixture and pan juices. Turkey is done when leg joints are loose or when a meat thermometer inserted in thickest part of breast registers 170F (75C). Remove wooden picks or skewers and untie legs. Place turkey on a platter. Strain pan juices into a gravy boat. Serve turkey with couscous and gravy. Makes 12 servings.

Duckling in Walnut-Pomegranate Sauce

Fesenjan (Iran)

Celebrate with this party dish during the winter holidays when pomegranates are in season.

1/4 cup butter or margarine
1 large onion, finely chopped
1 (4-lb.) duckling, cleaned
2-1/2 cups Chicken Broth, page 36
Juice of 1 lemon (3 tablespoons)
Salt and freshly ground pepper to taste

1/2 cup pomegranate juice
2 cups ground walnuts (about 10 oz.)
1 tablespoon sugar
Pomegranate seeds for garnish
Walnut halves for garnish

Melt butter or margarine in a large pot. Add onion. Sauté until tender. Rinse duckling thoroughly. Add to onion in pot. Cook until browned on all sides, about 10 minutes. Add broth, lemon juice, salt and pepper. Bring to a boil. Reduce heat and cover. Simmer over low heat 40 minutes or until duckling is barely tender. Remove duckling from pot. Set aside. Skim excess fat from pan juices. Stir in pomegranate juice, ground walnuts and sugar. Return duckling to pot. Bring to a boil. Reduce heat and cover. Simmer over low heat 1 hour, stirring sauce occasionally to prevent sticking. Place duckling on a platter. Spoon sauce over duckling. Garnish with pomegranate seeds and walnut halves. Makes 3 or 4 servings.

TIP

If pomegranates are unavailable, substitute pomegranate molasses, which may be purchased at Middle Eastern grocery stores, or Grenadine Syrup, page 179. Grenadine syrup is also available at supermarkets.

Chicken Oregano

Kotopoulo Reganato (Greece)

Katherine Fenady, who shared her recipe, serves this chicken with buttered noodles.

3 lbs. chicken pieces
1/2 cup olive oil or vegetable oil
1/4 cup lemon juice

2 garlic cloves
1 tablespoon crushed dried oregano
Salt and freshly ground pepper to taste

Place chicken pieces in a single layer in a large baking pan. Combine oil, lemon juice and garlic in blender. Process until mixture is smooth and creamy. Stir in oregano, salt and pepper. Pour over chicken pieces. Turn chicken to coat with marinade. Cover and marinate several hours or overnight in refrigerator. Preheat oven to 350F (175C). Bake chicken pieces, uncovered, 1-1/2 hours or until tender. Brown tops of chicken pieces under broiler, if desired. Makes 6 to 8 servings.

Fish Bake

Psari Plaki (Greece)

Plaki means cooked with herbs and vegetables. The result is irresistibly aromatic.

1 (2-1/2- to 3-lb.) whole fish such as
    white fish, sea bass, perch
    or other firm-fleshed fish, dressed
Juice of 1 lemon (3 tablespoons)
Salt and freshly ground white pepper
    to taste
3 large onions
1/2 cup olive oil
2 garlic cloves, minced
5 medium carrots, peeled, sliced diagonally
5 medium celery stalks, sliced diagonally

1 (8-oz.) can tomato sauce
1/2 tomato-sauce can dry red or white wine
1 tablespoon chopped fresh parsley
1 tablespoon chopped fresh dill or
    1 teaspoon dill weed
Salt and freshly ground black pepper
    to taste
1 medium lemon, thinly sliced
1 (1-lb.) can whole tomatoes, drained, or
    4 fresh tomatoes

Rinse fish. Pat dry. Sprinkle fish all over and inside cavity with lemon juice. Sprinkle lightly with salt and white pepper. Set aside. Cut onions in half lengthwise, then slice to make long, thin strips. Set aside. Preheat oven to 350F (175C). Heat olive oil in a large skillet. Add garlic, onion strips, carrots and celery. Sauté until vegetables are tender but not browned. Add tomato sauce, wine, parsley, dill, salt and black pepper. Bring to a boil. Reduce heat. Cook over medium heat 3 minutes. Place fish in a large baking pan or casserole. Spoon some of the vegetables into fish cavity. Spread remaining vegetables with liquid on and around fish. Overlap lemon slices across fish. Crush or chop canned tomatoes or dice fresh tomatoes. Spread over fish and vegetables. Cover and bake 1-1/4 to 1-1/2 hours or until fish flakes easily when pierced with a fork. Makes 6 to 8 servings.

Shrimp Pilaf

Garides Pilafi (Greece)

Clams or any shellfish with shells removed may be substituted for the shrimp.

1 lb. medium shrimp
1/4 cup olive oil
1 medium onion, chopped
1 garlic clove, minced

1 (8-oz.) can tomato sauce
Salt and freshly ground pepper to taste
3 cups Chicken Broth, page 36
1-1/2 cups long-grain rice

To butterfly shrimp, peel and devein. Slit each shrimp down back without cutting all the way through. Open slit. Heat olive oil in a large saucepan. Add onion and garlic. Sauté until onion is tender. Add shrimp. Sauté 2 minutes. Add tomato sauce, salt and pepper. Cook 1 minute. Add broth. Bring to a boil. Reduce heat. Add rice. Cover and cook over medium heat until rice is tender and liquid is almost absorbed, about 30 minutes. Makes 4 servings.

Latin Quarter Kebabs   Photo on cover.
(Greek-Style)

Inspired by seafood displays in Greek restaurants in Paris' Latin Quarter.

1 lb. large shrimp or prawns (about 12)
6 baby-lobster tails
12 scallops
1/2 cup olive oil
1/4 cup cider vinegar
1 garlic clove, minced
2 tablespoons chopped fresh parsley
1 tablespoon chopped fresh dill or
    1 teaspoon dill weed

1 tablespoon chopped fresh mint or
    1 teaspoon crushed dried leaf mint
Salt and freshly ground black pepper to taste
12 cherry tomatoes
6 green-pepper squares
6 red-pepper squares

If desired, remove shells from shrimp or prawns. Or partially remove shells, leaving tails intact. Remove veins. Remove shells from baby-lobster tails by cutting lengthwise through each shell. Rinse scallops. Combine olive oil, vinegar, garlic, parsley, dill, mint, salt and black pepper in a large bowl. Add shelled shrimp, lobster and scallops. Toss to coat well with marinade. Marinate in refrigerator 2 hours or longer. Prepare hot coals on barbecue grill. Or preheat oven to broil. Thread 2 shrimp or prawns, 1 lobster tail, 2 scallops, 2 cherry tomatoes and 4 pepper squares on each skewer. Place on grill or broiler rack 4 inches from heat source. Grill or broil, basting and turning frequently to cook evenly, until shellfish is tender, 8 to 10 minutes. To eat, remove any remaining shells. Makes 6 servings.

Shrimp Abu Dhabi
Murabyan (Arab Gulf States)

Pink Gulf shrimp are prepared simply and served plain or with rice.

1 lb. large shrimp or prawns (about 12)
Salt to taste
1/2 cup all-purpose flour
2 tablespoons butter or margarine
2 tablespoons olive oil

1 large onion, chopped
2 garlic cloves, minced
2 tablespoons chopped cilantro
Juice of 1 lime (3 tablespoons)
Cilantro sprigs for garnish

Clean and devein shrimp or prawns, removing shells but leaving shells on tails intact. Sprinkle shrimp or prawns with salt. Roll lightly in flour, shaking off excess. Melt butter or margarine with olive oil in a large skillet. Add onion and garlic. Sauté until onion is tender. Add shrimp or prawns and chopped cilantro. Sauté until shrimp or prawns are golden, about 7 minutes. Place on a platter. Sprinkle with lime juice. Garnish with cilantro sprigs. Makes 4 servings.

How to Make Latin Quarter Kebabs

1/Remove shells from baby-lobster tails by cutting lengthwise through each shell.

2/Alternate cherry tomatoes, pepper squares and marinated seafood on each skewer.

Sesame Fish Bake

Tajin Samak (Arabic)

Whole fish topped with Sesame-Seed Sauce and onions is elegant and tasty.

Sesame-Seed Sauce, page 64
1/2 cup toasted pine nuts, page 67
1 (2-1/2- to 3-lb.) whole fish such as
   white fish, sea bass, perch or
   other firm-fleshed fish, dressed

1/4 cup olive oil
1/4 cup lemon juice
Salt and freshly ground pepper to taste
1/4 cup vegetable oil
2 large onions, sliced, separated in rings

Prepare Sesame-Seed Sauce and toasted pine nuts. Set aside. Rinse fish and pat dry. Place in a baking dish. Sprinkle fish all over and inside cavity with olive oil, lemon juice, salt and pepper. Turn fish to coat well. Cover and marinate 2 hours or longer in refrigerator. Preheat oven to 350F (175C). Bake fish, uncovered, 40 to 50 minutes, basting frequently with pan drippings. Cooked fish will flake easily when pierced with a fork. Heat vegetable oil in a medium skillet. Add onions. Sauté until onions are golden brown. Pour Sesame-Seed Sauce over fish. Top with browned onion rings. Sprinkle with toasted pine nuts. Makes 6 servings.

Rice-Stuffed Mussels

Midye Dolması (Turkey)

Stuffed mussels or clams are enjoyed as an appetizer or a main dish.

6 dozen mussels or clams in the shell
1/2 cup olive oil
2 medium onions, chopped
2 cups short-grain rice
1/4 cup raisins
1/4 cup pine nuts
1/4 teaspoon ground cinnamon

1/4 teaspoon ground allspice
Salt and freshly ground pepper to taste
1 cup bottled clam liquor
1 cup Chicken Broth, page 36, or water
2 cups Chicken Broth, page 36, or water
Lemon wedges

Scrub mussel or clam shells thoroughly with a stiff brush to remove hairy tufts. Discard any already opened shells. This indicates they are not safe to eat. To open scrubbed shells for stuffing and cooking, freeze a few minutes until shells open; or pry open with a clam opener; or dip in warm (150F, 65C) water 2 to 3 minutes, depending on thickness of the shell. Discard any shells that are dry inside or those with an offensive odor. Rinse thoroughly in cool water. Heat olive oil in a large skillet. Add onions. Sauté until tender. Add rice, raisins, pine nuts, cinnamon, allspice, salt and pepper. Sauté until rice is glazed. Add clam liquor and 1 cup broth or water. Bring to a boil. Reduce heat and cover. Cook over medium-low heat 10 minutes or until liquid is absorbed. Spoon 1 tablespoon rice mixture into each mussel or clam. Close shell. Wind string several times around each shell to secure. Tie tightly. Place in a large casserole or Dutch oven with lid. Add 2 cups broth or water. Bring to a boil. Reduce heat and cover. Cook over medium-low heat 20 to 25 minutes or until rice is tender. Remove from heat and uncover. Let mussels or clams stand in pan juices until cool enough to handle. Arrange on a large platter. Untie or snip off strings to open shells. Serve with lemon wedges. Makes 6 to 8 servings.

Fish Sauté with Vegetables

Samak Ma'Khoudrah (Arabic)

Arab cooks often garnish this dish with Sesame-Seed Sauce and toasted pine nuts.

2 medium onions
1/2 cup all-purpose flour
1/4 teaspoon salt
1/8 teaspoon freshly ground black pepper
1-1/2 lbs. fish fillets
1/2 cup olive oil

1 green or red bell pepper, cut in long, thin strips
2 tablespoons chopped fresh parsley
Salt and freshly ground black pepper to taste
Lemon wedges for garnish

Cut onions in half lengthwise, then slice to make long, thin strips. Set aside. In a shallow pan, combine flour, 1/4 teaspoon salt and 1/8 teaspoon black pepper. Mix well. Roll fish in flour mixture to coat lightly. Heat 1/4 cup olive oil in a large skillet. Add fish. Sauté until browned on both sides, about 10 minutes. Cooked fish will flake easily when pierced with a fork. Remove fish from skillet. Place on a platter. Keep warm. Pour remaining 1/4 cup olive oil into skillet. Add onions, green- or red-pepper strips and parsley. Sauté until onions are tender. Add salt and black pepper to taste. Spoon onion mixture over fish. Garnish with lemon wedges. Makes 6 servings.

Sea Bass en Croûte

Levrek Buğulama (Turkey)

En croûte means wrapped in pastry. This fish is enclosed in buttery, flaky filo pastry.

1-1/2 lbs. sea-bass fillets or any
   firm-fleshed fillets, cut in
   6 (4-inch) squares
Salt and freshly ground pepper to taste
6 filo pastry sheets

1/4 cup butter, clarified, page 157, or
   margarine, melted
6 teaspoons butter or margarine
6 (1/4-inch) tomato slices
Juice of 1 lemon (3 tablespoons)

Preheat oven to 350F (175C). Butter a large baking sheet. Set aside. Rinse fish. Pat dry. Sprinkle with salt and pepper. Stack filo pastry sheets. Cover with plastic wrap to prevent drying out. Brush 1 filo sheet with clarified butter or melted margarine. Fold filo lengthwise into thirds, making a rectangle. Place 1 fish piece near bottom of rectangle. Place 1 teaspoon butter or margarine on fish. Top with a tomato slice. Sprinkle with 1-1/2 teaspoons lemon juice. Fold in sides of rectangle. Roll up. Repeat with remaining filo and fish. Place rolls on prepared baking sheet. Brush with clarified butter or melted margarine. Bake 35 to 40 minutes or until golden brown. Makes 6 servings.

Onion-Stuffed Fish

Mashkul (Arab Gulf States)

Cinnamon, turmeric and cumin are a traditional flavor blend in North Africa and the Gulf States.

6 (3/4- to 1-lb.) porgies, trout or
   other frying fish, dressed
Salt and freshly ground pepper to taste
2 tablespoons butter or margarine
2 tablespoons olive oil
4 medium onions, chopped
2 teaspoons ground cinnamon
1 teaspoon ground turmeric

1 teaspoon ground cumin
1 cup vegetable oil
1/2 cup all-purpose flour
Juice of 1 lime (3 tablespoons)
3 to 4 large lettuce leaves
1 medium tomato, cut in wedges
1/2 medium unpeeled cucumber, thinly sliced

Rinse fish and pat dry. Sprinkle all over with salt and pepper. Heat butter or margarine and olive oil in a large skillet until butter or margarine melts. Add onions, cinnamon, turmeric and cumin. Sauté until onions are tender. Spoon onion mixture into fish cavities, reserving 1 or more tablespoons. Pour 1 cup vegetable oil into skillet. Heat to 350F (175C) on a deep-fry thermometer. At this temperature, a 1-inch cube of bread will turn golden brown in 65 seconds. Carefully add reserved onion mixture to hot oil. Roll fish in flour to coat lightly. Carefully add to hot oil. Fry until golden on one side, 3 to 5 minutes. Turn to fry other side, 3 to 5 minutes, depending on size and thickness of fish. Cooked fish will flake easily when pierced with a fork but will be moist. Sprinkle with lime juice. Place lettuce leaves on a large platter. Arrange fish on lettuce leaves. Reheat any onion mixture remaining in skillet. Drain and spoon over fish. Garnish with tomato wedges and cucumber slices. Serve immediately. Makes 6 servings.

Swordfish Kebabs

Kılıç Şiş (Turkey)

Cook succulent fish on skewers for a treat on a hot summer evening.

1-1/2 lbs. swordfish fillets,
   cut in 1-1/2-inch cubes
1/2 cup olive oil
1/4 cup vinegar
1/4 teaspoon red-pepper flakes

Salt and freshly ground black pepper to taste
18 fresh or dried bay leaves
Boiling water, if needed
Lemon wedges for garnish

Rinse fish cubes. Drain on paper towels. In a large bowl, combine olive oil, vinegar, red-pepper flakes, salt and black pepper. Add fish cubes. Marinate in refrigerator 2 hours or longer. If using dried bay leaves, place in a small bowl and cover with boiling water. Let stand 5 minutes. Drain. Prepare hot coals on barbecue grill. Or preheat oven to broil. On long metal skewers, alternate swordfish cubes with bay leaves, allowing 3 or 4 fish cubes and 3 bay leaves for each skewer. Place on grill or broiler rack 4 inches from heat source. Cook, turning frequently, 8 to 10 minutes or until fish cubes are tender and browned on all sides. Do not overcook. Serve with lemon wedges. Makes 6 servings.

Shrimp & Feta Bake

Garides Giouvetsi (Greece)

As a first course or a main dish, this flavorful seafood from the Greek islands is memorable.

1 lb. large shrimp or prawns (about 12)
1/4 cup olive oil
1 small yellow onion, minced
2 green onions, chopped
2 garlic cloves, minced
2 large tomatoes, diced

1/4 cup dry white wine
2 tablespoons chopped fresh parsley
1 teaspoon crushed dried leaf oregano
Salt and freshly ground pepper to taste
1/4 cup crumbled feta cheese (1 oz.)
Chopped parsley for garnish

Clean and devein shrimp or prawns, removing shells but leaving shells on tails intact. Refrigerate. Heat olive oil in a large skillet. Add yellow onion, green onions and garlic. Sauté until onions are tender. Add tomatoes, wine, 2 tablespoons chopped parsley, oregano, salt and pepper. Cook over medium heat 30 minutes or until sauce thickens. Preheat oven to 350F (175C). Spoon half the tomato sauce into a medium casserole. Cover with shrimp or prawns. Top with remaining sauce. Sprinkle cheese evenly over sauce. Bake 15 to 20 minutes or until shrimp is pink and cheese is golden brown and slightly melted. Garnish with parsley. Makes 4 servings.

Desserts

Probably the best-known category of Middle Eastern desserts are the pastries made with filo dough. Although known by numerous names, nut-filled filo pastries are generally classified as *baklavas*. There is no end to the variety of their shapes and sizes. Syrians make Pistachio Baklava, shaping nut-filled rolls into nests topped with pistachio nuts. Armenians have a weakness for crinkled Walnut Rolls. A dowel is required to make these nut-filled baklavas. Other baklavas are rolled, formed into cigarette shapes, folded into triangles, stacked or coiled. Don't be afraid to try your hand at several different shapes. Once you have become acquainted with filo, using it is easier than making pie. Look through Filo Main Dishes, pages 110 to 121, for further information on working with this paper-thin pastry.

All Middle Eastern cuisines boast a version of layered baklava filled with one or more mixtures of nuts. These rich desserts are cut into diamonds, a favorite Middle Eastern shape. Instructions for layering and cutting filo pastries are on page 113.

Most baklavas require steeping in syrup. The general rule to remember is to add cooled syrup to hot pastry or hot syrup to cooled pastry. This will prevent syrup from crystallizing and keep filo from becoming soggy.

An ingenious cook devised Shredded-Pastry Dessert. It is an airy, feather-light pastry made with shredded filo. It requires no skill at all. After baking, the pastry is steeped in syrup. You can also use up leftover dough by cutting squares, bow ties, rectangles or circles. Shape them into butterflies, bows or knots and fry them until golden. Pile them into a linen-lined basket to serve with after-dinner coffee.

Filo pastries keep well at room temperature for several days or even weeks, although I do not recommend prolonged storage. They are surprisingly economical. Because baklavas are so rich, small portions go a long way. A single large pan of baklava, using 1 pound of filo and 1 pound of nuts, makes 40 or more pieces. To accommodate a party crowd, cut filled and rolled-up filo into bite-size pieces. Fold single strips of dough into bite-size triangles or roll up to make cigarette shapes.

A deceptively simple filo pastry is Sweet Baste-la, an elegant Napoleon-like Moroccan dessert. Double circles of filo are fried into puffed golden saucers and stacked with a cream filling between layers.

Of all the cookies, Wedding Cakes are the most famous. They are known as *kourabiedes* in Greek, *kurabiye* in Turkish and *graybeh* in Arabic. Every Middle Eastern country has its own version. Greek cooks coat tiny rounds or crescents heavily with powdered sugar. Cookie balls may be dimpled or pinched, decorated with whole cloves, shaped into rings, letters, figures or fashioned with cookie cutters. Date Domes are an Arabic filled variation.

Sponge cakes are a Middle Eastern tradition. Sponge Cake and Walnut Cake are versions which may be steeped in syrup or not. ✄

How to Clarify Butter

Place butter in a skillet over low heat until melted. Simmer over low heat until the milky residue disappears and butter is clear and shiny, about 15 minutes. Skim off any milky residue. Use clarified butter as directed in recipe. Can be kept refrigerated for several weeks.

Menu

Thanksgiving Dinner

Flaming Fried Cheese,
page 24
Zucchini Soup, page 37
Roast Turkey with
Bulgur Stuffing, page 96,
or Rice Stuffing for
Turkey or Lamb, page 103
Pumpkin Custard Pie,
page 114
Sweet-Potato Salad, page 57
Greek Holiday Bread, page 79
Pistachio Ice Cream, page 187
Coffee or Tea

New Year's Eve Buffet

Steak Tartar, page 23
Cracker Bread, page 69
Macaroni Casserole, page 107
Greek Village Salad,
page 60
New Year's Bread, page 78
Mixed-Vegetable Casserole,
page 82
Date Domes, page 158
Turkish Delight, page 185

Date Domes   Photo on page 173.

Ma'amul (Arabic)

Festive cookies are shaped in a special wooden mold called a tabi.

Date Filling, see below
1 cup unsalted butter or margarine,
  room temperature
1-1/2 cups granulated sugar
1-1/2 teaspoons brandy
1-1/2 teaspoons orange-blossom water
1 egg

1/2 teaspoon ground black-cherry kernels
  (mahlab), if desired
3 cups all-purpose flour
1 cup fine-grade semolina
Dash of salt
Powdered sugar for sprinkling

Date Filling:
1/2 lb. pitted dates
1 tablespoon butter or margarine,
  room temperature

1 teaspoon orange-blossom water, if desired

Prepare Date Filling. Set aside. Butter baking sheets. Set aside. Preheat oven to 350F (175C). Combine butter or margarine and granulated sugar in a large bowl. Cream until light and fluffy. Stir in brandy and orange-blossom water. Beat in egg. Add cherry kernels, if desired. Gradually add flour, semolina and salt until dough pulls away from side of bowl. Knead until smooth, about 5 minutes. Pinch off pieces of dough 1-1/2 inches in diameter. Shape into balls. Pat into 3-inch circles. Place 1 tablespoon date mixture in center of a circle. Pull edges of circle over filling and pinch together to enclose filling. Place cookie in decorative mold, or *tabi*. Pat down gently in mold. Knock molded cookie out of mold dome-side up onto greased baking sheet. Repeat with remaining dough circles and filling. Bake 20 minutes or until bottom of cookies are pale golden. Do not let tops of cookies brown. Cool on a rack. Sprinkle with powdered sugar while still warm. Makes 16 to 20 cookies.

Date Filling:
Cut up dates. Place in food processor or blender. Process to a paste. Add butter or margarine. Add orange-blossom water, if desired. Process until blended.

TIP

The tabi, a dome-shaped mold with a handle, is generally available at Middle Eastern grocery stores. If no mold is available, use your hands to shape filled dough into balls, patties or bars.

How to Make Date Domes

1/Pat dough into 3-inch circles. Place 1 tablespoon date mixture in center of each circle. Pull edges of each circle over filling and pinch together to enclose filling.

2/Place filled cookie in decorative mold. Pat down gently in mold. Knock molded cookie out of mold dome-side up onto greased baking sheet.

Rice Pudding

Rizogalo (Greece)

A creamy pudding to serve from a pretty bowl or in your most-delicate dessert dishes.

4 cups milk (1 qt.)
3 cups water
3/4 cup short-grain rice
1 cup sugar

2 or 3 egg yolks
1/2 cup milk
1 teaspoon vanilla extract or almond extract
Ground cinnamon for sprinkling

In a large saucepan, combine 4 cups milk, water and rice. Bring to a boil over medium heat. Reduce heat. Simmer, uncovered, over low heat until rice is soft and mixture is slightly thickened. Add sugar. Simmer over medium-low heat 5 minutes. In a small bowl, slightly beat egg yolks. Beat in 1/2 cup milk. Stir a small amount of hot rice mixture into yolk mixture. Add yolk mixture to rice mixture in saucepan. Stir over low heat until blended. Stir in extract. Pour into custard cups or dessert bowls or a large serving bowl. Pudding will be thin but will thicken as it cools. Garnish with a sprinkle of cinnamon. Refrigerate several hours. Makes 6 to 12 servings.

Variation

Egyptian Rice Pudding (Roz bi-Laban): Substitute 1 teaspoon rose water for extract. Garnish with chopped toasted almonds, page 67.

Shredded-Pastry Dessert

Kataifi (Greece)

Easy-to-use shredded filo, or kadaif, is usually available at Middle Eastern grocery stores.

Medium Syrup, page 184
2 cups coarsely chopped walnuts
   (about 10 oz.)
1 teaspoon ground cinnamon
1/4 teaspoon ground cloves

1 lb. fresh or thawed frozen shredded
   filo dough
1/2 cup unsalted butter, clarified, page 157,
   or margarine, melted

Prepare Medium Syrup. Set aside to cool. In a small bowl, combine walnuts, cinnamon and cloves. Set aside. Preheat oven to 350F (175C). Butter a 13" x 9" baking pan. Set aside. Separate shredded dough to loosen and fluff. Spread a third of the shredded dough in prepared baking pan. Sprinkle with a third of the clarified butter or melted margarine. Spread a third of the walnut mixture over dough. Spread with half the remaining shredded dough. Sprinkle with half the remaining butter or margarine. Sprinkle with remaining walnut mixture. Top with remaining shredded dough. Sprinkle with remaining butter or margarine. Bake 30 to 40 minutes or until golden brown. Pour half the cooled syrup over pastry. Let stand 10 minutes. Pour remaining syrup over pastry. Cut into 2-inch diamond or square shapes without removing from pan. Let stand 1 to 8 hours before serving. Makes 24 pieces.

Variations

Shredded-Pastry Rolls: Pull off a 4" x 2" piece of shredded dough. Place flat, fluffing to loosen dough. Place 1 tablespoon nut mixture at bottom of rectangle. Roll up jelly-roll fashion, tucking in sides. Place roll in a buttered baking pan. Sprinkle with butter or margarine. Repeat with remaining shredded filo, nut mixture and butter or margarine. Bake at 350F (175C) 20 to 30 minutes or until rolls are golden. Add syrup as directed above. Makes 20 to 25 pieces.

Arabic Cheese-Filled Pastry: Substitute the following cheese filling for the walnut filling: Combine 3/4 pound ricotta cheese, 1/4 cup sugar and 1 teaspoon orange-blossom water in a small bowl. Mix well.

Christmas Pudding

Anushabur (Armenia)

This festive dessert is prepared in huge batches for large gatherings during the holidays.

1 cup fine- to medium-grade bulgur
Water
12 cups water (3 qts.)
1-1/2 cups golden raisins
2 cups dried apricots

2 cups sugar
1 teaspoon rose water
Ground cinnamon for garnish
Blanched almonds for garnish
Candied cherries for garnish

Place bulgur in a large saucepan. Add water to cover. Drain in a fine sieve. Discard water. Pour 12 cups water into saucepan. Add drained bulgar. Stir well. Bring to a boil. Remove from heat. Let stand 1 to 2 hours. Again, bring to a boil. Reduce heat and cover. Simmer over very low heat, stirring frequently to prevent sticking, 1-1/2 hours or until thickened. Fold in raisins, apricots and sugar. Cover. Simmer over very low heat 30 minutes longer, stirring frequently. Remove from heat. Add rose water. Turn pudding into a serving bowl. Refrigerate to chill. Sprinkle with cinnamon or decorate with almonds and cherries. Makes about 20 servings.

Shredded-Pastry Dessert

Pistachio Baklava

Spread a third of the shredded dough in pan. Sprinkle with a third of the butter or margarine. Spread a third of the walnut mixture over dough. Repeat layering twice, ending with buttered shredded dough. Bake.

Coil walnut-filled filo rolls and brush with clarified butter or melted margarine. Bake until golden. Pour syrup over pastries and let stand. Spoon 1 tablespoon pistachio nuts into center of each coil.

Pistachio Baklava   Photo on page 173.

Swareh (Syria/Lebanon)

This version of individual baklavas is shaped like a rosette and topped with pistachio nuts.

Medium Syrup, page 184
15 filo pastry sheets
2 cups coarsely chopped walnuts
   (about 10 oz.)

1/2 cup unsalted butter, clarified,
   page 157, or margarine, melted
2 cups coarsely chopped pistachio nuts
   (about 1/2 lb.)

Prepare Medium Syrup. Set aside to cool. Preheat oven to 325F (165C). Stack filo pastry sheets. Cut through center to make 2 stacks. Stack again. Trim to measure 15 inches on the 2 long sides. Working with 1 filo sheet at a time, place on a flat surface. Cover remaining filo sheets with plastic wrap to prevent drying out. Spoon about 1/4 cup walnuts 3 inches from bottom of filo to within 1/2 inch of edges. Fold in edges. Fold bottom over walnuts. Roll up tightly jelly-roll fashion. Coil the roll, using your thumb as a guide. Coil should be about 3 inches in diameter. Place on an ungreased baking sheet. Brush top and sides of coil with clarified butter or melted margarine. Repeat with remaining filo, nuts and butter or margarine. Bake 45 to 50 minutes or until golden. Pour cooled syrup over warm pastries. Let stand 1 hour. Spoon 1 tablespoon pistachio nuts into center of each coil. Tap nuts lightly to secure them to pastry. Makes 30 pastries.

Walnut Cake

Karitopita (Greece)

My friend, Ann Pappas, kindly shared her mother's recipe for this holiday cake.

Cinnamon Syrup, see below
7 eggs, separated
1-1/2 cups powdered sugar
1/4 cup all-purpose flour
1/2 teaspoon ground cinnamon
1/2 teaspoon ground cloves
1/2 teaspoon ground nutmeg

1/4 teaspoon baking soda
2 cups finely chopped walnuts (10 oz.)
6 Zwieback crackers, crushed, or
   1-1/2 cups crushed Zwieback or
   graham-cracker crumbs
2 tablespoons Cognac or brandy

Cinnamon Syrup:
1-1/2 cups sugar
3/4 cup water
1 cinnamon stick

5 whole cloves
1 lemon slice

Prepare Cinnamon Syrup. Set aside. Preheat oven to 350F (175C). Grease and flour a 9-inch square pan. Set aside. In a large bowl, beat egg yolks and powdered sugar until light and fluffy. Into a medium bowl, sift together flour, cinnamon, cloves, nutmeg and baking soda. Add nuts and cracker crumbs. Mix well. Gradually beat crumb mixture into egg mixture until blended. Add Cognac or brandy. Beat egg whites until stiff but not dry. Fold into cake batter. Pour into prepared pan. Bake 35 to 40 minutes or until a wooden pick inserted in center of cake comes out clean. Pour cooled syrup over warm cake. Let soak 20 minutes. Cut into 2-1/4-inch diamond or square shapes. Makes 16 servings.

Cinnamon Syrup:
Combine all ingredients in a medium saucepan. Bring to a boil. Boil until candy thermometer registers 212F (100C) or until a thin syrup is formed. Cool before pouring over warm cake. Or pour hot over cooled cake.

Berry Parfait

(Adapted Turkish)

Any berries or cut fruit may be used with any flavor ice cream.

2 (1-pint) baskets strawberries, raspberries or
  blackberries
1/4 cup brandy or raki

1 pint vanilla ice cream
1/4 cup honey
Mint sprigs for garnish

Rinse and hull berries. Place in a large bowl. Pour brandy or raki over berries. Toss lightly. Refrigerate at least 1 hour. When ready to serve, place a scoop of ice cream in each serving dish. Top with about 2 teaspoons honey and some of the berries. Spoon some juice over berries. Garnish with mint sprigs. Makes 6 to 8 servings.

Sponge Cake
Revani (Turkey)

A classic holiday dessert—especially for weddings.

1 cup Thin Syrup, page 184	**1 cup semolina**
1 cup unsalted butter or margarine,	**4 eggs**
room temperature	**Whole blanched almonds for garnish**
1 cup sugar	

Prepare Thin Syrup. Set aside to cool. Preheat oven to 350F (175C). Generously grease an 8-inch square baking pan. Set aside. Combine butter or margarine and sugar in a large bowl. Beat until light and fluffy. Gradually add semolina. Beat until blended. Add eggs, one at a time, beating well after each addition. Turn into prepared pan. Bake 30 minutes or until golden. Cut into 2-inch squares or diamond shapes without removing from pan. Press an almond into the center of each piece. Pour half the cooled syrup over warm cake. Let stand 10 minutes or until syrup is absorbed. Pour remaining syrup over cake. Let stand 20 minutes before serving. Makes 12 servings.

Variations
Arabic Sponge Cake: Add 1/2 cup coarsely chopped blanched almonds or 1 cup shredded unsweetened coconut to batter.
Cheese-Filled Sponge Cake: In a small bowl, mix 2 cups ricotta cheese, 1/4 cup sugar and 1 teaspoon orange-blossom water. Mix well. Pour half the cake batter into a greased 11" x 7" baking pan. Cover with cheese mixture. Top with remaining batter. Bake and continue with recipe as directed.

Honey-Dipped Cookies
Melomacarona (Greece)

An expected treat whenever Greeks gather for a celebration.

2 cups vegetable oil	**About 4 cups all-purpose flour**
1/2 cup powdered sugar	**1 cup honey**
1/2 cup milk or half and half	**1/2 cup water**
1/2 teaspoon baking powder	**1 cup coarsely chopped walnuts**
1/4 teaspoon baking soda	**(about 5 oz.)**

Preheat oven to 350F (175C). Pour oil into a large bowl. Beat in powdered sugar until creamy, about 5 minutes. Beat in milk or half and half, baking powder and baking soda. Gradually beat in flour until dough pulls away from side of bowl. Turn out onto a floured surface. Knead 5 minutes or until dough is soft and pliable. Pinch off pieces of dough 1-1/2 inches in diameter. Mold into oval finger-like shapes. Place on ungreased baking sheets. Bake 20 to 30 minutes or until golden underneath. Cookies will not brown on top. Cool on baking sheets. Combine honey and water in a small saucepan. Bring to a boil. Remove from heat. Cool slightly. Using a spatula, dip each cookie in warm honey mixture. Place on waxed paper. Sprinkle with walnuts. Makes 24 cookies.

French Cigarettes   Photo on page 10.

Cigarettes au Miel (Tunisia)

These short-cut honey-dipped pastries were shared by Mrs. Robert Robaire.

Almond Paste, page 182, or 2 cups marzipan
1 tablespoon grated orange peel
Honey Syrup, page 184
1 (1-lb.) pkg. wonton wrappers,
    about 75 (3-1/2-inch square) skins

Oil for frying
1/2 cup coarsely chopped pistachios,
    blanched almonds or walnuts

Prepare Almond Paste, if using. Place Almond Paste or marzipan in a medium bowl. Stir in orange peel. Prepare Honey Syrup. Set aside to cool. Place 1 tablespoon Almond Paste or marzipan across bottom of 1 wonton wrapper to within 1/4 inch of sides. Fold edges in 1/2 inch. Roll up jelly-roll fashion. Moisten seams to seal well. Pour oil 1 inch deep into a medium skillet. Heat oil to 350F (175C) on a deep-fry thermometer. At this temperature, a 1-inch cube of bread will turn brown in 65 seconds. Carefully place rolls in hot oil. Do not crowd in skillet. Fry until golden, about 3 minutes. Remove from hot oil. Drain on paper towels. Place in a shallow dish or large baking sheet with rimmed sides in a single layer. Pour cooled syrup over pastries. Let stand 1 hour. Sprinkle with pistachios, almonds or walnuts. Makes 75 rolls.

Variation

Israeli Cigars: Substitute the following filling for Almond Paste or marzipan: Combine 2 cups ground almonds or unsalted peanuts, 2 tablespoons sugar and 1 teaspoon cinnamon. Mix well.

Wedding Cakes

Kourabiedes (Greece)

These cookies are part of almost every Balkan and Middle Eastern cook's holiday repertoire.

1 cup unsalted butter or margarine,
    room temperature
1/4 cup granulated sugar
1 egg yolk
2 tablespoons brandy or orange juice,
    if desired

2-1/2 cups sifted all-purpose flour
1/2 teaspoon baking powder
1/2 cup ground blanched almonds
    (about 2 oz.)
About 30 whole cloves, if desired
Powdered sugar for sprinkling

Combine butter or margarine and granulated sugar in a large bowl. Beat in egg yolk until mixture is smooth and light. Beat in brandy or orange juice, if desired. Sift together flour and baking powder. Add to egg mixture, a little at a time, beating well after each addition. Stir in almonds. Turn out onto a floured surface. Knead with floured hands until dough is no longer sticky. Preheat oven to 350F (175C). Pinch off pieces of dough 1 inch in diameter. Shape into balls or crescent shapes. If desired, insert 1 whole clove in center of each ball or crescent. Or use your fingers to press 1 or 2 dimples into each cookie. Place on ungreased baking sheets. Bake 30 to 35 minutes or until cookies are pale golden. Cool on baking sheets. Sprinkle heavily with powdered sugar while still warm. Cookies are extremely fragile. Remove from baking sheets with a spatula. Store in an airtight container between sheets of waxed paper. Makes about 30 cookies.

Floating Islands

Muhalebi (Albania)

Floating islands of egg-white puffs on silky rice custard.

4 cups milk (1 qt.)	**1/2 cup cold milk**
1/3 cup sugar	**1/4 cup rice flour**
3 eggs, separated	**1/2 cup sugar, if desired**

Combine 4 cups milk and 1/3 cup sugar in a shallow saucepan or skillet. Bring to a simmer. Reduce heat to maintain a low simmer. Place egg whites in a medium bowl. Beat until stiff, but not dry. Use a large spoon to shape egg whites into egg shapes. Place a few at a time in simmering milk mixture. Do not crowd in pan as egg whites will expand during cooking. Cook 2 minutes on each side, turning carefully with a slotted spoon. Remove carefully with slotted spoon. Drain on paper towels. Beat egg yolks in a medium bowl. Beat in cold milk. Gradually stir in rice flour until mixture is smooth. Gradually stir into hot milk mixture. Stir constantly over medium-low heat until thickened to custard consistency, 5 to 7 minutes. Do not overcook or custard will curdle. Turn custard into a large, shallow bowl. Top with egg-white puffs. If desired, prepare caramel topping by heating 1/2 cup sugar in a small aluminum skillet over low heat until sugar melts and turns golden brown. Do not allow to caramelize to candy. Immediately pour caramel topping over egg-white puffs to create a lacy pattern. Makes 6 to 8 servings.

Variation

Rice-Flour Custard: Omit egg-white puffs. Reserve egg whites for another use.

Rice flour is available at most Oriental or health-food stores. If not available, substitute 1 cup plus 1 tablespoon all-purpose flour for 1 cup rice flour.

Penelope Twists

Koulouria (Greece)

Melt-in-your mouth cookie twists are served during the holidays.

1 cup unsalted butter or margarine, room temperature	**1/2 teaspoon vanilla extract**
	3-1/2 cups all-purpose flour
1/2 cup sugar	**1-1/2 teaspoons baking powder**
1/4 cup vegetable oil	**2 tablespoons orange juice**
2 eggs	**1 egg, beaten**
3 tablespoons Cognac or brandy	**Sesame seeds for garnish**

Place butter or margarine and sugar in a large bowl. Beat until pale and creamy. Add oil. Beat until blended. Add 2 eggs, one at a time. Beat until smooth. Stir in Cognac or brandy and vanilla. Sift together flour and baking powder. Gradually add to egg mixture alternately with orange juice, beating until mixture is smooth. Knead by hand until dough is soft and pliable. Preheat oven to 350F (175C). Butter baking sheets. Pinch off pieces of dough 1 inch in diameter. Shape into balls. Roll each ball between your palms into a 6-inch rope. Fold in center. Hold each end and twist. Place on prepared baking sheets. Brush with beaten egg. Sprinkle with sesame seeds. Bake 20 to 25 minutes or until golden. Makes 16 to 20 twists.

Walnut Rolls

Burma (Armenia)

If you don't have a long, 1/2-inch wooden dowel, use a curtain rod or extra-long chopstick.

Medium Syrup, page 184
1-1/2 cups finely chopped walnuts
   (about 1/2 lb.)
2 tablespoons sugar

10 filo pastry sheets
1/2 cup unsalted butter, clarified, page 157,
   or margarine, melted

Prepare Medium Syrup. Set aside to cool. Combine walnuts and sugar in a small bowl. Set aside. Stack filo pastry sheets. Cover with plastic wrap to prevent drying out. Preheat oven to 350F (175C). Place 1 filo sheet on a flat surface. Brush with clarified butter or melted margarine. Sprinkle 2 tablespoons nut mixture across pastry 3 inches from bottom to within 1 inch of sides. Fold in sides. Fold bottom over filling. Place dowel on top of filling. Roll up jelly-roll fashion. Gently push dough on both ends of dowel toward center, creating a crinkled effect. Do not crinkle too tightly. Gently pull out dowel. Place crinkled roll carefully on an ungreased baking sheet. Brush with butter or margarine. Repeat with remaining filo, nut mixture and butter or margarine. Cut rolls into 2-inch diagonal slices without removing from baking sheet. Bake 25 to 30 minutes or until crisp and golden brown. Pour cooled syrup over warm pastry. Let stand 2 hours or longer before serving. Makes 10 rolls or about 60 pieces.

Variation

Walnut Rolls in a Skillet: Use half the recipe, preparing 5 rolls. Form a coil with rolls in a generously buttered 8-inch skillet. Start coil at side of skillet, winding toward center. Cook over very low heat, shaking pan occasionally to prevent sticking, about 20 minutes until golden brown underneath. Slip coil from skillet onto a large plate. Invert back into skillet. Cook over low heat 20 minutes longer to brown other side. Cut into 2-inch diagonal slices. Pour cooled syrup over hot pastry. Let stand 2 hours. Makes about 24 pieces.

Bananas Wrapped in Filo

Mutabbaq ma' Moze (Saudi Arabia)

Maylasian Moslems shared this unusual dessert on their pilgrimages to Mecca.

3 large bananas, peeled
1/4 cup any kind of jam
1/2 cup coarsely chopped nuts or coconut
6 or 12 filo pastry sheets

1/4 cup unsalted butter, clarified, page 157,
   or margarine, melted
Honey for garnish
Powdered sugar for sprinkling

Preheat oven to 350F (175C). Butter a baking sheet. Set aside. Brush each banana with jam. Roll in nuts or coconut. Stack filo pastry sheets. Cover with plastic wrap to prevent drying out. Use 1 filo sheet for each banana roll or use 2 sheets if pastry is very thin. Brush filo sheet or sheets with clarified butter or melted margarine. Place 1 banana crosswise near bottom of buttered filo sheet. Fold in sides. Fold bottom of filo over to cover banana. Roll up jelly-roll fashion. Place on prepared baking sheet. Brush with butter or margarine. Repeat with remaining bananas, jam, filo and butter or margarine. Bake 20 to 30 minutes or until golden. Let stand 10 minutes before slicing. Cut into 1-1/2- to 2-inch diagonal pieces. Top with honey or sprinkle with powdered sugar. Makes 3 to 6 servings.

Walnut Rolls

Persian Almond Rolls

Roll up filled filo and dowel jelly-roll fashion. Gently push dough on both ends of dowel toward center, creating a crinkled effect. Carefully pull out dowel.

Stack 2 filo sheets, brushing each with butter or margarine. Sprinkle 1/4 cup almond mixture across bottom of filo. Fold in sides and fold bottom over filling. Roll up jelly-roll fashion and place on baking sheet. Brush with butter or margarine.

Persian Almond Rolls

Baklava (Iran)

Cardamom and almonds give easy dessert rolls a typically Persian flavor.

Medium Syrup, page 184
2 cups finely chopped blanched almonds (about 10 oz.)
1 teaspoon ground cardamom

1/4 cup sugar
16 filo pastry sheets
1/2 cup unsalted butter, clarified, page 157, or margarine, melted

Prepare Medium Syrup. Set aside to cool. In a small bowl, combine almonds, cardamom and sugar. Set aside. Preheat oven to 350F (175C). Butter a large baking sheet. Stack filo pastry sheets on a flat surface. Cover with plastic wrap to prevent drying out. Stack 2 filo sheets, brushing each with clarified butter or melted margarine. Sprinkle 1/4 cup almond mixture across filo sheets 3 inches from bottom to within 1 inch of sides. Fold in sides. Fold bottom over almond mixture. Roll up jelly-roll fashion. Place on prepared baking sheet. Brush top with butter or margarine. Repeat with remaining filo sheets, butter or margarine and almond mixture. Bake 30 to 35 minutes or until crisp and golden. Pour cooled syrup over warm pastry. Let stand several hours, turning occasionally to coat pastry with syrup. Cut rolls into 2-inch diagonal slices. Makes 8 rolls or about 30 pieces.

Sweet Bastela

Ktefa (Morocco)

Here is one of the most-delectable and attractive company desserts.

Egg Custard, see below
1/2 cup coarsely chopped blanched almonds
   (2 oz.)
2 teaspoons ground cinnamon
Pinch of ground cardamom

1 tablespoon sugar
30 filo pastry sheets
Oil for frying
Powdered sugar for sprinkling
1 (8-oz.) jar raspberry preserves

Egg Custard:
3 egg yolks
1/4 cup sugar
1 cup milk

Pinch of salt
1 teaspoon orange-blossom water or
   vanilla extract

Prepare Egg Custard. Refrigerate until ready to use. Combine almonds, cinnamon, cardamom and sugar in small bowl. Set aside. Cut filo into circles using a 7- or 8-inch pan lid as guide. Stack circles and cover with plastic wrap to prevent drying out. Pour oil 1/2 inch deep into a 10-inch skillet. Heat to 350F (175C) on a deep-fry thermometer. At this temperature, a 1-inch cube of bread will turn golden brown in 65 seconds. Layer 2 filo circles. Carefully place in hot oil. When filo puffs, quickly turn with tongs. When filo is pale golden, remove from skillet. Drain on paper towels. Filo will continue to brown as it cools. Continue to fry filo circles in pairs, until all sheets are used. There will be 15 pairs. Set aside until ready to serve. To assemble pastry, place 1 pair of filo circles on a platter. Sprinkle with some of the almond mixture. Top with another pair. Sprinkle with more almond mixture. Top with a third pair. Spread with some of the Egg Custard. Continue to stack remaining pairs, sprinkling 2 layers with almond mixture and spreading custard on the third, until all ingredients are used, ending with filo. Sprinkle pastry with powdered sugar. Stir preserves. Spoon evenly around pastry. Cut into wedges to serve. Makes 8 servings.

Egg Custard:
In the top of a double boiler, blend egg yolks with sugar. Stir in milk and salt. Stir constantly over boiling water until custard coats a metal spoon, about 20 minutes. Remove from heat immediately. Stir in orange-blossom water or vanilla. Place pan in a bowl of ice water until cool. Makes about 1 cup.

Variation

Short-Cut Sweet Bastela: Omit Egg Custard. Prepare 1 (3-ounce) package instant vanilla-pudding mix as directed on package. Fold in 1/2 cup whipped cream and 1/2 teaspoon vanilla. Substitute pudding mixture for the Egg Custard.

How to Make Sweet Bastela

1/Cut filo into 7- to 8-inch circles. Place 2 stacked circles at a time in hot oil. When filo puffs, quickly turn with tongs. Remove from skillet when filo is pale golden. Drain on paper towels.

2/To assemble pastry, layer filo circles, almond mixture and Egg Custard. Repeat layering until all ingredients are used, ending with filo. Spoon preserves around pastry.

Butterflies

Parnaveh (Iran)

Leftover pieces of filo may be used to make both Butterflies and Golden Dollars, below.

1 cup sifted powdered sugar
1 teaspoon ground cardamom or cinnamon

2 filo pastry sheets or 24 (4" x 2") filo strips
Oil for frying

Combine sugar and cardamom or cinnamon in a small bowl. Mix well. Set aside. Stack filo pastry sheets or any leftover filo strips. Cut into 4" x 2" rectangles. Cover with plastic wrap to prevent drying out. Pour oil 1-1/2 inches deep into a large skillet or shallow saucepan. Heat to 375F (190C) on a deep-fry thermometer. At this temperature a 1-inch cube of bread will turn brown in 50 seconds. Work with 1 filo rectangle at a time, keeping remaining filo covered. To shape a butterfly, moisten your fingers with water and pinch or twist together the 2 long sides of a rectangle across the center. Carefully place in hot oil. Do not crowd in pan. Fry up to 30 seconds until pale golden. Do not let brown in oil. Butterflies will continue to brown while cooling. Remove from skillet with a slotted spoon. Drain on paper towels. Repeat with remaining rectangles. Sprinkle with sugar mixture. Serve warm or cool. Makes about 24 butterflies.

Variation

Golden Dollars: Cut filo sheets into 2- to 2-1/2-inch circles. Fry and sprinkle with sugar mixture as directed.

Fried Curls

Deples (Greece)

Crisp honey-dipped fried cookies are similar to Italian crostoli and Chinese bow ties.

Honey Syrup, see below
1 cup coarsely chopped walnuts (about 5 oz.)
2 tablespoons sugar
1/4 teaspoon ground cinnamon
3 eggs

1 teaspoon lemon juice
1/2 teaspoon baking powder
1-1/2 to 1-3/4 cups all-purpose flour
Oil for frying

Honey Syrup:
1 cup honey
1/2 cup water
1 small cinnamon stick

1 teaspoon grated orange peel or lemon peel
1/2 teaspoon lemon juice

Prepare Honey Syrup. Set aside to cool. In a small bowl, combine walnuts, sugar and cinnamon. Set aside. Beat eggs in a large bowl. Add lemon juice and baking powder. Mix until blended. Gradually add flour until dough pulls away from side of bowl. Flour your hands and knead dough until smooth and no longer sticky. Divide into 4 equal portions. Shape each portion into a ball. Cover with a dry cloth towel. Use a rolling pin or pasta machine to roll out each portion of dough into a paper-thin 30'' x 4'' strip. If using pasta machine, roll in settings suggested by manufacturer for paper-thin dough. Cut dough into 6'' x 4'' strips. Cover with towel until ready to fry. Pour oil 1-1/2 inches deep into a large shallow saucepan or skillet. Heat oil to 375F (190C) on a deep-fry thermometer. At this temperature, a 1-inch cube of bread will turn golden brown in 50 seconds. Working with 1 dough strip at a time, carefully place in hot oil. Curl strip around a fork, using another fork as a guide. Cook and turn until curled strip is crisp and golden. Drain on paper towels. Cool. Dip 1 curl at a time into cooled syrup. Drain on a rack over waxed paper. Sprinkle with walnut mixture. Makes 20 cookies.

Honey Syrup:
Combine all ingredients in a small saucepan. Bring to a boil. Reduce heat. Cook, uncovered, over medium heat 10 minutes. Pour into a small bowl.

Cheese Turnovers

Mutabbaq ma'Jebneh (Arabic)

Simple to make and simply delicious. Crisp turnovers with a moist filling.

1 cup ricotta cheese (8 oz.)
2 tablespoons sugar
1 teaspoon orange-blossom water

16 (3-1/2-inch square) wonton wrappers
Oil for frying
Powdered sugar for sprinkling

In a small bowl, combine ricotta cheese, sugar and orange-blossom water. Mix until blended. Set aside. Place wonton wrappers on a flat surface. Spoon about 1 tablespoon cheese mixture in center of each wrapper. Moisten edges around wrapper. Fold bottom right corner to top left corner, making a triangle. Pour oil 1 inch deep into a large skillet. Heat to 375F (190C) on a deep-fry thermometer. At this temperature, a 1-inch cube of bread will turn golden brown in 50 seconds. Carefully place turnovers in hot oil. Fry, turning once or twice to brown evenly, until golden brown on both sides, about 3 minutes. Drain on paper towels. Sprinkle with powdered sugar. Makes 16 triangles.

Filo with Cream Filling

Galaktoboureko (Greece)

I found this popular pastry sold at fast-food counters in Boston at Faneuil Hall Market Place.

Medium Syrup, page 184
8 egg yolks
1-1/2 cups sugar
6 cups warm milk (1-1/2 qts.)
6 tablespoons cornstarch

1 cup whipping cream
1 tablespoon vanilla extract
12 filo pastry sheets (about 1/2 lb.)
1/2 cup unsalted butter, clarified, page 157,
**   or margarine, melted**

Prepare Medium Syrup. Set aside to cool. Preheat oven to 350F (175C). Lightly butter a 13" x 9" baking pan. Set aside. Combine egg yolks and sugar in a 2-quart saucepan. Beat until thickened and pale. Stir in warm milk alternately with cornstarch. Stir constantly over low heat until mixture simmers and begins to thicken. Remove from heat. Stir in cream and vanilla. Stir until blended. Stack filo pastry sheets on a flat surface. Trim or fold to fit baking pan. Cover with plastic wrap to prevent drying out. Layer half the filo in pan, brushing each sheet with clarified butter or melted margarine. Pour cream mixture over layers. Top with remaining filo, brushing each sheet with butter or margarine. Brush top sheet with butter or margarine. Lightly score in 2-inch diamond or square shapes with a sharp knife. Do not cut all the way through. Bake 40 to 50 minutes or until golden brown. Pour cooled syrup over warm pastry. Let stand until custard is set. Makes about 24 pieces.

Coins

Thriba (Morocco)

Moroccan Sephardic Jews celebrate the end of Passover with plates of sweets, including these cookies.

1/2 cup unsalted butter or margarine,
**   room temperature**
1 cup sugar
1 cup vegetable oil

1 cup ground walnuts (about 5 oz.)
3-1/2 to 4 cups all-purpose flour
Few drops of water
Ground cinnamon for garnish

Preheat oven to 350F (175C). Butter large baking sheets. Set aside. Cream butter or margarine and sugar in a large bowl until light and fluffy. Beat in oil until mixture is smooth. Stir in walnuts. Add flour a little at a time, mixing well after each addition, until dough pulls away from side of bowl. If dough is too dry, add a few drops of water. Knead slightly and shape into a smooth ball. Turn out onto a floured surface. Roll out until dough is 1/2 inch thick. Cut into rounds with a 1-inch cookie cutter. Place cookies on prepared baking sheets. Bake 25 to 30 minutes or until golden underneath. Tops of cookies will not brown. Remove from baking sheets and place on a plate or rack. Sprinkle hot cookies with cinnamon. Makes about 48 cookies.

Deluxe Baklava

(Greek-Style)

My daughter, Marya, prepares this luxurious baklava as a Christmas gift for special friends.

Medium Syrup, page 184
4 cups finely chopped walnuts
   (about 1-1/4 lbs.)
1 tablespoon ground cinnamon
1/2 teaspoon ground allspice
1/2 teaspoon ground nutmeg

1/4 teaspoon ground cloves
1/4 cup sugar
40 filo pastry sheets (about 2 lbs.)
1-1/2 cups unsalted butter, clarified,
   page 157, or margarine, melted

Prepare Medium Syrup. Set aside to cool. Preheat oven to 350F (175C). Lightly butter a 13" x 9" baking pan. Set aside. In a medium bowl, combine walnuts, cinnamon, allspice, nutmeg, cloves and sugar. Set aside. Stack filo pastry sheets on a flat surface. Trim to fit pan. Cover with plastic wrap to prevent drying out. Layer 12 filo sheets in baking pan, brushing each sheet with clarified butter or melted margarine. Spread 1 cup nut mixture over layered filo sheets. Top with 8 more filo sheets, brushing each with butter or margarine. Spread with 1 cup nut mixture. Layer 8 more filo sheets, brushing each with butter or margarine. Spread with remaining nut mixture. Top with 12 remaining filo sheets, brushing each with butter or margarine. Brush top sheet with remaining butter or margarine. Cutting all the way through pastry, cut into 1-inch diamond shapes without removing from pan. Bake 30 minutes. Reduce heat to 200F (95C). Bake 30 minutes longer. Pour cooled syrup over warm pastry. Let stand several hours before serving. Makes about 110 pieces.

Butter Rings

Graybeh (Syria)

Julie Nassraway's tender cookies won't overcook when baked on double baking sheets.

3 cups all-purpose flour
1-1/2 cups fine-grade semolina
Dash of salt
1 cup sugar

About 1-1/4 cups butter or margarine,
   room temperature
24 to 30 toasted whole blanched almonds,
   page 67

Preheat oven to 250F (120C). Place 1 baking sheet on top of another. Set aside. Combine flour, semolina, salt and sugar in a large bowl. Mix well. Add 1 cup butter or margarine. Beat with electric mixer, adding more butter or margarine to make a soft pliable dough. Knead dough with your hands until no longer sticky. Pinch off 1-inch pieces. Roll each piece with your palms on a clean surface to make an 8-inch rope. Form into a circle, overlapping ends. Press an almond into overlapping ends to fasten. Place on ungreased double baking sheets. Bake 20 minutes. Increase temperature to 350F (175C). Bake 10 minutes longer or until cookies are firm, but not brown. They should be slightly golden underneath. Makes 24 to 30 cookies.

From the top: Orange-Peel Preserves, page 178; Pistachio Baklava, page 161; Deluxe Baklava; and Date Domes, page 158.

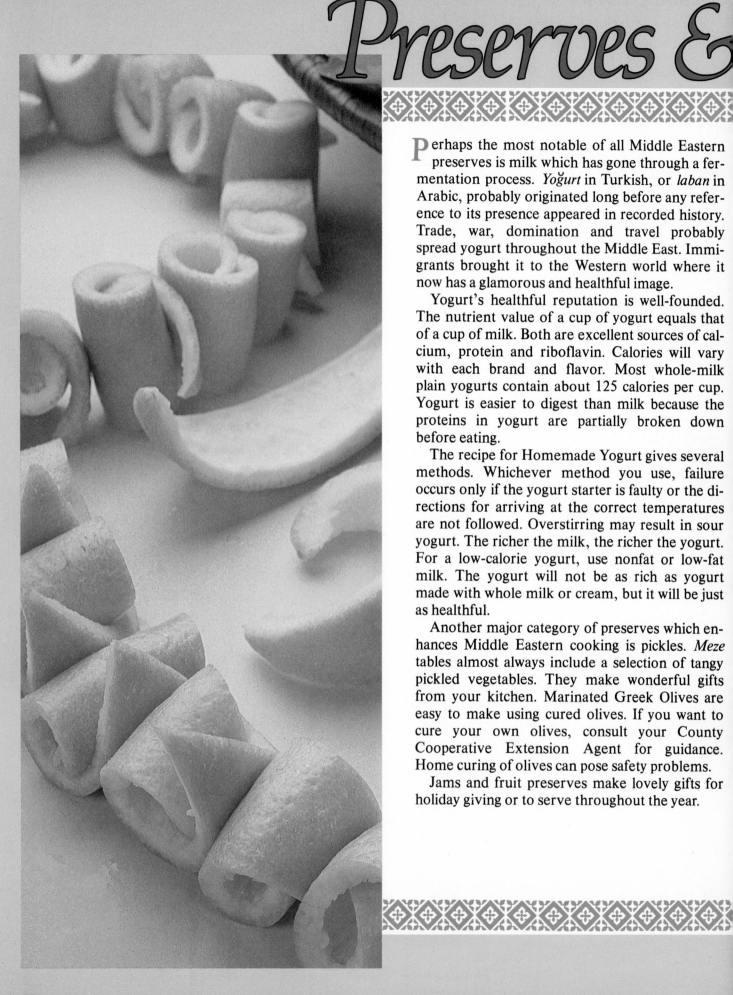

Perhaps the most notable of all Middle Eastern preserves is milk which has gone through a fermentation process. *Yoğurt* in Turkish, or *laban* in Arabic, probably originated long before any reference to its presence appeared in recorded history. Trade, war, domination and travel probably spread yogurt throughout the Middle East. Immigrants brought it to the Western world where it now has a glamorous and healthful image.

Yogurt's healthful reputation is well-founded. The nutrient value of a cup of yogurt equals that of a cup of milk. Both are excellent sources of calcium, protein and riboflavin. Calories will vary with each brand and flavor. Most whole-milk plain yogurts contain about 125 calories per cup. Yogurt is easier to digest than milk because the proteins in yogurt are partially broken down before eating.

The recipe for Homemade Yogurt gives several methods. Whichever method you use, failure occurs only if the yogurt starter is faulty or the directions for arriving at the correct temperatures are not followed. Overstirring may result in sour yogurt. The richer the milk, the richer the yogurt. For a low-calorie yogurt, use nonfat or low-fat milk. The yogurt will not be as rich as yogurt made with whole milk or cream, but it will be just as healthful.

Another major category of preserves which enhances Middle Eastern cooking is pickles. *Meze* tables almost always include a selection of tangy pickled vegetables. They make wonderful gifts from your kitchen. Marinated Greek Olives are easy to make using cured olives. If you want to cure your own olives, consult your County Cooperative Extension Agent for guidance. Home curing of olives can pose safety problems.

Jams and fruit preserves make lovely gifts for holiday giving or to serve throughout the year.

Confections

Confections are usually confined to street food in the Middle East. Confectioners sell Turkish paste, which are tiny squares of powdered paste-jellies eaten like candy. Sesame candy is sold on Turkish streets. Candied fruits are displayed in colorful array in huge oak tubs in the market-places, or *souks,* in North Africa. In the cuisines of Iran, the Arab Gulf States and North Africa, candied fruits are an especially important ingredient.

Ice cream is sold everywhere, even in the most remote villages. Most ice creams are forms of ices made with flavorings, such as rose water, orange-blossom water, almond extract and pomegranate juice. These flavorings may also be added to vanilla ice cream to create a different flavor. If you want to go all the way back to basics, make home-made ice cream with cream, adding fresh-fruit puree such as persimmon for an exotic touch.

Dates, the staple food of Bedouins—actually survival food in lean times—are high-calorie, nutritious confections eaten for breakfast, snacks and served with tea. Moslems break fasts with dates, following the example supposedly set by the prophet Mohammed. Dates grow in the desert oases and marshes of Southern Iraq. In fact, Iraq is responsible for three-fourths of the world's date supply. In Saudi Arabia, date syrup, called *dibs,* is collected from the bottom of date bins. It is considered the rarest of treats.

Stuffed Dates filled with homemade Almond Paste make delectable gifts from your kitchen. Many of the confections in this section will be enjoyed as holiday gifts.

Syrups are included in this section. Many are essential for making filo pastries. Thin Syrup is used on porous cakes and cookies. Medium Syrup is the standard syrup for most sweet filo pastries.

Fresh-fruit syrups are used to make drinks. Some fruit syrups such as the one made from pomegranates, commonly called *grenadine syrup,* can also be used in sauces. ✄

Menu

Easter Dinner

Egg & Lemon Soup, page 41
Roast Lamb with Potatoes, page 136
Greek Village Salad, page 60
DeLuxe Baklava, page 172
Greek Coffee, page 32
Naturally Dyed Eggs, page 52
in a Basket Centerpiece

Preserved Grape Leaves

Warak Arish Makboos (Arabic)

Preserve your own grape leaves for Stuffed Grape Leaves.

50 to 70 grape leaves
8 cups water (2 qts.)
1/4 cup salt

Lemon wedges
3 cups water
3 cups vinegar

Sterilize two 1-quart canning jars and lids according to manufacturer's instructions. Rinse grape leaves. Use only young leaves that have not been exposed to chemicals or pesticides. Pour 8 cups water into a large saucepan. Add salt. Bring to a boil. Add grape leaves. Boil 30 seconds. Drain, discarding water in pan. Let leaves stand until cool enough to handle. Place leaves shiny-sides up in stacks of 10 or 15 with largest leaves on bottom. Roll up each stack and tie with string. Pack vertically into hot sterilized jars. Trim edges of rolls to fit jar, if necessary. Tuck in several lemon wedges. Pour 3 cups water and 3 cups vinegar into a large saucepan. Bring to a boil. Pour over leaves in jars, covering completely. Seal jars according to manufacturer's instructions. May be stored in refrigerator up to 6 months. For longer storage, process filled jars 15 minutes in a hot-water bath, page 186, according to manufacturer's instructions. Makes about 2 quarts.

Preserved Lemons or Limes

Citron Confits à la Marocaine (Morocco)

Preserved citrus fruits add zest and flavor to Lemon Chicken or to a favorite stew.

10 ripe medium lemons or limes
   (about 3 lbs.)
4 to 5 tablespoons salt

1 tablespoon coriander seeds
1 teaspoon whole cloves
About 8 cups water (2 qts.)

Sterilize canning jars and lids according to manufacturer's instructions. Wide-mouthed jars are necessary to accommodate whole lemons. Make a deep slit on 4 sides of each fruit, starting from bottom and ending short of stem end, so cut fruit will keep its shape. Sprinkle salt into slits, making sure salt is packed in well. Place fruit in hot sterilized jars. Divide coriander seeds and cloves evenly among jars. Pour 8 cups water into a saucepan. Bring to a boil. Pour as much boiling water over fruit in jars as needed to cover fruit completely. If necessary, weight down fruit with a sterilized stone to keep submerged. Seal jars according to manufacturer's instructions. Store in a cool, dark, dry place 3 weeks before using. May be stored up to 6 months. For longer storage, process filled jars 20 minutes in a hot-water bath, page 186, according to manufacturer's instructions. To use Preserved Lemons or Limes, skim off harmless residue on top of liquid. Use tongs to remove required amount of fruit. Wash fruit and cut into quarters to eat as pickles. To flavor stews and other foods, remove and discard pulp and use only peel. Makes 2 quarts.

How to Preserve Grape Leaves

1/Place blanched leaves shiny-side up in stacks of 10 or 15 with largest leaves on bottom. Roll up each stack and tie with string. Pack vertically into hot sterilized jars.

2/Pour boiling water-and-vinegar mixture over leaves in jars, covering completely. Seal jars according to manufacturer's instructions.

Clotted Cream

Kaymak (Turkey)

A simplified version of the cream used to garnish sweet pastries. It closely resembles Devonshire cream.

1 cup dairy sour cream
2 cups whipping cream

Place sour cream in a large bowl. Stir until smooth. Gradually stir in whipping cream until blended. Cover with a clean cloth. Let stand at cool room temperature (65F, 20C) 24 hours. Line a bowl with several paper coffee filters or triple layers of cheesecloth with enough overhang to lift out easily. Transfer cream mixture to prepared bowl. Cover with a clean cloth. Refrigerate 24 hours. Cream will separate from whey. Lift cream out of bowl using overhanging filters or cheesecloth. Place on a plate. Spoon cream into a refrigerator container. Cover and refrigerate. May be stored up to 1 week. Makes 2 cups.

Orange-Peel Preserves   Photo on page 173.

Liko me Portokale (Albania)

My mother, Farfuri Rushit, served these with wooden picks as a confection with demitasses.

8 medium, thick-skinned oranges	**1 cinnamon stick**
8 cups water (2 qts.)	**4 or 5 whole cloves**
3 cups sugar	**2 teaspoons lemon juice**
2-1/2 cups water	

Remove stem end of oranges. To section peel, cut with a sharp knife, dividing peel only into 8 portions. Remove peels. Reserve fruit for another use. Trim any excess white membrane from peels. Tightly roll up each peel section, making a curl. Thread curls, using a needle and heavy thread or string. Thread 16 curls for each garland. Tie ends of each garland together. Place garlands on a clean towel in a dry place. Do not cover. Let dry 1 to 2 days, depending on humidity and temperature. Sterilize jelly glasses or canning jars according to manufacturer's instructions. Pour 8 cups water into a large saucepan. Bring to a boil. Drop garlands in boiling water. Reduce heat. Cook, uncovered, over medium-low heat 40 to 50 minutes or until peels are tender. Drain, discarding water in pan. Pat garlands dry with paper towels. Combine 3 cups sugar and 2-1/2 cups water, cinnamon, cloves and lemon juice in saucepan. Bring to a boil. Add garlands. Cook, uncovered, over medium-low heat until syrup is thickened or until jellying point, 220F (104C) on a candy thermometer. At this temperature, jelly dropped from a cold metal spoon will fall in a sheet. Remove from heat. Cool garlands in syrup. Remove cooled garlands from syrup using clean tongs. Snip and remove string. Drop loose curls back into hot syrup. Pour syrup and curls into hot sterilized jelly glasses or canning jars. Attach lids according to manufacturer's instructions. Immediately invert jars for a few seconds so hot preserves can destroy any mold or yeast that may have settled on lids. May be stored 3 to 4 months in refrigerator. For longer storage, process filled glasses or jars 15 minutes in a hot-water bath, page 186, according to manufacturer's instructions. Makes 2 pints.

Yogurt Cheese

Labanah (Arabic)

A traditional breakfast: sprinkle Yogurt Cheese with olive oil and serve with olives and pocket bread.

2 cups plain yogurt or Homemade Yogurt, page 180	**1 teaspoon salt**

Fold a large piece of cheesecloth into a square several thicknesses thick. Or use a clean, white, lint-free towel. Place yogurt in center of cheesecloth square or towel. Bring corners up and tie securely, making a bag containing yogurt. Hang bag from faucet over a bowl several hours or overnight at cool room temperature. Or place bag in a colander over a bowl and let stand in refrigerator or at room temperature several hours or overnight. Remove cheese from bag. Place in a medium bowl. Stir in salt. Place in a refrigerator container. Cover and refrigerate. Use within 1 week. Makes about 3/4 cup.

How to Make Orange-Peel Preserves

1/Section peel by cutting into 8 portions with a sharp knife. Remove peels and trim any excess white membrane.

2/Tightly roll up each peel section. Thread 16 curls for each garland, using a needle and heavy thread or string. Tie ends of each garland together.

Grenadine Syrup

Robb-e Anar (Iran)

Syrup made from pomegranates is used to flavor meats, poultry, soups, sauces and beverages.

4 cups pomegranate juice (1 qt.), see below   **2 cups sugar**

Sterilize jelly glasses or canning jars and lids according to manufacturer's instructions. Combine juice and sugar in a medium saucepan. Bring to a boil over medium heat. Continue to boil until a medium-thin syrup is formed or a candy thermometer registers 205F (95C). Skim off foam. Pour syrup into hot sterilized jelly glasses or canning jars, leaving 1/4 inch headroom. Seal according to manufacturer's instructions. May be stored up to 1 month in refrigerator. For longer storage, process filled glasses or jars 15 minutes in a hot-water bath, page 186, according to manufacturer's instructions. Makes 3 cups.

TIP ✖✖✖✖✖✖✖✖✖✖✖✖✖✖✖✖✖✖✖✖✖✖✖✖✖✖✖✖

You will need 8 to 12 fresh pomegranates to make 1 cup juice. To squeeze juice from pomegranates, use a plastic or porcelain orange juicer. Do not use metal or juice may darken. Cut each pomegranate in half. Squeeze on juicer. Seeds that remain unpressed may be placed in a cheesecloth bag and squeezed by hand. Wear rubber gloves to prevent staining your hands. Strain juice through several thicknesses of cheesecloth before using.

Eggplant Pickles

Turshi (Albania)

These pickles are usually served before dinner with appetizers or as a condiment with a main course.

3 lbs. Japanese eggplants (9 or 10)
Water
1 cup chopped fresh parsley
1 tablespoon chopped fresh oregano or
   1 teaspoon crushed dried leaf oregano

2 large tomatoes, chopped
1-1/2 garlic heads, minced
2 hot yellow peppers, minced
Olive oil
1/4 cup salt

Sterilize two 1-quart canning jars and lids according to manufacturer's instructions. Wash eggplants. Leave stems on. Peel lengthwise strips from eggplants to make stripes. Place eggplants in a large saucepan. Add water to cover. Bring to a boil. Continue to boil 3 minutes. Set aside until cool enough to handle. Starting from bottom and ending short of stem end, make a deep slit in each eggplant almost all the way through to the opposite side. In a medium bowl, combine parsley, oregano, tomatoes, garlic and peppers. Mix well. Fill eggplant slits with tomato mixture. Squeeze gently to close slightly. Place stuffed eggplants upright in hot sterilized jars. Pour in olive oil to cover eggplants completely. Divide salt equally among jars. Process filled jars 40 minutes in a pressure canner at 10 pounds pressure according to manufacturer's instructions. Seal according to manufacturer's instructions. Shake jars to distribute salt evenly around eggplants. Store upright in refrigerator, turning occasionally, 2 to 3 weeks before using. May be stored up to 6 months. Makes 2 quarts.

Homemade Yogurt

Choose one of several methods for making yogurt easily and inexpensively at home.

4 cups nonfat, low-fat or
   regular milk (1 qt.)

2 tablespoons plain yogurt

Heat milk in a 2-quart saucepan to 185F (85C) or until bubbles appear around edges. Let cool to 110F (45C), or lukewarm. Place yogurt in a small bowl. Stir about 1/2 cup lukewarm milk into yogurt. Pour yogurt mixture into milk, stirring gently to blend. Do not stir vigorously or mixture will become tart. **If using a yogurt maker,** follow manufacturer's instructions. **If using a thermos bottle,** fill with warm water (115F, 45C). Discard water and refill thermos with yogurt mixture. Replace cap and let stand 4 hours. **If using a saucepan or ceramic or plastic bowl,** rinse in warm water. Place yogurt mixture in pan or bowl. Cover with lid or plastic wrap. Cover completely with a double-thickness of bath towel. Keep covered at least 6 hours or until yogurt is set. **If using oven,** preheat to 150F (65C). Turn off heat. Cover yogurt and place in warm oven. Let stand several hours or overnight. Cool. Store yogurt in refrigerator. Makes 1 quart.

Variations

Rich Yogurt: Substitute 2 cups whipping cream (1 pint) for 2 cups of the milk.
Fruit Yogurt: Sweeten 1-1/2 cups pureed or mashed fruit with 1/4 cup sugar. Blend in 1 teaspoon lemon juice. Stir into Homemade Yogurt.
Frozen Yogurt Sticks: Spoon Fruit Yogurt, above, into 1/3-cup paper cups. Insert wooden sticks in centers. Freeze. Tear off paper to serve.

How to Make Eggplant Pickles

1/Peel lengthwise strips from washed eggplants to make stripes.

2/Fill eggplant slits with tomato mixture. Squeeze gently to close slightly. Place upright in hot sterilized jars.

Marinated Greek Olives

Elies Marinates (Greece)

Plain cured olives are dressed up with spices and vegetables.

1 qt. canned pitted or unpitted, black or green olives
1 cup olive oil
1/2 cup red-wine vinegar
1 teaspoon crushed dried leaf oregano

1 leek stalk, white part only, sliced
2 orange slices
1 lemon, sliced
2 small hot red peppers
1 bay leaf

Make a slit in 1 side of each olive. Place in a large clean bowl or jar. Add remaining ingredients. Mix well. Cover. Marinate several hours before eating. Place in jars to store. It is not necessary to seal jars. Olives may be stored in refrigerator up to 1 month. Makes 1 quart.

Stuffed Dates

Les Dattes Farcies (Morocco)

Friends and family will appreciate a gift of home-stuffed dates.

1 cup Almond Paste, below   **1 lb. pitted dates**

Prepare Almond Paste. Pinch off small pieces and shape into ovals. Stuff ovals into each date. Reserve any remaining Almond Paste for another use. Makes up to 2 pounds.

Variation

Substitute whole blanched almonds dipped in rose water or orange-blossom water for Almond Paste.

Almond Paste

Dhaw'k Allawz (Arabic)

The Arabs take credit for this confection used to fill dates, pastries and cookies.

1 cup blanched almonds   **2 teaspoons almond extract**
1-1/2 cups powdered sugar   **2 or 3 drops rose water**
1 large egg white

Preheat oven to 300F (150C). Spread almonds on a baking sheet. Bake 10 to 15 minutes or until almonds appear oily but not browned. Cool slightly. Place almonds in blender or food processor. Process until ground. Add powdered sugar, egg white and almond extract. Process until a paste is formed. Add rose water. Process a few seconds longer. Scrape side of container with a rubber spatula. Turn paste into a plastic or glass container. Cover and refrigerate 4 days to blend flavors. May be stored up to 4 months. Makes 1 cup.

Almond Ice Cream

Bademli Dondurma (Turkey)

Here's a short-cut version of a favorite ice cream.

1 pint vanilla ice cream   **2 or 3 drops almond extract**
1/4 cup ground toasted blanched almonds,
**   page 67**

Soften ice cream slightly at room temperature. Place in a cold medium bowl. Stir in almonds and almond extract until blended. Pack into a freezer container, leaving 1/2 inch headroom. Cover and freeze solid. Makes 1 pint.

How to Make Almond Paste & Stuffed Dates

1/Spread almonds on a baking sheet. Bake 10 to 15 minutes or until almonds appear oily but not browned.

2/Process almonds until ground. Add powdered sugar, egg white and almond extract. Process until a paste. Add rose water and process a few seconds longer.

3/Shape small pieces of Almond Paste into ovals.

4/Stuff an oval of Almond Paste into each pitted date.

Thin Syrup

Thin syrups are usually poured over sponge cakes. Try one of the flavored variations.

3 cups sugar   **1/2 lemon**
4 cups water (1 qt.)

Combine all ingredients in a large, heavy saucepan. Bring to a boil, stirring frequently. Reduce heat. Once mixture boils and sugar is dissolved, do not stir or syrup may cloud or crystallize. Cook, uncovered, over medium-low heat until a candy thermometer registers 205F (95C). At this temperature, syrup dropped from a cold metal spoon will fall in a thin stream. Discard lemon half. Cool syrup. Use immediately or refrigerate in a plastic container with lid. May be refrigerated up to 1 month. Makes 3 cups.

Variations

Cinnamon Thin Syrup: Add 1 cinnamon stick with lemon half.
Rose-Water Thin Syrup: Stir 1/2 teaspoon rose water into cooked syrup.
Orange-Blossom Thin Syrup: Stir 1/2 teaspoon orange-blossom water into cooked syrup.

Medium Syrup

This syrup is most commonly used on baklava and other sweet filo pastries.

3 cups sugar   **2 tablespoons lemon juice**
1-1/2 cups water

Combine all ingredients in a large, heavy saucepan. Bring to a boil, stirring frequently. Reduce heat. Once mixture boils and sugar is dissolved, do not stir or syrup may cloud or crystallize. Cook, uncovered, over medium-low heat until a candy thermometer registers 212 to 218F (100 to 102C). At this temperature, syrup dropped from a cold metal spoon will fall in a sheet. Remove from heat. Cool. Use immediately or refrigerate in a plastic container with lid. May be refrigerated up to 1 month. Makes about 2 cups.

Variations

Honey Syrup: Stir in 2 tablespoons honey after removing from heat.
Rose-Water Medium Syrup: Stir 1/2 teaspoon rose water into cooked syrup.
Orange-Blossom Medium Syrup: Stir 1/2 teaspoon orange-blossom water into cooked syrup.

Turkish Delight

Lokum (Turkey)

Somewhat different from what you buy in candy stores but equally delicious.

3 envelopes unflavored gelatin
1/2 cup water
2 cups granulated sugar
1 cup water

1 cup citrus, apple or pomegranate juice
Food coloring, if desired
Powdered sugar

Oil an 8-inch square pan. Dissolve gelatin in 1/2 cup water. In a medium saucepan, combine granulated sugar and 1 cup water. Bring to a boil over medium heat. Add dissolved-gelatin mixture. Stir until blended. Simmer over medium heat 30 minutes. Add fruit juice. Add food coloring, if desired. Simmer 5 minutes longer. Pour into prepared pan. Refrigerate until firm. Use a sharp, wet knife to cut into 1-inch cubes. Spread powdered sugar on a large piece of waxed paper. Drop cubes onto powdered sugar and toss to coat well. Makes 64 pieces.

Apricot Fruit Leather

Pestil (Turkey)

Fruit leathers from Turkey and Syria have been sold in candy stores in New York City for generations.

12 apricots (about 2 lbs.)
Few drops of orange food coloring, if desired

Line a large rimmed baking sheet with plastic wrap. Set aside. Peel, pit and slice fruit to measure about 4 cups. Place in food processor and process until pureed. Add food coloring, if desired. Pour puree onto prepared baking sheet, spreading 1/4 inch thick. **To dry outdoors,** place in direct sunlight or behind a pane of glass. Cover or bring inside at night if night temperatures vary more than 20F (11C) from daytime temperatures or if fog or humidity is possible. Ouside drying will take 1 to 3 days, depending on humidity and temperatures. Check fruit leather frequently for dryness. **To oven-dry,** set oven thermostat at lowest setting. On most ovens this is 150F (65C). Place puree on baking sheets in oven and leave oven door open. Fruit leather will be dry within several hours or overnight. **To dry in food dehydrator,** follow manufacturer's instructions. When fruit leather is completely dry, loosen edges and peel off plastic. Place on clean plastic wrap and roll up loosely. May be stored up to 3 weeks at room temperature, 3 to 4 months in refrigerator or 1 year in freezer. Makes about 1 pound.

Sesame Candy

Pastelli (Greece)

For thousands of years, this candy has been made in many Middle Eastern countries.

1 (1-lb.) jar honey (2 cups)
1 lb. hulled sesame seeds

Butter an 8-inch square pan. Set aside. Heat honey in a medium saucepan over medium heat until a candy thermometer registers 280F (140C). At this temperature, syrup dropped into cold water will separate into threads which are hard but not brittle. Stir in sesame seeds. Immediately pour into prepared pan. Cool slightly. While still soft, cut into diagonal 2" x 1" strips or diamond shapes. Do not remove from pan until candy is firm. Makes about 3 pounds.

Sesame Ice Cream

(Adapted)

Especially developed for those who love the flavor of halva candy.

1 pint vanilla ice cream   **1 tablespoon honey**
1/4 cup sesame-seed paste (tahini paste)

Soften ice cream slightly at room temperature. Place in a cold medium bowl. Stir in sesame-seed paste and honey until blended. Pack into freezer container, leaving 1/2 inch headroom. Cover and freeze solid. Makes 1 pint.

Canning Methods

Use a **hot-water bath** for canning fruits, tomatoes and other acidic foods, butters, conserves, preserves and jams. The foods must be immersed in boiling water (212F, 100C) in a canner or large kettle. Process from 10 to 45 minutes, depending on the type of food and size of jars.

The **steam-pressure method** is used for low-acid foods. A steam-pressure canner is a heavy kettle with a lid that can be clamped down to make a steam-tight seal. Lids are fitted with a safety valve, vent and pressure gauge. Steam-pressure canners are fitted both with dial gauges and weighted gauges. Foods are processed at high temperatures (240F, 115C) for control of bacteria.

If you have any questions about safety, make inquiries. Your County Cooperative Extension Agent will be able to answer questions on canning foods. A catalogue of publications including those with canning information may be obtained by writing to U. S. Government Publications, Consumer Information, Pueblo, CO 81009. For further information and recipes, see *Canning*, published by HPBooks.

How to Make Sesame Candy

1/Cut slightly cooled mixture into diagonal strips or diamond shapes.

2/When candy is firm, remove from pan and serve.

Pistachio Ice Cream

Fistikli Dondurma (Turkey)

Do not let ice cream melt while softening or it will contain ice crystals after it's refrozen.

1 pint vanilla ice cream
1/4 cup coarsely ground pistachio nuts

1 drop orange-blossom water
Green food coloring, if desired

Soften ice cream slightly at room temperature. Place in a cold medium bowl. Stir in remaining ingredients until blended. Place in freezer container, leaving 1/2 inch headroom. Cover and freeze solid. Makes 1 pint.

Rose-Petal Jam

Moraba-ye Barg-e Goll (Iran)

An exotic spread for biscuits or toast.

1 cup packed fresh rose petals　　　　**3 cups sugar**
2 cups water　　　　　　　　　　　　**Juice of 1 lemon (3 tablespoons)**

Sterilize jelly glasses or canning jars and lids according to manufacturer's instructions. Rinse rose petals and pat dry. Use only fresh, young rose petals that are unblemished and have not been exposed to chemicals or pesticides. Place dried rose petals in a medium saucepan. Add water. Bring to a boil. Petals will discolor. Remove petals with a slotted spoon. Set aside. Add sugar to liquid in pan. Bring to a boil. Continue to boil 15 minutes. Add lemon juice. Add rose petals to boiling syrup. Boil until jellying point, or 220F (104C) on a candy thermometer. At this temperature, jelly dropped from a cold metal spoon will fall in a sheet. Pour into hot sterilized jars, leaving 1/4 inch headroom. Attach lids according to manufacturer's instructions. Immediately invert jars for a few seconds so hot jam can destroy any mold or yeast that may have settled on lids. Jam may be stored 3 to 4 months in refrigerator. For longer storage, process filled glasses or jars 15 minutes in a hot-water bath, page 186, according to manufacturer's instructions. Makes about 1 pint.

Black-Pepper Spice

Huwait (Yemen)

All-purpose Yemenite spice may be added to soups, sauces and even yogurt.

2 tablespoons freshly ground black pepper　　**1 tablespoon ground cumin**
2 tablespoons ground turmeric

Combine all ingredients in a jar with a tight-fitting lid. Shake to mix well. May be stored up to 1 year. Makes about 1/4 cup.

Mixed Spice

Baharat (Arabic)

Arab housewives purchase this all-purpose spice mix by the bagful.

2 tablespoons freshly ground pepper　　**1/2 teaspoon ground cardamom**
1 tablespoon ground coriander　　　　　**1 nutmeg, grated**
1 tablespoon ground cloves　　　　　　**Pinch of ground cinnamon**
2 tablespoons ground cumin

Combine all ingredients in a jar with a tight-fitting lid. Shake to mix well. May be stored up to 1 year. Makes about 1/2 cup.

Index

Regional Index

Many of the recipes in this book have crossed regional boundaries. The following classifications are given as a guide to recipe origins.

8.34627902331